50 *Hikes*

In the Tennessee Mountains

Hikes and Walks from the Blue Ridge to the Cumberland Plateau

DORIS GOVE

Countryman Press

Woodstock, Vermont

An Invitation to the Reader

With time, access points may change, and trails, signs, and landmarks referred to in this book may be altered. If you find that such changes have occurred on the trails described in this book, please let the author and publisher know so that corrections may be made in future editions. Other comments and suggestions are also welcome. Address all correspondence to:

Backcountry Guides
P.O. Box 748
Woodstock, VT 05091

Library of Congress Cataloging-in-Publication Data

Gove, Doris.
50 hikes in the Tennessee Mountains: hikes and walks from the Blue Ridge to the Cumberland Plateau/Doris Gove. −1st ed.
    p. cm.
Includes index.
ISBN 0-88150-432-7 (alk. paper)
1. Hiking−Tennessee−Guidebooks. 2. Tennes-see−Guidebooks.
I. Title: Fifty Hikes in the Tennessee Mountains.
II. Title.
GV199.42.T2 G68 2001
917.68−dc21   00-064160
                    CIP

Maps by Mapping Specialists Limited,
    © 2000 by The Countryman Press
Interior photographs by Doris Gove
Cover photograph of Great Smoky Mountains
    National Park © Jim Hargan
Cover and text design by Glenn Suokko

Copyright © 2001 by Doris Gove

First Edition

Published by Backcountry Guides
A division of The Countryman Press
PO Box 748
Woodstock, Vermont 05091

Distributed by W. W. Norton & Company, Inc.
500 Fifth Avenue
New York, NY 10110

Printed in the United States of America

10 9 8 7 6 5 4

Acknowledgments

I would like to thank the staffs of state and national parks, nature centers, private hiking lands, the Cumberland Trail Conference, the Cherokee National Forest, and area experts for their help and information.

Ann Kraybill and the staff at The Countryman Press guided me through this project with patience and encouragement.

Past, present, and future trailbuilders, maintainers, conservation activists, wilderness advocates, park and greenway friends groups, and many other volunteers work hard—any trail we hike on represents their love for nature.

My hiking friends kept me from getting lost, showed me their favorite spots, and helped with car shuttles.

50 Hikes at a Glance

HIKE	NEAREST TOWN	RATING
1. Backbone Trails	Shady Valley	Easy
2. Holston Mountain	Elizabethton	Easy
3. AT: Watauga Dam to Vandeventer Shelter	Elizabethton	Difficult
4. AT: Laurel Falls	Hampton	Difficult
5. Beauty Spot Bald & Stamping Ground Ridge	Erwin	Easy
6. Rattlesnake Ridge (USFS 26)	Erwin	Difficult
7. Rock Creek Falls (USFS 148)	Erwin	Difficult
8. Smokies Elevation Sampler	Gatlinburg	Easy
9. Porters Creek	Gatlinburg	Easy/moderate
10. Trillium Gap and Brushy Mountain	Gatlinburg	Moderate
11. AT: Newfound Gap to Clingman's Dome	Gatlinburg	Difficult
12. Little River	Gatlinburg	Easy
13. Meigs Creek	Townsend	Moderate/difficult
14. Fodderstack Loop	Tellico Plains	Very difficult
15. Jeffrey Hell (USFS 196)	Tellico Plains	Easy/difficult
16. Falls Branch (USFS 87)	Tellico Plains	Moderate/difficult
17. Bald River (USFS 88)	Tellico Plains	Moderate
18. John Muir Trail at Reliance (USFS 152)	Reliance	Easy
19. Copper Road	Cleveland	Easy
20. Bays Mountain Park: Lakeside Trail	Kingsport	Easy
21. Sycamore Shoals	Elizabethton	Easy
22. House Mountain	Knoxville	Moderate/difficult
23. Ijams Nature Center	Knoxville	Easy
24. North Ridge	Oak Ridge	Moderate
25. Audubon Acres	Chattanooga	Easy

DISTANCE	VIEWS	WATERFALL	CAMPGROUND NEARBY	CAMPSITE ON TRAIL	KIDS	NOTES
0.5		★	★		★	One of the shortest tunnels in the world
4–5	★				★	A stroll; good fall colors
9.0	★			★		Steep hike to AT shelter
4.4		★	★	★		Deep rocky gorge; AT shelter
2–3	★		★	★	★	Compare grassy and heath balds
6.0	★		★			Remote wilderness hike
4.5		★	★			Dogleg waterfall
3.0			★		★	Three hikes: samples of elevation zones
7.4		★		★	★	Spring wildflowers; Smokies homesite
6.2	★	★			★	Wildflowers; Grotto Falls; heath bald
8.4	★			★		Little-used AT section to highest point in state
8–10	★	★	★		★	Wide, easy trail; beautiful river
7.0	★					Steep, remote valley; 18 creek crossings
9.9			★			Citico Wilderness Area; remote
4.4			★			Thick rhododendron; rushing creeks
2.6		★				High waterfall; virgin forest
10	★			★	★	Steep climb past waterfall, then easy walk
6.0		★			★	Gentle walk along Hiwassee River
4.6					★	Swim in Ocoee River; learn some history
2.1					★	Best hike for kids; pretty lake
2.0					★	Learn how the American Revolution was won
4.8	★				★	Rocks; flowers; great fall colors
1.5					★	Boardwalk along Tennessee River; bat cave
7.5	★					National Recreational Trail; part of city greenways
3.0	★				★	Native American village site; peaceful walk in city

50 Hikes at a Glance

HIKE	NEAREST TOWN	RATING
26. CG: Tri-State Peak and Cumberland Trail	Cumberland Gap	Moderate
27. CT: LaFollette to Cove Lake	LaFollette	Difficult
28. Hidden Passage	Jamestown	Moderate
29. Slave Falls & Twin Arches Loops	Jamestown	Moderate
30. Angel Falls Overlook	Oneida	Moderate/difficult
31. Leatherwood Loop	Oneida	Moderate
32. CT: Nemo Bridge to Alley Ford	Wartburg	Moderate
33. Honey Creek	Elgin	Difficult
34. Colditz Cove	Rugby	Easy/moderate
35. Gentlemen's Swimming Hole	Rugby	Easy/moderate
36. North Old Mac & Panther Branch	Wartburg	Moderate
37. Judge Branch and South Old Mac	Wartburg	Easy/moderate
38. Piney River Pocket Wilderness	Spring City	Moderate
39. Laurel Falls Pocket Wilderness	Dayton	Easy/moderate
40. North Chickamauga Creek Pocket Wild.	Soddy-Daisy	Difficult
41. Virgin Falls	DeRossett	Moderate
42. Fall Creek Falls: Woodland, Gorge, & Falls	Pikeville	Easy/difficult
43. Fall Creek Falls: Pawpaw Trails	Pikeville	Easy
44. Stone Door–Big Creek	Beersheba Springs	Difficult
45. Savage Day Loop	Palmer	Moderate
46. Foster Falls	Tracy City	Easy/moderate
47. Fiery Gizzard Trail and Dog Hole Loop	Tracy City	Difficult
48. Lone Rock Trail at Grundy Lakes	Tracy City	Easy
49. Shakerag Hollow	Sewanee	Easy/moderate
50. CT: Signal Point to Edwards Point	Signal Mountain	Difficult

DISTANCE	VIEWS	WATERFALL	CAMPGROUND NEARBY	CAMPSITE ON TRAIL	KIDS	NOTES
7.0	★				★	Cumberland Trail terminus; history
9.9	★		★			Steep climb to exposed ridge; views
8.0	★	★	★		★	Rockhouses; bluffs; fall colors
11.2	★	★	★	★	?	High arches; mile-long bluff; old homesite
6.0	★		★	★	?	Wildflowers; swimming spots; and the views
3.3	★		★		?	Wildflowers; frog pond; river views
5.0					★	Bluffs; magnolias; swimming
5.6	★	★				Maze of boulders; creeks; bluffs
1.5	★	★			★	Big trees; rock shelter; waterfall
2.2					★	Clear Creek
4.2		★	★	★	★	Spring wildflowers, especially trilliums
7.3	★		★	★	★	Easy creekside walk with option to climb to tower
10	★	★		★	?	Spring wildflowers; bridges; cascades
5.0	★	★		★	?	Deep rushing creek; rocks to climb under
8.0	★	★	★	★		Rocks! and bluffs; beautiful creek
8.0	★	★		★		Vanishing creeks; wildflowers; vista
2.8	★	★	★			Highest waterfall in East
4.6	★	★	★		★	Views of gorge; cable trail
9.0	★	★	★	★	?	Rim and floor of Savage Gulf; remoteness
8.4	★	★			★	Plateau walk with views into Savage Gulf
5.0					★	Falls; view of gorge
8.8	★	★				Fruit Bowl boulder field; wild creek; flowers
1.5					★	Hundreds of coke ovens
3.0	★				★	Spring flowers; view of Highland Rim
5–6	★	★		★		View of Tennessee Gorge; swimming

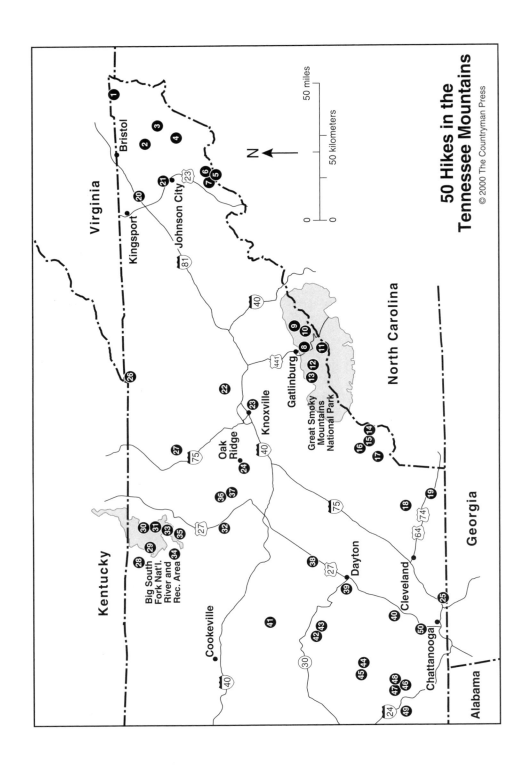

50 Hikes in the
Tennessee Mountains

© 2000 The Countryman Press

CONTENTS

V. NORTHERN CUMBERLAND MOUNTAINS

VI. SOUTHERN CUMBERLAND MOUNTAINS

Introduction

The Mountains of Tennessee

Based on geology and geography, East Tennessee has three regions: the high-elevation western Blue Ridge on the border with North Carolina (mostly Cherokee National Forest and Great Smoky Mountains National Park and collectively called the Unaka Range); the low-elevation Valley and Ridge Province between two mountain ranges, containing the Tennessee River and most of the cities; and the Cumberland Mountains, which form plateaus and gorges. These three sections run roughly parallel to each other and to the eastern border of Tennessee.

For millions of years, tectonic movement thrust the Appalachian Mountains up, and then erosion carved them down again—at least three times. An inland sea collected layers of sand and pebbles from the erosion, and seashells settled as layers of limestone. Marshy areas around the sea produced masses of organic matter that was pressed into deposits of coal, oil, and natural gas—resources that affect the cultural history and politics of the region today.

The eastern mountains along the North Carolina border, made of solid hard sandstone, have long backbones and deep-sloped side valleys. The Ridge and Valley Province has sharp sandstone ridges and limestone valley floors, while the Cumberland Mountains have a hard sandstone rock cap with softer rock underneath, often eroded into deep overhangs called rockhouses.

The creeks and rivers, responsible for valleys, gorges, and scenic beauty, flow from their respective high points, collect in the valleys, and then swing north; all of East Tennessee drains into two great rivers, the Tennessee and the Cumberland, which merge and flow into the Ohio River at Paducah, Kentucky.

Selecting Hikes

There are hundreds of wonderful hikes in East Tennessee, and it was difficult to choose only 50. The ones that made the cut for this book are well established, have adequate parking, are fairly easy to find (though some are remote and on gravel roads), and are beautiful. Some of the trails are popular and heavily used, but I have tried to include more that receive little use and can provide true wilderness experiences. Even in the Smokies, with an annual visitation of more than 10 million, many of the best trails have a private feel. New trails and trail extensions, such as sections of the Cumberland Trail, are emphasized here. Several wilderness areas in the Cherokee National Forest provide excellent hiking with no crowds. Please use these descriptions as introductions to hiking opportunities and to the natural and cultural history of the mountainous regions of Tennessee.

Maintained trails from less than 1 to more than 10 miles are included; most are easy to follow, but a few are more complicated. The trail narratives are intended as much as possible to help you choose. Some hikes have sections that are barrier-free and are appropriate for handicapped people and baby strollers. Others may be challenging—take the teenagers who think they can do anything. In many of the hike descriptions only a portion of a trail will be featured, and there will be a brief description of the longer possibilities or trail connections.

In general I have omitted trails that see heavy horse or mountain bike use, though some trails are included on which sharing is no problem.

Maps

The maps in this book are meant to be an introduction to the area and a guide to the specific hike described. To explore further, you should get more detailed maps. The forest service, state parks, and other managing agencies usually provide maps for hikers showing trail connections and landmarks. The information block at the head of each hike contains the names of the pertinent USGS maps—available at ranger stations, visitors centers, map stores, and hiking stores, and possibly from the Internet. The DeLorme *Tennessee Atlas and Gazetteer* is useful for finding trailheads and roads.

Landmarks, signs, exact routes, levels of maintenance, and blazes or other trail markers may change after the publication of this book. For the better, we can hope.

Always take a compass, a guidebook, and the best maps available. Pack maps and guidebooks in plastic bags; if you want to reduce weight, photocopy relevant pages.

Safety and Equipment

Check the weather forecast. Hikes along ridgetops can be dangerous in thunderstorms, and heavy rain can swell creeks. Rocky or steep hikes can be dangerous in icy conditions. In summer weather, even if you're in great shape, a hot, humid pull uphill can be exhausting. In many cases cautions will be listed in the hike narratives, but plan ahead with safety in mind. Always be prepared to retreat if weather or other conditions become dangerous. If a creek crossing looks too hard, it probably is.

Carry more water than you think you'll need. Take frequent water breaks, and make sure that everyone in your group has enough to drink. Don't count on creek or springwater unless you're prepared to boil or filter it. Don't substitute sugary drinks for water, and if you do want to take fruit juice, dilute it by about half. Fruit, sandwiches, and healthy trail snacks provide all the energy, potassium, and other electrolytes needed for normal or even strenuous hiking, but don't skimp on the water.

Other safety equipment that should be in your pack: rain gear, a first-aid kit, a jackknife, matches, spare clothes (in a plastic bag), a hat and mittens in cold weather, a flashlight, and extra food. A single-use space blanket (about the size of a small notebook) and a roll of duct tape could also be useful. And take a waterproof mat to sit on: You lose a lot of body heat from your head, but after you sit on a cold, wet log for a lunch break, you may question that piece of wisdom. (Wear the hat, too, though.) On very cold days eat lunch with your mittens on; fuzz on a sandwich is better than fingers that can't get warm again.

Wear layers and wicking fabrics, especially next to your skin. Hypothermia is often more of a danger in above-freezing wet weather. Put on rain gear before you get wet, and put on another layer of clothes before you get cold, especially if you're stopping for lunch after a vigorous walk. If your clothes are wet with sweat, it's better to take off the damp layers (well, most of the layers, anyway) before putting on dry layers. Watch children and other hiking companions for signs of problems.

Remember that higher elevation may mean colder, wetter, windier, and wilder weather.

A waterfall near Woodson Gap, near the proposed route of the Cumberland Trail

➤ Cumberland Trail

By 2008 the Cumberland Trail (CT) will run along the Cumberland Mountains from Signal Point National Military Park near Chattanooga to Cumberland Gap National Historic Park on the Kentucky border. Tennessee's 53rd state park and its first linear park, the CT will run for 280 miles through public and private lands. White blazes mark the trail, and campsites allow for extended backpacking trips. This book includes most of the completed sections of the CT, but workers build trails too fast for a guidebook to keep up with. The CT Conference provides maps and updates on an excellent web page: http:/www.cumberlandtrail.org.

Founded by the Tennessee Trails Association in 1997, the CT Conference has an office in Crossville, about halfway along the trail. Staff members plan trails, write grants, organize work crews, recruit volunteers, and negotiate with landowners. When they have nothing else to do, they go out and build rock steps.

Many university students participate in Breakaway programs—instead of lying on the beach for spring break, they come to Tennessee to build trails. Recent participants include Michigan State, Florida State, Emory, and Northwestern. More than 100 students worked on the trail in 2000, along with members of the Boy Scouts, Americorps, hiking and environmental organizations, crews from correctional institutions, and individuals.

In 2000 Hillary Rodham Clinton designated the CT as one of 16 Millennium Legacy Trails.

Always stay within sight distance of your group and tell someone if you need a bathroom break or if the group is going too fast for you. A whistle can help if someone gets separated, but be aware that creek noise, heavy vegetation, and contour can block sounds.

Don't Get Lost

Many trails are blazed with paint marks or designs, and some have signs at intersections. Blazes may be faint or fresh; signs may have been knocked down or burned in a campfire. On a blazed trail, always keep track of the blazes; it's easy to get off-course. If you don't see a blaze for a while, turn around and look for one behind you; make sure you know how to backtrack if necessary. Some trails use double blazes at sharp turns or road crossings.

If branches hit you in the face or the treadway disappears, take the hint: You need to reconsider. You may have missed a turn or followed a path from someone else's mistake. In fall when the leaves are fluffy the trail may be harder to follow, and it's easy to lose the trail when it crosses piles of boulders.

If you get lost, stop, relax, consult guidebooks and maps, and develop a strategy to get back to the trail. Have the group stay put while one person looks for the trail, by either backtracking or circling. Stay in voice contact. Be prepared to go back to your starting point and call it a day if the trail is too difficult to follow.

Trail Narratives

Hiking is the best exercise in the world (hey, I'm not biased!), but it should be more than that. Every hike has special features that will be described in the narratives. But in some narratives I describe detail trees, rocks, or animals that may occur throughout a region

A typical rockhouse in the Cumberland Plateau

or on almost all the trails. For example, pawpaw trees may grow throughout the Cumberlands and the Ridge and Valley Province; they may be mentioned in one place but described in greater detail in another. Consult the index to find natural history information on certain features.

The hikes are loops, backtracks, or shuttles. I have described what I think of as manageable day hikes that include the best features of a trail. Obviously, you can adapt them to your group's needs—hike part of a loop or shuttle and backtrack, or create a loop with trail connections beyond the described trail segment. Or hike 10 miles farther.

Some trails have easy sections, great for a stroll, and then more challenging parts. I have tried to provide enough information to allow you to design your own outing.

Backcountry campsites are available on many trails. In the Smokies, most state parks, and some other areas, permits are required. Practice Leave-No-Trace camping, and carry a plastic bag to carry out trash left by others.

Hike Ratings and Times

The hikes are rated easy, moderate, or difficult, with more details in the descriptions. These are subjective judgments, but I have tried to be consistent, so after you hike a few of these trails, you'll be able to see if you agree with my ratings.

The same goes for the subjective estimates of hiking time—I assume an average of 2 miles per hour, with added time for difficult or steep terrain. This does not include lunch or swim stops. Again, you'll have to use your own experience as a guide. Please don't trust my estimates if you are starting late in the day and have the same amount of daylight hours as the estimated hiking time. (Check your local newspaper for the time

of sunset on each hiking day.) Vertical rise is also an estimate—ups and downs along the way (some steep) may not be reflected. Also, easy does not mean "no hills."

In other words, YMMV—your mileage may vary.

➤ Hiking with Children

- *Make it fun!*
- *Allow for plenty of rest and exploration stops.*
- *Provide good snacks; perhaps get the kids to help make or buy them.*
- *Make sure they drink water or juice— children often don't see the need. (Babies seem to do better in that department.)*
- *Make rules that reduce the risk of getting lost or hurt: Don't run, cut switchbacks, leave the trail, or pass the (adult) leader. Make sure the kids know that new rules may be issued for strange things they think up.*
- *Give each child a whistle. Have them practice with it, but tell them not to use it for fun.*
- *Emphasize that if they get separated from the group or feel lost, they must sit down, hug a tree, pretend they are fawns waiting for their mother, pretend to grow roots, or whatever seems to work. And then they should blow the whistle.*
- *Make it fun!*

Giving Back

Most of the trails you hike on are maintained by volunteers; some were designed and built by volunteers. Hiking clubs from Georgia to Maine take responsibility for maintenance of the Appalachian Trail, and local clubs and individuals adopt trails in their areas.

50 Hikes in the Tennessee Mountains

Here are some ways to help:
- The Smokies has a Volunteers in the Park program (and they'll call you a VIP). You could adopt a trail, work in the library, or help backcountry campers plan trips. The forest service and state parks also recruit volunteers.
- Most hiking clubs maintain trails. Contact Tennessee Trails Association, the Smoky Mountains Hiking Club, or local clubs.
- National Trails Day, the first weekend in June, features organized work parties in all parts of the state. Contact clubs in your area for information.
- Pay up. Many places ask for donations, and more and more facilities charge use or parking fees.
- The Smokies, Cherokee National Forest Wilderness Areas, Big South Fork, and

many other areas wouldn't exist without citizen activism. When you hear of conservation projects to protect public or private lands, consider helping. Every wilderness area in Tennessee represents months or years of citizen advocacy, and the same groups continue to work for greater protection of beautiful places.

Key to Map Symbols

— — — main trail

• • • • • alternate or side trail

(P) parking

view

Appalachian Trail

campground

shelter

Northern Unaka Mountains

Heath Bald on Stamping Ground Ridge

1

Backbone Trails

Total Distance: 0.5 mile

Hiking Time: 40 minutes

Vertical Rise: 60 feet

Rating: Easy

Map: USGS Laurel Bloomery

Two short trails from the Backbone Rock Recreation Area feature a waterfall, a creek-side picnic area, and a climb over one of the shortest tunnels in the world. Most of this hike involves steps or rock scrambling, but it's safe except when icy. All the high parts—except the second half of the water-fall loop—have protective fences.

How to Get There

From US 19E in Elizabethton, take TN 91 north into Shady Valley to the intersection of TN 91, US 421, and TN 133. Drive north on TN 133 (straight ahead) for 10 miles to USFS Backbone Rock Recreation Area. Or from the junction of US 58 and VA 716 in Damascus, Virginia, drive south 3.7 miles on VA 716, which becomes TN 133 at the state line.

The Hike

Mountains surrounding Shady Valley pre-vented harvesting of valuable resources—iron, manganese, and timber—until 1900, when the Norfolk and Western Railroad blasted a 50-foot tunnel through Backbone Rock and ran a rail line to Crandull. With this break-and-enter line in place, loggers and miners quickly took just about everything they wanted. Then the residents of the valley got back to farming, and the forest service took over 20,000 acres along Bea-verdam Creek. The mountainside between TN 133 and the Appalachian Trail (AT) is protected from here to the Virginia border as a forest service primitive area. Shady Valley itself is a cove with limestone bed-rock surrounded by sandstone mountains

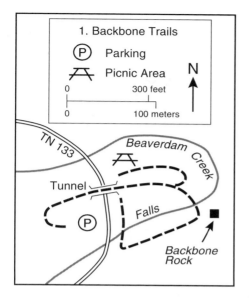

1. Backbone Trails

Ⓟ Parking

🅰 Picnic Area

N

0   300 feet

0   100 meters

TN 133

Beaverdam Creek

Tunnel

Falls

Ⓟ

Backbone Rock

of lichens indicates decades of protection. One lichen looks like mustard splashed on the vertical rock faces.

At the top of the steps a blue-blazed trail goes left toward the Appalachian Trail on the ridgetop. But turn right to skirt boulders and walk out to a fenced sandstone bridge over the road. From here, you can look down on the tops of rhododendron, mountain laurel, yellow birch, witch hazel, and road traffic. Asphalt on the rock protects you from slipping, and wire fences keep the kids from falling off.

Go all the way across, catch an open view to the right, and descend more stone steps to the picnic area along Beaverdam Creek. Picnic shelters built by the Civilian Conservation Corps feature massive tree trunk supports and cement tables. This is a good place to eat, play in the water, and look at the jagged end of the rock barrier that kept loggers out until 1900.

From the picnic area, go right toward the road and the other parking lot. Climb the other stone steps into thick rhododendron that muffles traffic noise. The steps curve to the right above the road, and then to the left to a fenced cement platform where you can hear the falls and get a glimpse of them to the left. Continue up rock steps past a huge erosion-pitted boulder and cross a culvert over a creek with Backbone Falls on the right and some pretty cascades on the left. You can lean out—very carefully—to see the falls. This is a good place to turn back if you want to avoid unprotected trail along a precipice. There's another great view of the falls if you backtrack down the steps and walk up the road a bit.

But if you choose to go on, cross the culvert to a narrow, densely shaded trail as it swings to the right to parallel the falls. Watch for slippery spots and uneven steps. The waterfall (actually a cascade, since the

(similar geologically to Cades Cove in the Smokies) and, at 2,800 feet, is the highest cove in Tennessee. Cranberries grow in bogs here, and the town of Shady Valley puts on a cranberry festival in September. Because of the presence of rare plants and animals, The Nature Conservancy owns and protects several bogs along Beaverdam Creek.

Two trails, connected by a route across the top of Backbone Rock, are included in this description, which starts on the scramble up to the west side of the rock overpass. The big rocks on this end are easier to go up than down. From the large parking area west of TN 133 (left if you're coming from the south), hike to the right toward the rock face and stone steps. (A small trail straight from the parking lot leads to the cement platform of a former pit toilet.) Witch hazel flanks the trailhead, but gives way to sourwood trees and mountain laurel. Stone steps and handrails were built in the 1930s, and the almost solid growth

Rosebay rhododendron

water slides along a rock face) looks like a white snake slipping down a crack in the rock. Yellow birch, Fraser magnolia, and tulip tree grow along the steep slope to the left, and a mass of rhododendrons follows the course of the falls. The fractured rock face on the right looks like layers of blocks; it seems that if you pulled out one block, the whole wall would topple into a heap. Pink, green, cinnamon brown, and black lichens grow here.

There's a mini falls near the road, and, after all that excitement, the creek slides through a culvert to Beaverdam Creek to flow north into Virginia. A fenced walkway leads along the road back to the picnic area.

From Backbone Arch you can look down into the tops of yellow birches that cling to a hillside you wouldn't want to climb. Look for oval-with-a-point leaves with double-toothed margins—that is, tiny teeth between small teeth. Then look down the twigs to branches or the main trunk to find the yellow-to-silver bark curls that give the tree its name. Horizontal ringlets alternate with clumps of split ends. Old trees may have blocky bark on the lower trunk, but the branches will still show the curls; just look up. Once you learn this bark, you will see yellow birches on many of the hikes in this book, usually on moist, north-facing slopes with good soil. They also grow well on ridgetops, where wind whips them into weird shapes.

At the end of winter twigs hold male catkins, about 1 inch long and stiff. In spring, at about the time cricket frogs start singing, the catkins grow to 3 or 4 inches and dangle, releasing clouds of yellow pollen. Demure female catkins grow farther back on the twig; they expand a little to receive the pollen. Male catkins fall off and look like fat yellow caterpillars on the ground, while females grow into conelike fruits that scatter tiny winged seeds late in the year.

These seeds often germinate on a rotting log or in a soil pocket on top of a boulder. As the sapling grows, it must send roots, like tangled tentacles, out and down to search for real soil. If the log rots completely, the yellow birch appears to be standing upon twisted stilts.

Other Hiking Options

The 2.1-mile blue-blazed Backbone Trail leads from the top of Backbone Rock through the Beaverdam Primitive Area to the Appalachian Trail. Though not terribly steep, it's a relentless climb to the ridgetop. To the left is Abingdon AT Shelter in 3.4 miles, and to the right is Damascus, Virginia, in 4.6 miles. Shinleaf, a somewhat rare flower related to pipsissewa, can be seen blooming in summer near the AT. Once when I was coming down Backbone Trail, a young black bear and I startled each other. The bear fled.

2

Holston Mountain

Total Distance: 4–5 miles

Hiking Time: 2½–3 hours

Vertical Rise: 50–150 feet

Rating: Easy

Map: USGS Carter

Trail Marking: Yellow or orange blazes

This hike follows a ridgetop where you will probably be the only hikers. The gate near Blue Hole closes in winter; spring and fall are the best times for this outing. Bring the kids, a picnic lunch, and bathing suits in summer for a stop at Blue Hole.

How to Get There

From US 321/US 19E east of Elizabethton, turn north onto TN 91 and drive 10.5 miles to Panhandle Road, with a brown USFS sign for HOLSTON MOUNTAIN AND BLUE HOLE. Turn left onto a paved road that changes to gravel at 1 mile. At 1.5 miles enter the Cherokee National Forest (now on USFS 202), pass the Blue Hole parking area on the left, and drive to a fork at 3.2 miles. Park on the roadside of the gated right fork (the left fork goes to Holston Mountain Campground).

The Hike

The Appalachian Trail (AT) used to run along this ridgetop but was relocated in 1954 because the route passed through private land in the valley between Holston and Iron Mountains. Now the AT runs along Iron Mountain and crosses (on Cross Mountain!) to Holston Mountain at the north end of this hike. Still beautiful, and still connected to the AT farther north, Holston Mountain sees little hiker traffic these days. Use this description for a quiet, private hike.

Go around the gate to USFS TRAIL 44, marked by a HIKERS ONLY sign and blue blazes (it's also USFS 56A). Hike up less than a mile on a stony road that circles Holston

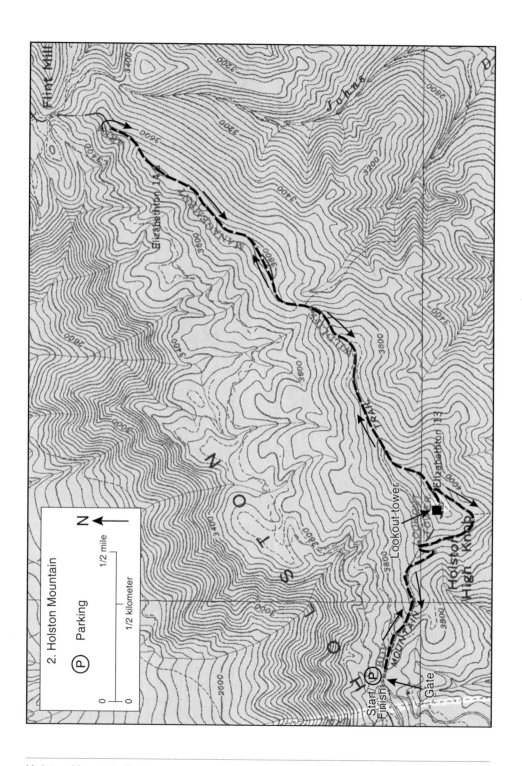

2. Holston Mountain

Ⓟ Parking

N ←

0 ——— 1/2 mile

0 ——— 1/2 kilometer

Flint Mill

Johns

Elizabethton 1A

HOLSTON MOUNTAIN

Elizabethton 113

Lookout tower

Holston High Knob

Start/Finish Ⓟ

Gate

MOUNTAIN TRAIL

High Knob (4,140 feet and usually breezy). Stop near the top to look back at the view of the valley you just drove from and Iron Mountain across the way. At the top you can walk left and look at the lookout tower, but it's fenced in and bristling with communications equipment; from the fence you might get a winter view of Holston Reservoir and farm fields. Return from the tower and look for the USFS 44 sign and blazes to the right of the road.

From the valley, you could see this as an undulating ridgeline. Now on top, you'll descend and climb gently through hickory, oak, tulip tree, and yellow birch. Shagbark hickory, with its shreds of bark peeling up from the bottom, stands in clusters along the trail. Shagbark hickory nuts are delicious, but squirrels find most of them first.

On the tops of rises look for dry-adapted flowers: bee balm, milkweed, agrimony. In the more sheltered saddles squawroot, anise root, violets, rue anemones, and ferns grow. In the deeper saddles hemlock and rhododendron get enough moisture, along with puffballs, turkey tail, and other fungi. If it's dry and windy, lie in the shelter of a hemlock and watch the treetops sway. You might hear the eerie moaning of two branches rubbing together.

The trail slides off the ridgetop to bypass a high point and then regains the crest of the ridge. Another, somewhat deeper saddle has a thick growth of rhododendron at the bottom and more spring flowers: hepatica and bloodroot in March, and mandarin, trillium, and blue cohosh later in April. At the next high point look for American chestnut snags and possibly shoots that come up from roots that weren't killed by the blight. Seventy years ago chestnuts dominated high-elevation ridges like this one; no other tree approaches their size, though chestnut oaks give it a try.

Turkey tail fungus

The trail now seems to be descending more, and you may want to choose a turnaround place. On the way back you will notice that, even with all the gentle ups and downs, the net elevation change is now upward and the climb back takes a little more energy.

Other Hiking Options

1. For a 13-mile hike or backpack on this trail and the AT (not quite the relaxed stroll described above), arrange a car shuttle at Cross Mountain Road (8.5 miles past the Panhandle Road turn, turn right onto Cross Mountain Road to a small parking lot for the AT). Hike on Holston Mountain Trail for 9.5 miles, turn right onto the AT (good white blazes), pass (or sleep in) Double Springs Shelter 0.1 mile from the junction, and hike 3.5 miles to TN 91. Cross it and reenter the

woods to get to your car.

2. Stop at Blue Hole on your way down the mountain. From the parking area, descend past a gate and turn left through rhododendron to some steps built for very tall people. Blue Hole isn't large, but it's deep and cold. It has a perfect shower-waterfall on one side and impressive rock faces all around.

3

Appalachian Trail: Watauga Dam to Vandeventer Shelter

Total Distance: 9 miles

Hiking Time: 5–6 hours

Vertical Rise: 1,200 feet

Rating: Difficult

Map: USGS Watauga Dam

Trail Marking: White blazes (AT)

This long, hard climb is not for small children, but take older kids who have too much energy. You'll reach the level ridge of Iron Mountain, with wonderful views and spectacular rhododendron blooms in June. You won't see many other people except in through-hiking season (March through May). It's a good fall hike, and it will warm you up in winter, but it may be too hot in summer. Steep parts can be slippery in the rain and dangerous when snowy or icy.

How to Get There

From the junction (and merger) of US 321 and US 19E in Elizabethton, go south on US 19E/US 321 for 0.6 mile and turn left onto Siam Road. At a traffic light and right curve look for TVA WATAUGA and WILBUR DAM signs. Stay on Siam Road—which twists around and passes a residential area, then farms—for 3.4 miles. Turn right onto Wilbur Dam Road and drive 1.8 miles to a TVA WELCOME sign. Pass Wilbur Lake (look for bufflehead ducks, scaup, and teal), cross the lake, turn left at the fork, and reach Iron Mountain Gap and the Appalachian Trail (AT) crossing at a small parking lot 2.4 miles past the TVA welcome (8.2 miles from US 19E/US 321). Just downhill from the gap is a TVA visitors center with bathrooms and more parking.

On the return drive keep track of your mileage: It's easy to miss the left turn from Wilbur Dam Road to Siam Road.

The Hike

From Iron Mountain, you can look east to the somewhat jumbled Unaka Mountains along the state line and west to the straight line of

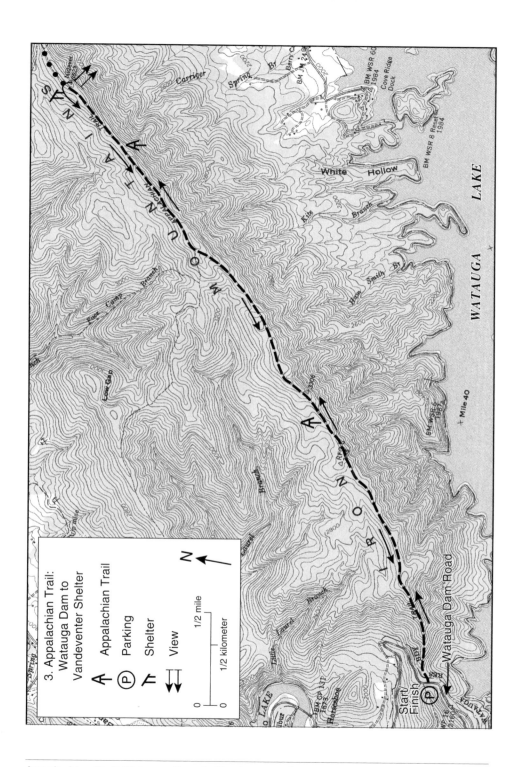

Holston Mountain and perhaps to the broad Tennessee Valley beyond. Iron and Holston Mountains, lying parallel and connected like an H by Cross Mountain, form the western part of the Unaka Mountains and the transition to the Tennessee River Valley. The Appalachian Trail climbs north from a small ridge above Watauga Lake (2,245 feet) to the top of Iron Mountain (actually a long ridge with an average elevation of 3,550 feet), providing the challenge of this hike. This is part of a 16-mile segment of the AT. People hiking from Georgia to Maine have come 417 miles to get to Vandeventer Shelter; hikers going the other way have done 1,743 miles.

From the parking area at the gap, look for a few steps up to an entrance sign for Big Laurel Branch Wilderness, designated in 1986. Extensive logging and a 1963 fire denuded this area, but regrowth and wilderness protection have made it excellent for hiking now. After registering, climb steeply for about 0.5 mile (it may feel like more; imagine what it's like for the long-distance hikers carrying 40-plus pounds) to two rock overlooks on the right and a short, welcome level spot. You can see blue-green Watauga Lake below and Pond Mountain to the southeast.

Continue up through oak and hickory forest with dogwood, mountain laurel, and serviceberry undergrowth. A few sourwoods grow here, and trailing arbutus covers the trailbank. Mountain laurel and blueberry thrive along this open, rocky stretch, but higher up you'll see small and then larger Carolina hemlocks.

As you continue to climb, larger overthrust rocks appear on the right, providing shelter and moist soil that supports rhododendrons, halberd-leaved violets (yellow blooms), Solomon's seal, and mayapples. The trail reaches a saddle and goes left

Hanging a pack to avoid mice in Vandeventer Shelter

➤ *Though hemlocks grow along almost every hike in this book, the common ones are eastern hemlocks; Carolina hemlocks are relatively rare. Here's how to tell them apart: On eastern hemlocks, the needles stick out flat from the twigs like neatly parted hair, while Carolina hemlocks have twigs with needles coming out at different angles, giving the twigs a fuller, even fluffy look.*

of the rocky crest. Rue anemone and blue cohosh bloom here, and squawroot pushes up through the soil in early April. This yellow plant looks like a scruffy ear of corn and

50 Hikes in the Tennessee Mountains

has no chlorophyll—it lives as a parasite on tree roots, usually oaks. The little white "kernels" are the flowers, but you will need a hand lens to see the flower structure. A common small tree in the saddle is striped maple, recognizable by its green bark with light green or ivory-colored vertical stripes.

Returning to the crest of the ridge at about 1 mile, the trail reaches a rock overlook of Watauga Lake and the boat docks on its opposite shore. After this, the ridge becomes wider; you can see a parallel ridge to the left, with a broad valley in between. After another open view on the right, the trail levels off in an area that features wildflowers in spring and blackberries in late summer. Tangles of greenbrier and grape may reach onto the trail. Wildflowers here include violets, spring beauty, bloodroot, and turk's cap lilies, and you may see signs of wild hogs digging for bulbs to eat.

The trail rises out of the saddle and, if there aren't too many leaves, you can see the last climb of the ascent of Iron Mountain. Swing right and then left to descend to the valley. A seasonal spring starts just to the right of the trail at the bottom; water seeps across the trail and down the valley to feed the waterfall that tumbles down a rock face to Wilbur Lake (look for it on the drive out). From the spring, take a few switchbacks up the hill to the other ridgeline and then descend beside the best rocks of the hike: high, slanted, and covered with thick moss. Rattlesnake plantain orchid and ferns grow along the base of the rocks. Just past them the trail enters a rhododendron tunnel.

A final short climb beside more ridgetop rocks and then a descent into a hollow brings you to the blue-blazed side trail to a spring and then Vandeventer Shelter, partially hidden behind a large rhododendron. Read the AT Trail Register (a notebook in the shelter where hikers leave messages or record their experiences; a recent entry: "I'm here, I'm cold, I'm leaving!"). Then climb the rocks behind the shelter for another good view of Watauga Lake and the mountains beyond. October views show the scarlet foliage of sourwood and blackgum, the yellows of hickory and tulip tree, and the darker reds of oak.

Backtrack to the parking area, downhill almost all the way.

Other Hiking Options

1. Arrange a car shuttle and hike south from TN 91 to the Watauga Dam Trailhead—a 16-mile hike, but it's mostly level or downhill. In mid-June the ridgetop rhododendrons put on a spectacular display, and fall colors are best in October. There are two AT shelters and several campsites along the trail.

2. From the Watauga Dam Trailhead, walk back along the road about 75 yards to find the steps up the roadbank of the AT going south. After a steep climb over a small ridge, the trail crosses Watauga Dam, which is open only to AT hikers (this includes you, if you made the climb). Return the same way for a 2.2-mile round-trip. This makes a nice side trip if you have some energy left after hiking to Vandeventer Shelter.

4

Appalachian Trail: Laurel Falls

Total Distance: 4.4 miles

Hiking Time: 3–4 hours

Vertical Rise: 400 feet

Rating: Difficult

Map: USGS Watauga Dam

There's a lot to look up to in this gorge: balanced boulders, ancient hemlocks, thundering water, a canopy of rhododendron, mountain laurel, and flame azalea. On this difficult hike you will squeeze along ledges over a creek and climb a steep boulder field. Spring and fall hiking are best here; winter hiking is possible but risky if the weather is changing. Do not attempt this hike in high water or if there is any possibility of ice.

How to Get There

From Elizabethton, take US 19E south to its junction with US 321. Turn left onto US 321 and drive 1.4 miles, passing through the small town of Hampton. After two concrete bridges, turn right into a USFS parking lot for Laurel Falls.

The Hike

The Appalachian Trail (AT) swings through Laurel Fork Gorge and then climbs Pond Mountain to head north to Maine. In this loop you'll hike about 2 miles of the AT and hike the 1-mile blue-blazed Hampton Blue Line connector trail twice. The gorge, part of the Pond Mountain Wilderness Area, conveys a feeling of remoteness and wildness. Many rare plants and animals survived in this gorge when their habitats in surrounding areas were farmed or logged.

Pass between boulders at the back of the parking area beside a small rocky side creek. Honeysuckle, dandelion, and other exotics grow along the trail, increasing the contrast with the special world of the gorge. Soon a bluff rises on the left that supports real native plants: columbine, walking fern,

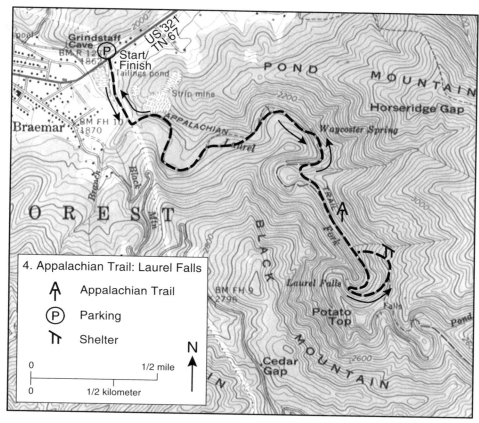

4. Appalachian Trail: Laurel Falls

Ⱥ   Appalachian Trail

Ⓟ   Parking

Ⱦ   Shelter

N

0   1/2 mile

0   1/2 kilometer

stonecrop, and a few spicebushes at the base. Large pits to the right are the only reminder of the iron mining that took place here after the Civil War.

The trail turns left up a steep climb on a rutted road; a glimpse to the right of Laurel Fork and big hemlocks offers some promise, but you should ignore a narrow trail on the right and continue up the road under a power line. Then turn right down the hill to a POND MOUNTAIN WILDERNESS sign. After the sign, veer right and descend on the rocky trail to a peaceful grove of hemlocks. There are some blue blazes, but they may be hard to see.

After the sign-in box, the magic of this hike begins to assert itself. Continue to

the right on the sandy trail to Laurel Fork. The sand, doghobble, rhododendron, and hemlock are all thick, and in summer a creek breeze will probably feel welcome. Spur trails to the right lead to swimming or wading spots in-season.

Buckled Rock rises across the fork. The waves in the rock striations (or the buckles—think of the way a highway buckles in an earthquake) reveal the force that pushed these mountains up and westward; this is hard rock, and it did not go willingly. Moss, poison ivy, hemlock, ferns, rock tripe, and lichens find a precarious living in cracks of the buckle, some of them growing in contorted positions to hang on to spots protected from most herbivores.

With the buckle on one side and steep, uncompromising Pond Mountain on the other, you are now in the gorge. Continue upstream and merge with an old road with good supporting rock work. It was hard to get into this gorge, but loggers did their valiant best—you'll see their roadbeds down here at the valley floor and their rail lines blasted through ridges on the hillside. They didn't want hemlock trees, however, so some massive old-growth eastern hemlocks still stand beside the rhododendron thickets. A flat area has served as a campsite where another road joins from the left; on your way back, remember to keep track of the blazes. Then you leave the security of the woods and scramble out to the creek's edge on rocks; in some spots you'll be climbing with hands and feet. This is a good place to judge ice and snow danger; if the trail is somewhat dangerous here, it will be worse farther on. Still, this is only a short rock scramble. Then you turn left away from the creek. Watch for the AT merging from the left. Your best hint will be the first white blaze; look back to see the double blaze that tells AT hikers to make a switchback to climb Pond Mountain. Continue along an old road and look left for views of Pond Mountain. Also to the left is a massive boulder pile—it probably once matched the buckle but then fell apart, as the buckle will someday. This south-facing wealth of crevices and shelters must be home to a thriving assortment of snakes, lizards, chipmunks, and other apartment-complex dwellers. Good hibernation opportunities, too.

In an especially thick rhododendron tangle the trail turns right to cross the first bridge over Laurel Fork. Floods here make extra work for trail maintainers; this new bridge replaces one that recently washed away, and it's high enough that it should last a few years longer. Power tools are not allowed in wilderness areas; maintainers must work with hand tools or assemble materials outside the area and carry them in. Stop to admire the beautiful rock base, probably built by early loggers and then repaired by trail maintainers. The trail turns upstream in a rhododendron boulevard to the next bridge, even more impressive. The boulder hillside gets higher as you ascend the gorge.

Look for a double white blaze signaling a sharp turn left up a hill. If you miss it and come to an unbridged creek crossing (again, remnants of an old logging road), turn back for about 100 yards and try again. There is a small campsite between the trail and the creek.

The trail becomes rough with rocks and exposed roots. It climbs to a dry ridge that's unusual because it runs from the steep side of Pond Mountain to the creek, somewhat like the flying buttress of a cathedral. From a rock promontory, you can see across to the mountain walls of this gorge. Table Mountain pine hangs out over the precipice; look for its apple-sized cones with sharp, curved spines. Mountain laurel, flame azalea, sourwood, menziesia (minniebush), rosebay rhododendron, and Catawba rhododendron thrive in the sun. From here it is possible to see all these members of the heath family blooming—white, pink, orange, and lavender—at the same time, since this view covers a wide range of elevations. Carolina hemlocks grow along the left side of the trail.

After a bit of rocky descent, the trail forks. A blue-blazed side trail goes left to an AT shelter, and this is the route you must take in high water. It's longer to the falls, but you won't get swept away by Laurel Fork. The right trail fork, white blazed, plunges down over large rocks that have been only slightly rearranged to provide steps; you will find

Honeysuckle azalea

yourself grabbing trees. At the bottom there is a slight confusion of trails; you want to basically head upstream and look for the blazes. The trail goes through open woods with a solid bank of rhododendron on the right. Look for a black locust that has fallen and been cut but continues to grow bushy sprouts from the trunk.

The gorge closes in on the trail now, disguised by the rhododendron, forcing you over a small ridge and then right to the creek edge. Here you'll know if you should have heeded the high-water advice (don't say you weren't warned)—the trail goes along a narrow ledge just above (or below) the water level. The ledge is short; pretty soon you round the nose of the vertical bluff face and step onto safe, level ground. Look up at buckled rock on both sides of the gorge, and especially at some boulders hanging over the top.

Continue along more rocky trail toward the sound of Laurel Falls—and there they are, at the bottom of a spur trail. Climb down to a level spot inside the bowl of this rock bluff amphitheater. People swim in the large, deep pool at the base of the falls, but keep in mind that it is full of the same kind of jagged rocks you just climbed over, complicated by currents near the base. Don't forget to look downstream to see Laurel Fork curve away against the high mountains—an excellent view in autumn. The falling water creates a cool breeze, which you'll need for the next part of this hike.

You may think you came for the waterfall, but just as memorable is the climb out of the waterfall basin. Of course, you could go back the way you came; that's the shortest way. But straight up the hill is one of the best (and hardest) staircases you've ever climbed—big steps, small steps, tippy steps, hand-and-foot steps, but steps all the same, wrestled into place by trail builders. There's a little relief at a left curve, and then you finally haul out onto level ground and a trail junction. The white-blazed AT goes right on its southerly course toward Dennis Cove, and a blue-blazed AT shelter trail heads left. Turn left onto the rocky former railbed and walk between vertical walls where loggers blasted through a side ridge to lay level rails. Stroll along for less than 0.5 mile, passing through more evidence of the rail lines (admire the lichens that have colonized the rock faces), then climb a knoll to the stone shelter. There should be a trail register for you to read and see who's been through on their way to Maine, and you can add comments about your day hike.

From here, the quickest way back is to follow the blue-blazed trail from the front of the shelter down to the AT along the creek. It drops down steeply, but it's only 0.5 mile long. At river level turn right, look for white blazes, and return the way you came.

Other Hiking Options

1. Add on a trip to Pond Mountain, which provides excellent views of the gorge, some aerobic exercise, and a remote campsite on the summit. A woodland pond near the campsite might have frogs or salamanders in spring. Follow the white AT blazes from the Blue Line Trail.

2. A rough and adventurous blue-blazed trail leads from the AT shelter to the trail up Pond Mountain; follow the old rail line behind the shelter, past a small cascading creek, and up to another overgrown rail line. At the junction of the blue-blazed trail with the AT, turn left to return to Blue Line Trail to Hampton or turn right to climb Pond Mountain.

3. Leave one car at Dennis Cove (4.1 miles on USFS 50—Dennis Cove Road—from Hampton) and hike the gorge one way.

5

Beauty Spot Bald and Stamping Ground Ridge

Total Distance: 2–3 miles

Hiking Time: 1½ hours

Vertical Rise: About 100 feet

Rating: Easy

Map: USGS Unicoi

These two easy hikes feel like the top of the world—excellent for a good-weather picnic and spectacular views anytime. Bring children, a blanket, binoculars, and maybe even a kite. Avoid this area, however, if there is any chance of thunderstorms. Summer is the best time for these two hikes; the elevation and breezes provide cool weather. Fall foliage and winter views are also good.

How to Get There

These two hikes start on USFS 230, a gravel road that runs between Indian Grave Gap on TN 395, and Iron Mountain Gap on TN 107.

From Johnson City, drive south on US 23 (soon to become I-26) to the Erwin Main Street exit. Turn right onto Main Street and drive three blocks to a traffic light at 10th Street (TN 395/NC 197). Look for a forest service sign for ROCK CREEK AND BEAUTY SPOT. Turn left at the light and drive 6 miles to Indian Grave Gap on the Tennessee–North Carolina state line. Turn right onto gravel USFS 230 and drive about 2 miles to the Beauty Spot parking area on the right. For Stamping Ground Ridge, continue on USFS 230 for about 4 miles to a parking area on the left.

The Hikes

Southern Appalachian balds have no trees— that's what makes them bald. Usually, balds form on the highest peaks of a ridge. However, from both balds on this hike, you can look up to Unaka Mountain—at least 500 feet higher—and see a full head of spruce

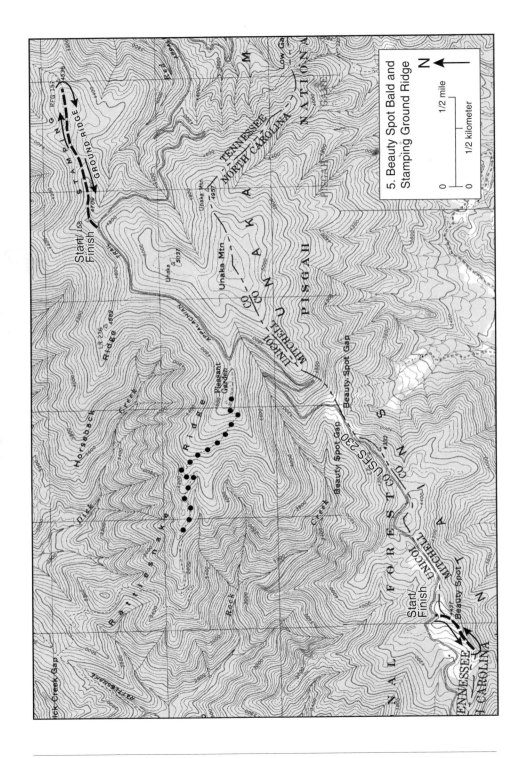

5. Beauty Spot Bald and Stamping Ground Ridge

trees. The two kinds of balds described here—grass bald and heath bald—have different origins and habitats, but both provide outstanding views and unusual plants. Grass balds in the southern Appalachians present two mysteries: How did they form and remain stable, and why are trees and bushes now encroaching from the edges? Some mountaintops and ridges that held grass balds for the last few hundred years are now completely forested. The forest and park services maintain others by mowing and cutting trees. Forest managers have also pastured cows and goats on the grass balds to keep them open. Grazing and fires may have served that purpose in the past, but ecologists still have differing theories about how the balds developed in the first place. Heath balds are less mysterious: The thin, acidic soil on steep or damaged high places simply cannot support tree roots. The shrubs that grow there specialize in conserving water; most of them have waxy or tough leathery leaves.

Beauty Spot Bald

From the fenced Beauty Spot parking area, walk up the hill on a path through the grass, which may be waist-high unless the forest service has mowed recently. At the high point (4,437 feet) a cleared area marks the spot where the Appalachian Trail (AT) crosses the bald. You should be able to see white blazes on posts in both directions. To the left, the AT descends to a forested path and then to Beauty Spot Gap. In the near view Unaka Mountain, covered with a dark growth of spruce trees, rises to 5,180 feet, and in the distance you can see Roan, Beech, and Grandfather Mountains. The rest of the horizon is filled with the waves and waves of Pisgah and Cherokee National Forests, with Erwin nestled in a valley to the west.

That's when it's clear, of course; in fog or light rain the bald can seem like another world. A note of caution, though: Heavy fog can disorient hikers who get just a few feet off the path.

Turn right and hike about half a mile on the open part of the bald until you reach thin trees and a path that leads right to USFS 230. Along the way look for goldenrod, yarrow, and wild sunflowers growing above the grass, and cinquefoil, violets, and gentians (which bloom in late summer) beside the trail. High patches of blackberries grow on the left, and clematis (virgin's bower) and dodder (a parasitic, non-chlorophyll plant with tiny white flowers and stringy yellow or orange stems) climb them. In spring you can find wild strawberries near the trail, but the real feast comes in August: highbush blueberries. About halfway between the summit and the trees, push through the grass on the right to 10-foot-tall blueberry bushes (with plenty of fruit within reach) and enjoy. Take a few home for blueberry pancakes. On a windy day the shelter of the blueberry bushes and a few hawthorns provides a good picnic spot. The blackberries taste just as good, and you may find more of them around the edges of the bald.

Return to the summit and either explore in the other direction or return to the parking area.

Stamping Ground Ridge

From the Stamping Ground Ridge parking area, you'll find a path between clumps of rhododendron to the right. Since this trail angles away from USFS 230, you will leave traffic noise behind and be surrounded by thick bushes. The gently descending trail over bare rock indicates the fragility of the heath bald community—wherever people have walked, nothing except a few flat lichens can grow. Beside the path lichens, club mosses, wintergreen, and trailing arbutus survive in thin soil. The ground cover looks and feels like a rug that could be rolled up from the bedrock. Try not to step on these plants—lichens serve as pioneers, holding bits of soil (made up partly of decayed fragments of their own bodies) that support the other plants. Lichens grow very slowly and can't recover from foot traffic. Several kinds of mosses and club mosses (including a furry, branched species) live with the lichens. They also grow slowly in this difficult environment; don't sit on them for your picnic.

Mountain laurels, blueberry bushes, rhododendrons, sand myrtles, and huckleberries tower over the carpet of ground plants. Most of the rhododendron here is Catawba rhododendron, which prefers high-elevation, open habitats. Its leaves are shorter and more rounded than those of the rosebay rhododendron that crowds creeks below; its pink-to-lavender flowers appear in June. The shrubs also depend on the pioneer lichens and mosses that created the soil in deeper pockets of the rock surface. Fire cherry, serviceberry, and a few other trees grow among the shrubs but stay small.

Views here, framed by rhododendron, include Roan Mountain ahead and Unaka Mountain to the right.

Walk down the bedrock path to an area of sandy soil (and trail erosion) with a tree cover of spruce, serviceberry, and beech. Less than a mile from the parking lot, Stamping Ground Ridge Trail meets Limestone Cove Trail in an open beech forest with billowy grass and soft moss patches. The grass is hardy and a fine place to sit for a picnic.

> *It's difficult to classify lichens, because each species contains one species of fungus and another of alga. The two have a relationship in which the fungi attach to a surface, absorb water and minerals, and hold (or perhaps capture) the algae, which make food through photosynthesis. Still, botanists have named more than 400 species in the southern Appalachians and divided them into three broad groups. Crustose lichens lie flat on a surface, almost as if they had been painted on, and include the gray-green ones seen here along with orange, pink, brown, and white versions seen on other hikes in this guide. Foliose lichens look like small leaves spreading out on the surface and can be seen between the edge of the trail and the thicker growth. Fruticose lichens have stalks that project above the surface; an example here is the reindeer moss that forms sea green mounds a little way back from the edge. These mounds feel sharp and brittle on dry days and soft and spongy in the rain. Another foliose lichen, British soldiers, has bright red tops on green stalks and grows in a few spots on this heath bald.*

Other Hiking Options

1. The Appalachian Trail goes south from Beauty Spot to Indian Grave Gap (2.3 miles). You could hike from Indian Grove Gap to Beauty Spot and back, or you could arrange a car shuttle and do it one way.

2. Going north, the AT reaches Unaka

A thru-hiker along the Appalachian Trail

Mountain in 3.3 miles with a 1,000-foot elevation gain. The spruce cover on the mountaintop provides a dark, secluded campsite or lunch spot for a hot day.

3. Limestone Cove Trail descends 2.8 miles from Stamping Ground Ridge Trail to the Limestone Cove Recreation Area, off TN 107. The trail is similar to Rattlesnake Ridge Trail (Hike 6), which also passes through the Unaka Mountain Wilderness Area and probably provides hiking privacy. You could hike it one way with a car shuttle or get some serious aerobic exercise by hiking both ways.

6

Rattlesnake Ridge (USFS 26)

Total Distance: 6 miles

Hiking Time: 4½ hours

Vertical Rise: 2,500 feet

Rating: Difficult because of elevation gain

Map: USGS Unicoi

Trail Marking: Yellow blazes, metal tags

This steep climb from the Rock Creek Recreation Area through the Unaka Mountain Wilderness Area passes mature forest that clearly reveals how vegetation changes with the elevation. It's rated difficult going up, but a car shuttle would make it a breeze coming down. An all-season hike, it might be best in fall and winter because of fall colors and the chance of snow scenes at the top. Northern exposure and high elevation make this area cool all summer. Mountain laurel and rhododendron bloom in June.

How to Get There

From Johnson City, drive south on US 23 (soon to become I-26) to the Erwin Main Street exit. Turn right onto Main Street and drive three blocks to a traffic light at 10th Street (TN 395). Look for a forest service sign for ROCK CREEK AND BEAUTY SPOT. Turn left at the light and drive 3 miles to Rock Creek Campground on the left. Hiker parking is by the bathrooms. In winter the campground is closed; park near the gate or at a small pullout just beyond the campground entrance.

The Hike

Designated in 1986, the Unaka Mountain Wilderness Area contains four excellent but little-used trails with nearby forest service campgrounds. Rattlesnake Ridge Trail climbs from near Erwin to the top of the state-line ridge and provides views of Unaka Mountain, Beauty Spot, and the North Carolina mountains.

From the campground bathroom building, walk up the road past campsites and a ONE WAY sign. Cross a gate into a grassy

EASTMAN CREDIT UNION
ECU BESIDE YOU

Eastman Credit Union
800-999-2328
www.ecu.org

Date: 05-28-2015

Time: 03:11:57 PM

Member Name:

Alexander Scott Williams

CB#: 1225 Branch: 722 Term: 4668

Teller#: 1320076

Member #: XXXXX00969

Acct #:XXXX38853

Seq #: 2358

EL   -$3,000.00

Item Count: 1

Transfer : 101938796

Total TXN: -$3,000.00

New Balance: $625.79

Memo: transfer 1 of 2

Authentication Used:Picture
                    ID/Scanned

Received	Disbursed
$1	$1
$2	$2
$5	$5
$10	$10
$20	$20
$50	$50
$100	$100
Coin	Coin
Total	Total

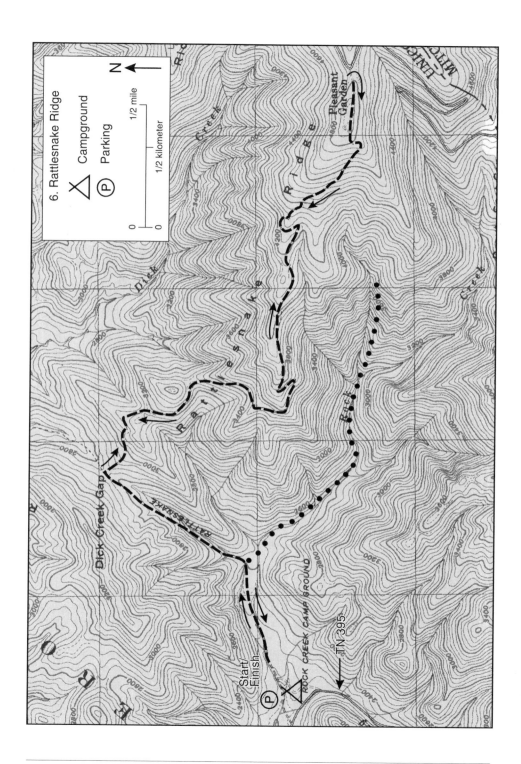

spot that has an information board with a map and regulations on the left. Continue on a gravel road and turn left to cross a wooden bridge, part of a bike trail. As soon as the bike trail goes on straight, Rattlesnake Ridge Trail swings right and enters the Unaka Mountain Scenic Area. After crossing a small creek and one of the few downhill sections on the hike, climb a bench above the creek through solid rhododendron, which will keep you cool. On the trailbank under the rhododendron and hemlock, look for gay wings. Sometimes called flowering wintergreen, these small, relatively rare flowers produce fringed pink flowers with rounded wings (petals sticking sideways from the main flower) in late April. The rest of the year the leaves lie flat and look like wintergreen or partridgeberry leaves.

Cross the creek again and ascend on the rocky trail through a more open area with doghobble along and possibly reaching into your pathway. A sign at the next creek crossing reassures you. Continue up to a switchback and ascend to a mostly deciduous forest of Fraser magnolia, chestnut oak, hickory, beech, and maple. A series of switchbacks leads through drier spots that host plants adapted to dry, southern exposure: mountain laurel replacing the rhododendron, and trailing arbutus and galax. At about 0.7 mile the trail leaves the scenic area; you'll know because 0.2 mile farther there is a five-way junction of horse, bike, and ATV trails. Find Rattlesnake Ridge Trail somewhat hidden in thick rhododendron to the right. A sign and registration box show the border of the Unaka Mountain Wilderness Area, and here the climbing begins in earnest. Wilderness trails have few blazes, but in this case no other trails branch off.

After a rhododendron tunnel, the trail repeats the pattern of sliding around to the south-facing slope, with its mountain laurels, pines, and blueberry bushes. Openings to the right provide views of other ridges. After a level spot (with a metal trail marking) the trail climbs an open, rocky hillside with bracken fern and ground pine alongside. Galax, wintergreen, and trailing arbutus leaves here have a deep burgundy color in fall and winter, the better to warm themselves by absorbing sunlight after the tree leaves have fallen. In late winter these burgundy leaves can start working on warm days and give new leaves a head start. A switchback sends you back to a rhododendron tunnel with moss and wood fern.

At about 2.5 miles the trail passes the first few spruce trees and then turns left into an open beech forest with long, billowy grass. A deciduous holly lives here: a multitrunked thin tree with red berries in winter and knobby blunt thorns on the twigs. A faint fork appears to the right; continue left through the beech grove and enter a rutted trail through a heath bald, which may be overgrown with greenbrier and laurel. Catawba rhododendron, with shorter, rounded leaves and pink-to-lavender flowers, replaces the rosebay rhododendron. Catawba rhododendron lives at higher elevations and drier conditions—it and the spruce trees tell you how much you have climbed. More blueberries and blackberries may provide snacks in season as the trail becomes more rutted, and soon an indication that you are nearing the end of your climb appears: trash. People visiting Pleasant Gardens from USFS 230 just above walk down a few hundred yards; why they drop trash when they are so close to their cars and a trash can cannot be explained.

Emerge into the large parking lot of Pleasant Gardens with a stone wall. Beauty Spot, a grassy bald, is visible to the right, and spruce-covered Unaka Mountain looms slightly to the left.

Heath bald with spruce trees

Rattlesnake Ridge (USFS 26)

Retrace your steps into the wilderness area. The return trip is easier on your lungs but harder on your knees.

Other Hiking Options

1. Arrange a car shuttle and hike this trail downward only.

2. The Appalachian Trail runs along the other side of USFS 230. The best places to get on it are at Beauty Spot (about 3 miles south of Pleasant Garden on USFS 230) and Indian Grave Gap (at the junction of TN 395 and USFS 230 on the state line). From Indian Grave Gap to the top of Unaka Mountain is 5.3 miles; from Beauty Spot to Unaka Mountain is 3.2 miles. Beauty Spot itself (a walk of 100 yards from the parking area; Hike 5) is worth a visit, especially in August when the blueberries are ripe.

3. Rock Creek Falls (Hike 7) is nearby.

4. Limestone Cove Trail descends 2.8 miles from Stamping Ground Ridge Trail to the Limestone Cove Recreation Area, off TN 107. The trail is similar to Rattlesnake Ridge Trail, which also passes through the Unaka Mountain Wilderness Area and probably provides hiking privacy. You could hike it one way with a car shuttle or get some serious aerobic exercise by hiking both ways.

7

Rock Creek Falls (USFS 148)

Total Distance: 4.5 miles

Hiking Time: 3–4 hours

Vertical Rise: 1,000 feet

Rating: Difficult

Map: USGS Unicoi

A dogleg waterfall and a long rippling cascade are just two of the payoffs for this steep aerobic climb. This all-season hike is relatively cool in summer and stunning in winter after a few subzero days. There are several creek crossings that can be dangerous in high water or thick ice and snow, however. Children will enjoy this hike if they're experienced hikers; if not, you'll end up carrying them.

How to Get There

From Johnson City, drive south on US 23 (soon to become I-26) to the Erwin Main Street exit. Turn right onto Main Street and drive three blocks to a traffic light at 10th Street (TN 395). Look for a forest service sign for ROCK CREEK AND BEAUTY SPOT. Turn left at the light and drive 3 miles to Rock Creek Campground on the left. Hiker parking is by the bathrooms. In winter the campground is closed; park near the gate or at a small pull-out just beyond the campground entrance.

The Hike

A Civilian Conservation Corps (CCC) crew built this campground and some of the trails in the 1930s. Visit the creek-fed rock swimming pool, sometimes occupied by albino trout, behind the bathroom building. Two hikes start from the campground—this one and Rattlesnake Ridge Trail (Hike 6)—and several others are nearby, so a camping-hiking trip here could be fun.

In 1986, Congress designated the Unaka Mountain Wilderness Area, approximately 1 by 3 miles. As a wilderness area, it can be used only for nonmotorized recre-

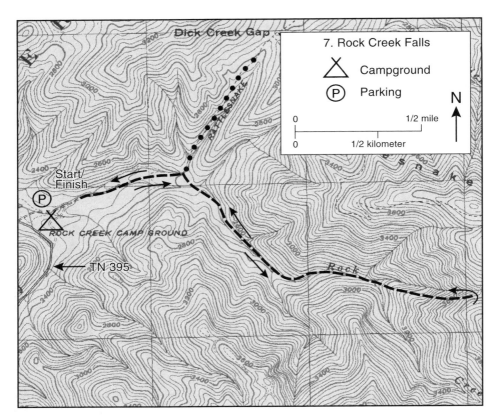

ation and is protected from logging, road building, and other intrusions. Rock Creek runs north, and the well-shaded valley may be cool and pleasant on hot summer days. This hike could be combined with a picnic and some foot cooling at the falls.

From the campground bathroom building, walk up the road past campsites and a ONE WAY sign. Cross a gate into a grassy spot that has an information board with a map and regulations on the left. Continue on a gravel road; soon a bridge crosses the creek to the left and Rock Creek Falls Trail continues straight. Mountain bikes share the trail until the bridge, but it's foot traffic only past there.

Trails in wilderness areas have entrance signs and usually registration boxes. The

forest service wants to know each trail's use pattern, so sign in. Hemlock and rhododendron cover the hillside and creekbanks here, but witch hazel branches hang right over the WILDERNESS sign. This shrub/tree grows throughout East Tennessee and can be seen on almost every hike in this guide. It blooms in late fall or winter when nothing else is flowering, but it usually chooses a warm spell when a few pollinators are on the job.

Ascend through more rhododendron into an open deciduous forest of yellow birch, striped maple, Fraser magnolia, and red oak. You'll soon swing left and descend to the creek, starting on the pattern for this hike. The old logging road that the trail follows crosses back and forth, while the creek

Red oak catkins

runs relatively straight down its valley. The first crossing may be the hardest; it should tell you if you've picked a good day for this hike. Bridges and cables were once here, probably built by the CCC, but the bridges have washed away and the cables can give you iron splinters. Find some good stepping-stones.

Climb up, drop down to cross the creek, climb again. The trail gets narrower and rockier as it climbs above creek level. From a higher perspective, you can see how difficult it must have been to build a logging road up here, and as you climb farther more large trees grow, apparently missed by the loggers. Also from up here, you can look down at the tops of trees; in spring you may get a view of Fraser magnolia flowers, with large creamy white petals. Rock Creek drops quickly with many cascades and small waterfalls.

From high on the right side of the creek at about 1.5 miles, look for the lower falls, actually a cascade. Large hemlocks frame the view. Apparently many hikers have stopped here, because the trail gets rougher as it twists around fallen trees and rocks. Blazes mark its course, which may have slippery muddy spots in wet weather. Lush vegetation may reach out and get your clothes wet, but continue on for less than half a mile to the upper falls in a horseshoe-shaped basin. Rock Creek tumbles off the edge of the rim, falls about a third of the way, takes a sudden right turn at a boulder, and then falls to a rock pool. You can approach the falls on boulders, but they may be slippery from spray. To the right of the falls, there is a small path that you can take along the rock face for a better view.

Jack-in-the-pulpit and a few small rhododendrons grow from cracks or tiny ledges. The sandstone here is blocky. The pile of boulders at the base of the falls shows that freeze-thaw action probably took place here for millennia.

Yellow birches, recognizable by their yellowish bark with horizontal curly peels, grow at the base of the falls. The view down the creek from here shows the solid green of rhododendron and hemlock, while a pretty deciduous forest grows down from the rock face on the other side.

Other Hiking Options

1. Rattlesnake Ridge (Hike 6) starts from the same trailhead.
2. The Appalachian Trail crosses TN 395/ NC 197 at Indian Grave Gap, 3 miles beyond Rock Creek Campground. From here, you can hike north to Beauty Spot (2.3 miles; Hike 5) or to the top of Unaka Mountain (5.3 miles).
3. Hike south on the Appalachian Trail from Indian Grave Gap for a downhill plunge to the Nolichucky River (7 miles). I recommend a car shuttle for this one, unless you prefer a very strenuous 14-mile round-trip.

Rime ice frosts the higher elevations in winter.

Smokies Elevation Sampler: Sugarlands Valley, Cove Hardwood, and Spruce-Fir Nature Trails

Total Distance: Less than 1 mile each

Hiking Time: 30–40 minutes each, with 30 minutes of driving between

Vertical Rise: Minimal; some climbing on Cove Hardwood

Rating: Easy

Map: Great Smoky Mountains trail map; USGS Gatlinburg; USGS Mount Le Conte; USGS Clingmans Dome

There are two ways to see Canadian vegetation zones: First, go to Canada, or second, climb to an elevation of 6,000 feet in the southern Appalachians. These three easy loop trails and the drives between them reveal the gradual habitat changes that go along with cooler temperatures and other elevation factors. This set of trails is best hiked in late April; all three have good wildflower displays. Clingmans Dome Road (access to Spruce-Fir) closes from December to March, but the other two trails would be delightful in snow. Spruce-Fir is cool in the hottest summer weather and doesn't attract the crowds headed for Clingmans Dome. Children will love these trails. Sugarlands Valley Nature Trail is paved and wheelchair accessible, with several rest benches.

How to Get There
All three nature trails are on the Newfound Gap Road through the Smokies. The following directions start at Sugarlands Visitor Information Center. For Sugarlands Valley Nature Trail, drive 0.5 mile and park on the left. For Cove Hardwood Nature Trail, drive 5 miles to the trailhead on the right (part of Chimneys Picnic Area). Park in the first set of parking places. For Spruce-Fir Nature Trail, drive 13 miles to Newfound Gap, turn right onto Clingmans Dome Road, and drive 2.7 miles to the trailhead on the left.

Sugarlands Valley Nature Trail
Relatively flat land, good soil, and plenty of clean water brought settlers to this land during the 1800s. They lived on corn and hogs, sold apples and moonshine whiskey,

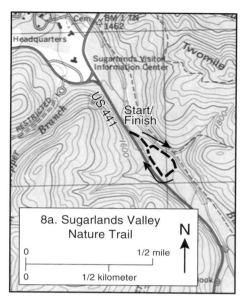

8a. Sugarlands Valley Nature Trail

N

0   1/2 mile

0   1/2 kilometer

and built schools and hotels. On this trail you can see reminders of their years in the Smokies: chimneys and forest-growth patterns that indicate old fields. Interpretive signs and photographs show that this valley was open farmland a century ago and looked much like other present-day valleys outside the park. The signs also discuss the successional changes as woods returned and describe plants and animals that live here now.

Enter the woods to the left of the parking lot and walk to the first creek. Turn left to go clockwise and approach the West Prong of the Pigeon River (named for the passenger pigeons that once flocked along lower parts of it). Large, well-made chimneys, some for two-story houses, indicate a prosperous community. In the late 1920s the park commission raised enough money to buy these homesteads, using government condemnation for the first time to create a national park now visited by millions.

The trail swings right to parallel the West Prong through a cool hemlock grove. Few flowers grow under hemlock, but you may see some galax, partridgeberry, and toothwort (which grows anywhere there is moisture and appears on all three of these trails). Note the clear water of the West Prong running between boulders; the mountains above hold water like a sponge, and creeks will run even during long droughts as that water slowly trickles out from many springs. You might also see bits of leaves and twigs stuck in trees above the banks from the last flood. This site provided ideal settlement land because the creek supplied water all year, but the fields and houses could be located above the flood zone. Look for sycamore trees leaning over the West Prong.

Near the next curve look to the right for the stars of this trail in May: pink lady's slippers under the hemlocks. Their leaves, a pair of dark green corduroy-lined ovals, can be seen all year. These orchids can grow in shade and acidic soil because they take most of their food from the roots of trees. But they can't take it directly—a fungus acts as the go-between and profits from transferring food from the host to the semiparasite.

The next curve returns you to the trail fork and the parking lot. Note the thin sweetgums, maples, tulip trees, and beeches here, interspersed with shorter hemlocks. The hardwoods can germinate on former fields, while the hemlocks have to wait until the other trees prepare the soil for them. In a few decades hemlocks may be taller than their benefactors. Several Fraser magnolia trees grow near the fork. These deciduous relatives of the waxy-leafed southern magnolia have 18- to 24-inch leaves with lobes (like earlobes) at their bases. Settlers in the Sugarlands Valley tapped maple trees for syrup.

Cove Hardwood Nature Trail

I have tried to avoid overused trails in this book; Cove Hardwood is an exception. Famous for its flowers, it attracts botany classes, school groups, photographers, and refugees from Michigan snow. Try to visit on weekdays, during rain, around sunrise (great for birdsong), or in winter. If you pull in and see five school buses, wait until later. On the other hand, you may enjoy watching kids finding nature awesome.

Drive into Chimneys Picnic Area and park as soon as you can on the right. Climb a steep bank to a group picnic area with a curved stone wall. Ascend to the right of the wall past a rock face with (if it's spring) hepaticas, jack-in-the-pulpits, phlox, and other flowers at eye level—a good place to use a hand lens and a flower book. Cross a tiny creek, ascend another hill with a bank of even more blooms, and then turn left for the spectacle of a carpet of flowers: phacelia, trillium, cohosh, dwarf ginseng, squirrel corn. If you don't have a flower book, usually someone (perhaps a fifth-grader) will be delighted to identify plants for you.

Cove hardwood refers to Appalachian habitats in which surrounding mountains protect a secluded valley; from here you can look down to the opening of the cove, and behind you (probably hidden by foliage) stand 5,000- to 6,000-foot mountains. The rich environment encourages a tremendous variety of trees, wildflowers, and other species. Coves that face north, as this one does, retain more moisture, giving them even more species diversity.

At a fork turn left to hike clockwise, and climb a modest hill with so many things to look at that no one will complain. If it's damp, 3- to 4-inch millipedes will be climbing tree trunks. In the rain red-cheeked salamanders may be out on the trail or on fallen logs. Silver bell, maple, and yellow buckeye trees

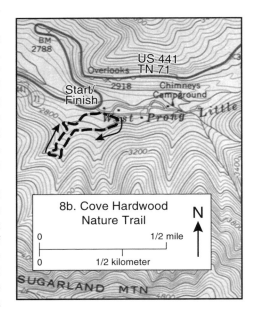

8b. Cove Hardwood Nature Trail

grow tall and straight in the mature forest. Deciduous trees don't shade the ground until May, and the spring flowers take advantage of the sun streaming through the branches. Compare the flower carpet on the left, under mostly deciduous trees, with the brown, needle-covered areas under hemlock stands on the right. A few summer and fall flowers grow here also, but the tree leaves grab most the sunlight.

At the top of the hill rest on the bench; the huge tree in front is a yellow buckeye, and the wavy or rippling pattern on its bark will help you pick out other buckeyes in the cove below.

Head down. More flowers, and long moss-covered logs. Where a small creek runs parallel to the trail, look for brook lettuce in the water or growing on rocks. Continuing down, you enter a hemlock grove, so you can stop identifying for a while. Large trees with dozens of root sprouts are American basswoods, relatives of the European linden.

To the right, next to the creek, is a large patch of wild ginger—lift some leaves gently to see if the maroon and cream flowers are out. You won't see this species on any other part of this trail. Continue down through a trampled section, cross the creek, and curve right again to pass boulders with flowers and ferns on top. The trail climbs a bit through open woods to reach the fork; turn left to return to your car.

If you're hiking this trail with children in spring, assign two or three kinds of flowers to each child and have them point out "their" flowers to the others. Jack-in-the-pulpits are the hardest.

Spruce-Fir Nature Trail

When glaciers covered most of the continent, northern animals retreated south, and when the glaciers melted, some of those northern species remained on the cool mountaintops. Plants also relocated—by scattering seeds ahead of the inch-by-inch advance of ice. Glacial periods thus left islands of northern ecosystems on high-elevation Appalachian habitats. Spruce-Fir Nature Trail, with plants and animals more typical of Canada than of Cove Hardwood Nature Trail, demonstrates one of these remnant habitats. Red spruce and Fraser fir, both evergreen trees that can withstand freezing and wind, dominate the forest, while a few smaller deciduous trees and shrubs live underneath them. In the last 30 years an exotic insect has killed many Fraser firs, which may also be weakened by air pollution. You will see dead fir trees and fallen spruce trees, a lot of blackberries taking advantage of the sun, and a crowd of young spruces and firs growing up.

Head into the woods from the parking area and turn right onto a trail of black soil that may have muddy spots. Spring beauty, toothwort, and trout lily bloom in April, and

small trees germinate on mossy nurse logs. A fork at a bench starts the loop; turn left in an open, grassy area and descend into thicker woods. There are no hemlocks here—most of them grow below 4,500 feet. Red spruce, appearing at about 4,000 feet, and Fraser fir, mostly above 5,000 feet, used to tower over ridgetops. The bottom part of this loop, away from the ridgeline, looks somewhat healthier with a lot of medium-sized spruce and fir, but as you start up the other side you enter tangles of blackberries and fallen tree trunks. Grab a blackberry cane; at this elevation they have very few thorns.

Botanists have identified study plots of relatively healthy Fraser fir in the park and hope to find some resistant forms or some conditions in which the trees can thrive. The balsam woolly adelgid—the insect that kills them—entered the park in the 1960s and spread slowly; botanists don't know if this forest will recover or what plant species will become dominant. Nesting birds, small

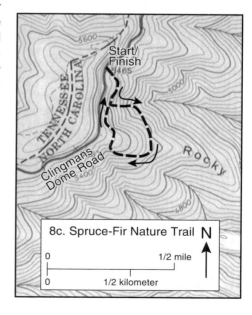

8c. Spruce-Fir Nature Trail N

0   1/2 mile

0   1/2 kilometer

This chimney made of river rocks can be seen along Sugarlands Valley Nature Trail.

50 Hikes in the Tennessee Mountains

mammals, salamanders, and other animals may be affected by the die-off of Fraser firs. Huge spruce trees fall during storms because they stand out over the dead firs, and also when the tangled root mats they once shared with the firs decay.

At the third bench notice exposed quartz. It feels smooth compared to the sandstone, mainly because it is igneous, or formed from melted materials. Extreme heat and pressure forced molten silicate crystals and water through cracks in the sandstone, leaving deposits like this or white veins and swirls across rock faces. Fire cherry and mountain ash, small high-elevation trees, live near the rocks.

Yellow birch, the most common deciduous tree here, becomes more frequent as you reach the top of the loop. One near the road takes the prize for weirdest stilt roots. These birches grow at all elevations (and can be seen on all three of these hikes). Look for the heart-shaped, crinkled leaves of witch hobble, or viburnum, a shrub found only at high elevations. It produces clusters of white flowers in May and orange berries in fall. The leaves turn a rich red or burgundy color in October.

Descend past mossy logs to the first bench and return to the parking lot in that muddy section (or walk along the road if the trail is too wet).

The three communities in this elevation sampler show very different responses to environmental disturbances from human activities. The spruce and fir community, with only two dominant tree species, changed dramatically when the firs started dying; these ridges may never recover. Cove hardwoods at lower elevations have more diversity and have weathered many

changes, including logging and the loss of the American chestnut. The Sugarlands Valley endured even greater disturbance—farming—and is quickly growing new forest. Air pollution from coal-fired plants, auto emissions, and industries affects all three communities, but the pollutants are most concentrated in high-elevation communities, which have the least resilience.

Other Hiking Options

1. Other nature trail loops start from Cosby Campground, Elkmont Campground, the Ogle Homestead on Cherokee Orchard Road, and behind Sugarlands Visitor Center.

2. Chimney Tops Trail, between the first tunnel and the loop of Newfound Gap Road, is a steep 2-mile (one way) hike to two huge lumps of exposed rock that tower over Cove Hardwood Trail and provide good views. The trail is overused on weekends because people think that it will be easy. (If you see buses in the parking lot, come back another time.) But on a quiet day it could make a good addition to the nature trails. Climbing out on the Chimney rocks can be dangerous; a park sign will remind you.

3. Another trail off the Newfound Gap Road, also busy but also beautiful, is Alum Cave, the shortest trail (5 miles) to Mount Le Conte. Even if you don't want to go that far, the trail offers a cascading creek, Arch Rock, Inspiration Point, and Alum Cave itself, all within 2.5 miles of the road.

4. The walk to Clingmans Dome tower offers a stark look at dead fir trees and, in contrast, a patch of relatively healthy firs just underneath the tower.

9

Porters Creek

Total Distance: 7.4 miles

Hiking Time: 4 hours

Vertical Rise: 1,600 feet

Rating: Easy, but moderate toward the end

Maps: Smokies map; USGS Mount Le Conte

Easy walking, old-growth forest, tumbling creeks, and famous spring wildflower displays make this an excellent introduction to Smokies hiking. Though heavily used on spring weekends, Porters Creek usually provides a refuge from crowded Gatlinburg, just a few miles away. This is a good all-season family hike, with the easier parts at the beginning. Take a flower book and hand lens.

How to Get There

From Gatlinburg, take US 321 east for 5.9 miles to the Greenbrier entrance to the park. Turn right and drive 4 miles to the end of the road; you can park near a gate. The road is first paved for a mile, then turns to gravel that's rough in spots and not open to buses or large campers. The park may close it in bad weather.

The Hike

European settlers crossed the Smokies soon after the Revolutionary War, making their homes in sheltered coves with abundant food, water, wood, and room to farm. To get to Greenbrier Cove they climbed through Dry Sluice Gap, and the route they took challenges today's hikers with high-tech boots and no livestock to worry about. Greenbrier Cove had schools, hotels, stores, roads, and many generations of families before the park commission bought their holdings in the late 1920s. This hike starts above the cove's community centers, but passes homesites and cemeteries.

After the gate, Greenbrier Road continues and rises higher above Porters Creek.

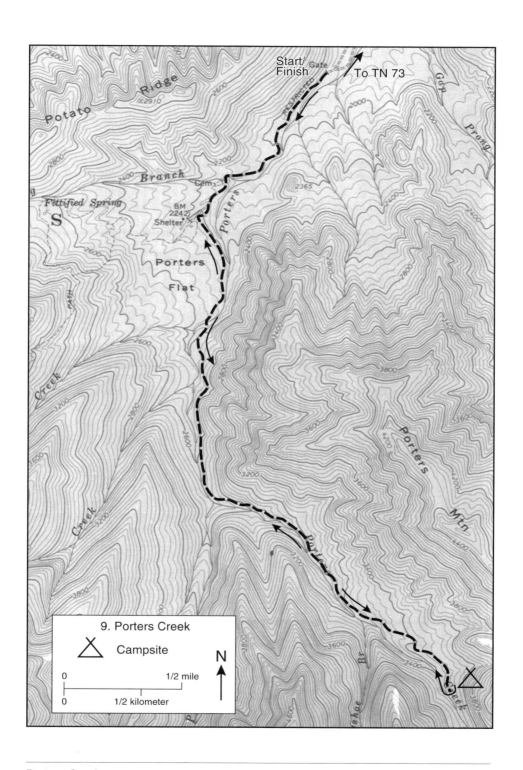

Mossy rocks and the roadbanks show off jack-in-the-pulpits, foamflowers, and violets in spring; as you proceed up the road, more flower species appear. In summer rhododendrons, asters, and goldenrods bloom.

At 0.4 mile look for stone steps on the right leading up to an old homesite. A faint trail passes a depression where the house stood, now filled with wood betony, shrubs of hearts-a-bustin', and poison ivy. Stone walls beyond surround former fields and outbuildings. Imagine sitting on the front porch here, watching wagons, horses, and your friends passing by on the road below.

Continue up the road, which is at about the same level as Porters Creek, and then cross a side creek on a footlog. The road curves left, passes a large patch of dwarf-crested iris, and rises into a hemlock forest with very little undergrowth. The scattered ground plants include partridgeberry and a few showy orchids. More stone steps to the right lead to a small cemetery in the hemlock shade. Descendants of Greenbrier Cove settlers come back to tend the graves, and some people have been buried here since the park was established in 1934.

Just past the cemetery, at 1 mile, the road splits to make a traffic turnaround. Porters Creek Trail goes left from the turnaround on a bank high above the creek. For a short side trip or lunch spot, turn right off the traffic circle to reach a restored typical homeplace. The cantilevered barn, springhouse, and two-story cabin represent a prosperous farm; boxwoods, daffodils, and a lilac bush show evidence of a well-tended yard. Native umbrella magnolias bloom in spring and cardinal flowers bloom in summer along the creek that runs through the springhouse. A new outhouse has been built behind the cabin. The area here and along the creek, known as Porters Flats, was once cleared for corn and potato fields, orchards, and pastures.

Return to Porters Creek Trail and enter a forest of tall trees on a real trail, though it may have been a narrow road at one time. Several mossy logs serve as nurse logs here, supporting saplings of hemlock, rhododendron, and yellow birch. Just before the trail curves left to descend to the creek, look for trillium leaves perched on these logs or rocks—these are painted trillium and have white flowers with deep pink designs painted across the inner surface of the petals. They prefer shaded woods like these and rarely associate with other trillium. Small single leaves of the same color and shape are young trillium; it takes a trillium plant several years to reach flowering age.

Then go down beside a boulder and cross Porters Creek on a high, angled log bridge (a lower one washed out in a flood in 1996) into the truly magical part of this hike—acres of wildflowers. (I can't help describing this as a spring wildflower hike, but it is beautiful in all seasons.) Hepatica, toothwort, spring beauty, and bloodroot make up the first wave of flowers, followed by trillium, Dutchman's-breeches, bishop's cap, squirrel corn, fringed phacelia, and rue anemone (all white so far). Geranium, buttercup, phlox, and fire pink add color. Metallic blue blister beetles, with swollen abdomens, useless wing, and spindly legs, may be stumbling through flower stems. Don't bother these inch-long insects—they produce a yellow oil that can causes blisters.

Swing to the right up the hill to find (of course) more flowers. At 1.9 miles from the start you'll reach Fern Branch Falls, a cascade on the right. Look for wild ginger and brook saxifrage in the creek as you cross on stepping-stones. Sitting stones are also available here. Look out to the left at mature

Using a hand lens to view a tulip tree flower

Porters Creek

forest with large tulip trees, basswoods, and buckeyes. Dutchman's pipe vine, with smooth, gray, tangled vines and plate-sized, heart-shaped leaves, climbs trees down the hillside, so you may get to see the curious pipe flowers. This vine is in the birthwort family, along with little brown jug and wild ginger; you can see the relationship in the heart-shaped leaves and fleshy flowers.

Past Fern Branch Falls the trail stays on a bench high above Porters Creek and passes through rhododendron and more hemlock. Even larger trees appear in the protected cove on the right. Look for a new flower, Clinton's lily (named for the first governor of New York), beside the trail. It produces a cluster of white flowers on top of an 8- to 18-inch stalk in May and blue-black berries in summer. Three or four broad, dark green leaves surround the base of the lily. Black cohosh, which has a long spike of white flowers, blooms in late summer. Its relative, doll's eyes, blooms in May but produces little round berries with a dark spot in each. The berries persist into fall and are poisonous, giving the plant another name: baneberry.

The trail keeps ascending gently (you may not even notice until you find how easy it is to return), and at 3.7 miles it reaches Backcountry Campsite 31, a spacious flat area shaded by hemlocks. A good spring and several sitting logs also make it comfortable, and once you see it you may want to plan a backpacking trip.

Return the same way, examining the flowers you missed on the way up.

Other Hiking Options

Greenbrier Cove is the access point for several Smokies trails, all beautiful: Brushy Mountain (4.2 miles; Hike 10), Ramsey Cascades (4 miles), Grapeyard Ridge (7.6 miles), and Old Settlers (15.6 miles).

10

Trillium Gap and Brushy Mountain

Total Distance: 6.2 miles

Hiking Time: 4 hours

Vertical Rise: 2,300 feet

Rating: Moderate

Maps: Smokies map; USGS Mount Le Conte

A waterfall, a boulder field, a beech gap, and a heath bald—this hike ranks high in habitat diversity and scenic variety. The first part, an easy walk to Grotto Falls, may attract crowds on nice weekends, but above the falls the hiking is a bit harder and much more private. You'll find abundant spring flowers, cool shade in summer, and outstanding fall colors from Brushy Mountain. It's just as beautiful in winter, and the extra 2 miles of hiking above the closed road will ensure privacy.

How to Get There

From Traffic Light 8 on US 441 in Gatlinburg, take Airport Road (Cherokee Orchard Road). At 1 mile bear right to enter the park, pass the Ogle Homestead, and bear right again to pass the Rainbow Falls Trailhead at 2.7 miles. Turn right onto Roaring Fork Motor Nature Trail (closed in winter) and drive 1.7 miles (4.4 miles from Traffic Light 8) to the Trillium Gap/Grotto Falls Trailhead. In winter, when Roaring Fork Road is closed, leave your car at the Rainbow Falls parking area, which adds 2 miles to each leg of this hike.

The Hike

Mount Le Conte, the third highest peak in the park at 6,593 feet, stands separate from the main crest of the Smokies, so the climb from its base is more than a mile. But the drive up to Cherokee Orchard takes care of part of the climb, and three long trails to the summit start here and meander up the north face of Le Conte. Rain clouds moving toward the Smokies from the west hit these

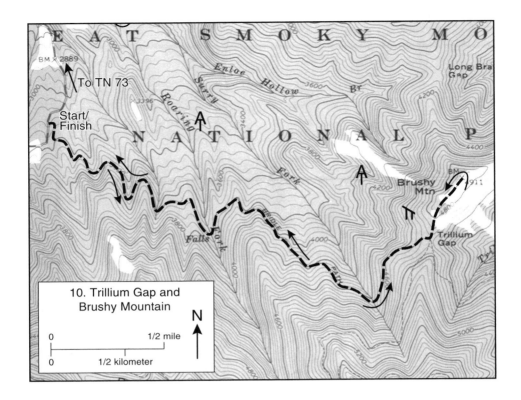

10. Trillium Gap and
Brushy Mountain

N

0   1/2 mile

0   1/2 kilometer

cool slopes and soak them; sunlight from the south has little chance of drying out hollows and valleys. So this hike provides moist habitats for plants, cool summer weather, and a good possibility of snow cover. The first part of Trillium Gap Trail heads southeast to cross creeks running from the mountaintop, and the largest of these, Roaring Fork, forms Grotto Falls. Until the 1930s the bases of these high, cool slopes were cultivated as apple orchards and landscape plant nurseries; near the Rainbow Falls Trailhead you can see old fruit trees and ornamental shrubs.

From the end of the parking lot, climb a well-worn bank to a wide trail through towering hemlocks. This area was too sheltered to serve as an orchard, but settlers nearby kept the big lumber companies from buying the

land, so this is a pocket of old-growth forest. Silverbells, beeches, Fraser magnolias, and sugar maples mix with the huge hemlocks. Rotting logs—a sure sign of mature forest—have moss, ferns, and saplings growing on them. Silverbell trees have tall, straight trunks with dark, flaky bark, but you are most likely to identify them in April when their white bell-shaped flowers carpet the trail.

Though it's possible to see bear or deer, they shy away from busy trails like this. But one local mammal, the red squirrel, announces its presence, probably because it knows what you have in that day pack. Red squirrels sit on high tree branches and make a surprising variety of chatters, chirps, and complaints. (Some people call them boomers.) If you stop for a picnic, they will invite themselves. You also may see chipmunks dashing across the trail, tails straight up, to and from holes between roots.

The trail rises out of the hemlock grove to a drier ridge with mountain laurel and galax, then returns to a shaded cove with a creek. Two hundred million years of erosion created a pattern of ridges and creeks that fan out from a summit. Here you are moving across the mountainside—over ridges and then across the creeks between them. Impenetrable tangles of rosebay rhododendron line the creeks but bloom sparsely in the north-facing, sheltered spots.

Each creek is a bit bigger than the last and has more white water, and then you round a larger ridge and descend to Roaring Fork and Grotto Falls. The water tumbles 30 feet over a ledge, and a grotto has been eroded out underneath where you can walk on slippery rocks. There are other stepping-stones in front of the falls, but high water can make this crossing dangerous. Roaring Fork loses more than a mile of elevation from a spring on Mount Le Conte to the West Prong of the Little Pigeon River in Gatlinburg.

Past the falls, the hiking becomes a bit steeper, but, since most people turn back at the falls, you'll have a private trail. Hillsides of deciduous trees—yellow buckeye, yellow birch, maple, silverbell—alternate with the dark hemlock, allowing a rich and varied ground cover of ferns and flowers. In September look for buckeyes on the trail. These shiny brown nuts grow in a plum-sized leathery fruit that splits to release three or four seeds—each with a flat side, a rounded side, and a pale spot (the buck's pupil?). Collect one and roll it between your hands to bring out the shiny red-brown grain pattern. Buckeyes grow mostly along creeks, and they cannot germinate on dry soil. The nuts are poisonous.

Becoming narrower and very rocky, the trail passes through a boulder field. Gaze up and down at a swath of rocks that look as if they had rolled down from a giant dump truck on the mountaintop. On north-facing slopes the extreme cold weather of the ice ages caused cracks in the bedrock; water then seeped into the cracks and froze, expanding them. Thousands of years of this broke off these great angular boulders, and later freezing and thawing brought them to the surface. Soil pockets between and on the rocks grow vigorous tangles of plants.

Cross a creek that cascades through and under the boulder field and continue up. Soon clumps of grass appear beside the trail—in the Smokies, grass usually means that you are getting near the top of something even when you can't see it yet. The land on each side of the trail flattens out, with grass as the main ground cover and beeches as the dominant trees. This beech gap (not a trillium in sight) formed between the high slopes of Mount Le Conte and the lower knob of Brushy Mountain, possibly because beech trees stand up to the wind that rushes through the gap. In early spring, spring beauty covers the ground; its small white flower has pink or red stripes inside like peppermint candy. Unfortunately, spring beauty bulbs taste good, and in some areas wild hogs dig them up, leaving a muddy mess and eroded soil.

To the right, Trillium Gap Trail heads up to the top of Mount Le Conte, and Brushy Mountain Trail down to Greenbrier Cove continues straight. To climb Brushy Mountain itself, turn left up a mossy trail that soon becomes a gully with rocks and poor footing. After a few hemlock and spruce trees, heath plants grow high above the trail and block any views. Members of the heath family (rhododendron, mountain laurel, sand myrtle, blueberry, and trailing arbutus) specialize in this environment of exposed, sandy

Painted trillium

soil. Some heath balds, or heath slicks, develop because a ridge is simply too steep to support the roots of trees; others, probably including this one, grow up on exposed rock after a fire. Mosses and mounds of fragile reindeer lichens, whose ancestors served as the soil-building pioneers of this heath bald, cover the ground. Try not to step on them. In May and June enjoy heath bald blossoms; in August eat the blueberries.

As you cross the summit of Brushy Mountain, you will be taller than the heath plants. You can look back at Mount Le Conte, and right to Charlies Bunion and the high crest of the Smokies, with several peaks over 6,000 feet. A spur trail to the left leads to an open area with a view of Greenbrier Cove and Mount Winnesoka, with the Tennessee River Valley in the distance.

Return the way you came, or explore part of upper Trillium Gap Trail.

Other Hiking Options

1. For a long, strenuous hike, turn right at Trillium Gap and hike the additional 3.7 miles to Le Conte Lodge. This rocky trail runs along the ridgeline that forms Brushy Mountain. Just before you reach Le Conte Lodge, you pass a spring that gives rise to Roaring Fork. Llamas use this trail to carry bed sheets and other supplies to Le Conte Lodge. If you meet them, be polite or they'll spit.

2. Continue along Roaring Fork Motor Nature Trail (not that you have a choice, since it's one way) and stop at the homesites and cemetery. About a mile down from the Trillium Gap parking area, Baskins Creek Trail leads left to a small waterfall in about 1 mile, and Grapeyard Ridge Trail sets off to the right for a 7.6-mile hike to Greenbrier Cove.

3. Arrange a car shuttle and hike from

Greenbrier Cove on Brushy Mountain Trail to Trillium Gap and then down to Roaring Fork Motor Nature Trail (8.2 miles).

4. On the way up to Cherokee Orchard, stop at the Ogle Homestead and take the Junglebrook Nature Trail—a loop past an old mill, two rocky creeks, hillsides of wildflowers, and the Ogle house and barn.

11

Appalachian Trail: Newfound Gap to Clingmans Dome

Distance: 8.4 miles (one way, including connection to Clingmans Dome parking lot)

Hiking Time: 5 hours

Vertical Rise: 1,500 feet

Rating: Difficult

Maps: Smokies map; USGS Clingmans Dome

Trail Marking: White blazes

Described here as a one-way hike, this trail has two access points along its route and good parking for car shuttles. This part of the Smokies is crowded on summer and fall weekends; though the trail receives little use, traffic jams may keep you from getting there. Mostly hilly and rocky, it probably won't suit young children, though sections make a good side trip (see "Other Hiking Options," below). The road from Newfound Gap to Clingmans Dome closes in winter (usually from December 1 to April 1, depending on weather); during winter you can hike on the trail or the road. Bring extra clothes and rain gear for this hike, even in summer.

How to Get There

From Sugarlands Visitor Center just outside Gatlinburg, drive 13 miles south on Newfound Gap Road (US 441) to Newfound Gap. To set up a car shuttle, pass Newfound Gap and turn right about 0.2 mile farther onto Clingmans Dome Road for the 8-mile trip to the parking lot. Leave one car here and return to Newfound Gap to begin the hike.

The Hike

The Appalachian Trail (AT) runs 70 miles along the highest peaks of the Smokies and neatly divides Tennessee from North Carolina. This section, about in the middle, has several distinctions: It is at least partly in Tennessee; it contains the highest point of the entire 2,160-mile AT (Clingmans Dome, at 6,643 feet, is 355 feet higher than Mount Washington); the whole section (except for a slight dip near the start) is above 5,000 feet; and its blackberries have no thorns. Though parallel to a busy road, it doesn't have many hikers (after all, why walk when you can drive?). In March and April many of the hikers you will meet have come 230 miles from Springer Mountain, Georgia, and intend to hike to Maine. If they're ready for a rest, they'll tell you about spring snowstorms, shelter mice, and life on the trail. They might also appreciate a home-baked brownie or two.

From Newfound Gap parking lot, cross US 441 (possibly the most dangerous part of the hike) to the end of a low stone wall, and look for the AT sign. The trail drops sharply left and passes between the highway retaining wall and a steep slope on the right. Sheltered below the wall and the high ridge, this hillside is covered with spongy mosses and ferns. Old-man's beard lichens hang from the trees like miniature Spanish moss. Yellow birch dominates the forest, with a few spruce and an understory of hobblebush. Spring beauty and trout lily bloom in April, sometimes under wet snow. The trail remains level for half a mile, then climbs 500 feet in the next half mile to warm you up. Then it descends into a beech gap— a shallow gap in the ridgeline that favors the growth of beeches and discourages spruces. A few yellow birches grow among the beeches, but they are easy to tell apart: Beeches have smooth gray bark, and yellow birches have curly yellow or brown bark. Thick grass carpets the beech gap, and spring beauties bloom above the grass. These flowers have edible tubers, and wild hogs will churn up the soil to eat them. A hog exclosure in the gap protects a part of this fragile environment; you can cross a metal grate stile, but the hogs can't. Nothing can protect these exposed beeches from a double threat, however—a scale insect that

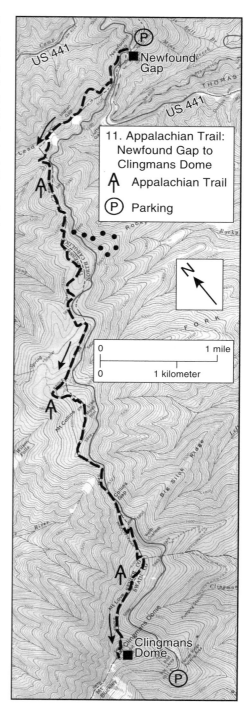

11. Appalachian Trail: Newfound Gap to Clingmans Dome

Ⱥ Appalachian Trail

Ⓟ Parking

feeds on the bark and brings with it a fatal fungus infection. Notice that many trees in this gap are dead.

From the other side of the hog exclosure, the trail rises into ridgetop evergreens—mostly red spruce, with a few Fraser firs. During most of the hike you will be between 5,500 and 6,500 feet—within the range of both these species, but the percentage of firs increases with the elevation. At Clingmans Dome (6,643 feet) firs outnumber spruces. All along this trail you will see skeletal dead firs, killed by the European balsam woolly adelgid (an insect related to aphids), which came to North America on imported plants and reached the Smokies in the 1960s.

After a little more climbing on log steps, descend through a patch of highbush blueberries into Indian Gap, where you'll see the road as you cross a grassy opening. Road Prong Trail, following the path of a cross-mountain trade road used until the 1920s, goes right to meet Chimney Tops Trail in 2.4 miles. Continue across the clearing to spruce woods and climb to 5,500 feet; you'll be above that elevation for the rest of the hike. At about 3 miles the trail runs along the side of the state-line ridge through muddy black soil. Trail workers built bog bridges here in the early 1980s; they're getting worn but will still keep your feet dry. A few springs flow from the left; look for one that comes out of a rock crack into a soup-bowl-sized basin of clear water. Continue through a thicket of young fir trees to the junction with Fork Ridge Trail to the left, which crosses Clingmans Dome Road and then drops into North Carolina (only 14 miles of hiking to the park's southern border). About 0.2 mile farther, on level, cushioned trail, the AT meets Sugarland Mountain Trail to the right; from here it's only 16.1 miles of hiking to the park's northern border. Half a mile down

> ## Trail Maintenance

Volunteers maintain the Appalachian Trail, organized by maintaining clubs and the Appalachian Trail Conference (ATC) in Harpers Ferry, West Virginia. The Smoky Mountains Hiking Club, based in Knoxville, is responsible for the AT in the park and also 30 miles of it in North Carolina. Trail riding clubs and hiking citizens (as well as co-opted families of club members) help. Maintenance jobs include building steps and waterbars (rock or log barriers that shunt water off the trail, preventing mud holes and erosion), cleaning the drains of waterbars, clearing the trail of blackberries and other brush, improving trail safety, and removing fallen trees. For dangerous jobs (such as cutting unstable piles of fallen tree trunks or repairing hurricane damage), the park service helps; to relocate severely eroded trails, an expert team from the ATC (also mostly volunteers) comes to work and supervise. Most of the AT shelters in the Smokies were built in the 1930s; volunteers raise money for materials and help remodel shelters. One of their jobs is to empty the composting privies and to dig new holes for pit toilets. Another frustrating job is carrying out hikers' trash.

You may notice many fallen logs that have been cut along the AT in the Smokies. Because dead fir trees and unstable spruce trees fall in winter storms, the first job of the year is to cut logs and push them out of the way. During a "chain-saw window," a few weeks in spring, the park allows maintainers to use chain saws; at other

A trail maintainer's artwork along the Appalachian Trail

Appalachian Trail: Newfound Gap to Clingmans Dome

times only hand tools can be used.

The Carolina Mountain Club, based in Asheville, North Carolina, and the Tennessee Eastman Hiking Club of Kingsport maintain the rest of the AT in Tennessee. As you hike, admire the work of these club members and many other trail volunteers.

Sugarland Mountain Trail is the AT Mount Collins shelter on the right.

After Sugarland Mountain Trail, the AT climbs Mount Collins—not all that steep but very rocky. Take a rest to enjoy long mountain views to the right. A sheltering ridge keeps this part of the trail cool, allowing ice or snow to hang on. The fir trees look a little healthier in this pocket, and the witch hobble shrubs more luxuriant. Look for turtleheads and gentians, which bloom in late summer.

This climb brings you above 6,000 feet, but you'll lose some of the elevation and have to regain it. The top of Mount Collins, at about 6,200 feet, was the site of Meigs Post, from which Return Jonathan Meigs surveyed Cherokee lands in 1802 to define new borders after the Holston Treaty of 1771 opened the fertile Tennessee River Valley for white settlers. An assistant waved a blanket from a mountain 15 miles northwest to give Meigs a survey point and Blanket Mountain its name. From Mount Collins, you may get a glimpse of Clingmans Dome and its two towers—one for communications and one for views.

From Mount Collins, make a long descent to Collins Gap, where the AT once more approaches the road. Here there's no doubt that you're in Tennessee, because in the gap the state line is the yellow line in the road. From here you make a long climb of nearly a mile on the rockiest part of this trail, with a few difficult steps for short people. Then the trail eases a bit, and good steps and waterbars keep it dry.

After a bit more climbing (after all, you're heading for the hike's highest point) you swing left and come out on a level trail underneath the Clingmans Dome observation tower. Go past the tower to a spur trail to the left to climb the tower; the AT continues straight at this point. From the tower a paved trail (usually crowded with families) goes 0.5 mile to the parking lot.

Other Hiking Options

1. For a short, easy AT visit, excellent for children and folks who just want to say they've hiked on the AT, park at the Fork Ridge trailhead 3.5 miles along Clingmans Dome Road. Cross the road to the AT connector (about 100 yards) and turn left at the AT sign. In 0.2 mile turn right onto Sugarland Mountain Trail and go 0.5 mile to the Mount Collins shelter to see where through-hikers (and other hikers with permits) sleep. Backtrack to return.

2. For a mostly downhill hike (but still with a long climb to Mount Collins), start at Clingmans Dome.

3. For a spectacular and private winter hike, start at Newfound Gap and go as far as you can, perhaps returning on the traffic-free road.

4. Hike west on the AT from Clingmans Dome to Silers Bald, or hike south from the parking lot on Forney Ridge Trail to Andrews Bald (both rocky trails).

12

Little River

Total Distance: 8–10 miles

Hiking Time: 5½ hours

Vertical Rise: 1,000 feet

Rating: Easy

Maps: Smokies map; USGS Gatlinburg and Silers Bald

This stroll along a gated road starts in a settled area and reaches to the base of the steep Smokies crest. The easy grade, the rich plant life, and the river with swimming holes, boulders, and cascades make it a great hike for families. Many Smokies visitors use this trail, but it provides room to spread out.

How to Get There

From Gatlinburg or the Gatlinburg bypass, enter the park on US 441 and drive to Sugarlands Visitor Center. Turn right onto Little River Road, drive 4.9 miles, and turn left into Elkmont. At 1.3 miles turn left before the entrance to the campground, and in 0.6 mile more bear left and park along the road near the gate.

The Hike

Early in the 20th century the Little River Lumber Company built rail lines up the gentle Little River Valley and the steeper side valleys to cut millions of big trees. Lumber milled near Townsend was sold widely; you've probably been in buildings made of Smoky Mountain wood. Signs of the lumbering operation include railbeds, cables, bits of machinery, and this trail itself. The forest here is 50 to 60 years old and has recovered from destructive logging and subsequent erosion and fires.

Little River Trail is 5.1 miles long (10.2 miles round-trip), but this description features the easy, gently climbing part. The last half mile climbs a bit more steeply and has three side-creek (called prongs here) crossings, difficult in high water.

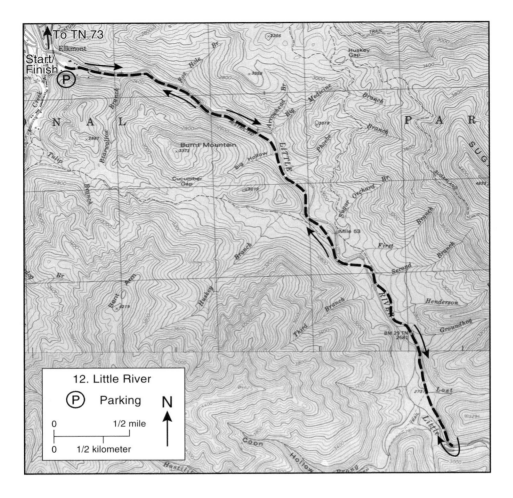

12. Little River

(P) Parking   N

0 — 1/2 mile

0 — 1/2 kilometer

Go around the gate and continue up the road past former summer cottages. A vacation community and club developed as the loggers finished their work, and, when farmers and other settlers were forced to sell and leave their land, the owners here negotiated the use of their plots for a limited time. The time ran out in the 1970s, was renegotiated, and ran out again 20 years later. Still a matter of controversy, the houses now stand abandoned; some may be torn down to allow the land to revert to forest, and some may be converted to park buildings. The houses are off-limits, but you can wander through yards where native and cultivated plants mix on pleasant lawns. This is a good place to find morel mushrooms in April.

Crowds of fireflies congregate on these lawns in June and flash mating messages to each other. The males synchronize their signals, and this has attracted the attention of researchers who want to know how bugs (beetles, actually) can do such a complex thing, and what we can learn about nervous system workings from it. The best way to

50 Hikes in the Tennessee Mountains

Morel mushroom and great chickweed

experience this light show is to camp in the campground and walk up this road at night. No flashlights!

But for normal daylight hiking, walk past the cottages and some two-story boulders to another gate. The mile of road between the gates was damaged in a flood and closed in 1996. You will see places where Little River took bites out of the old road surface. Doghobble and rhododendron hang down rock faces on the right, and mosses, flowers, and ferns live in wet places. Walking fern, which is more common in the Cumberlands than the Smokies, grows on these rocks: look for a colony of ferns with long, arrow-shaped fronds. Some fronds grow so long and pointed that the end looks like a thread; if the thread touches a good place to grow, it starts a new plant—this is how the fern walks. Very slow steps. One rock face drips enough water to form a large puddle

in the road, and tadpoles may hatch there in spring. Some amphibians need standing water to lay eggs in, and somehow they know where puddles are likely to form.

Several benches encourage rest stops to look at the river. At about 2 miles a wooden bridge crosses Huskey Branch, a vigorous cascade into a green pool. This is a good swimming hole with a pebble beach on the other side of the creek; you can scramble down rocks near the bridge or find an easier way just beyond the bridge.

Cucumber Gap Trail comes in from the right at 2.3 miles in a wide, open river valley. It runs across one of the ridges carved by the Little River and has good spring wildflowers.

Next is a wooden-plank bridge—once used by cars—over the Little River. Look up and down the river at the solid banks of rhododendron, which blooms best in places where it can lean out to get more sun. The young forest behind the rhododendron contains mostly tulip trees, which grow up fast on cleared or farmed land. Yellow birch, oak, and maple also do a good job of restoring forest habitats, while dogwoods spread their branches in the understory, making a lacy pattern when they bloom in spring. Small hemlocks scattered throughout the woods don't germinate until the other trees provide shade and moisture, and they grow more slowly. But in 100 years or so they may be as tall as the tulip trees.

From the bridge, you may also be able to see the high ridge of Sugarland Mountain on the left. Huskey Gap Trail, entering from the left, crosses that ridge; it runs 2.1 miles up to Sugarland Mountain Trail and then 2 more miles down to Newfound Gap Road. But Little River Trail continues on, a narrower track by now, along the river. Sycamore trees line the river. Their trunks and larger branches drop bark slabs and strips, leaving light and dark blotches. Pieces of bark on the trail have rounded, abstract shapes.

The next junction, at 3.7 miles, is a fork with a convenient quartz boulder to sit on. Little River Trail goes left, and Goshen Prong Trail goes right. This trail is well worth a side trip—it crosses an iron bridge into a creekside garden of ferns and wildflowers. It stays almost level for 3 miles before it starts the steep climb to the Appalachian Trail. Little River Trail continues left and merges with several creek channels and stepping-stones—for a while you will be surrounded by running water. Backcountry Campsite 24 appears on the right between the trail and Little River at 4.5 miles. And then Rough Creek Trail branches left for another steep route to Sugarland Mountain Trail. This is a good turnaround point, unless you want to try those unbridged creek crossings. The walk back will seem much easier; you may want to explore another of the side trails.

Other Hiking Options

Trails fork from Little River Trail like branches from a tree, and each junction has clear signs. Cucumber Gap Trail loops over a small ridge and drops to Jakes Creek Trail and a short road walk back to the Little River parking area. Huskey Gap Trail and Rough Fork Trail climb left to Sugarland Mountain Trail, which travels the spine of a 12-mile ridge. Goshen Prong Trail swings right and climbs, also pretty steeply, to the Appalachian Trail 2 miles from Clingmans Dome. These options may be too ambitious for a day hike, but the beginning of each branch trail offers more exploring. All have excellent wildflower displays.

The 1-mile Elkmont Nature Trail loops gently through a marshy area, several old homesites (look for daffodils and forsythia), and logging railroad beds.

13

Meigs Creek

Total Distance: 7 miles

Hiking Time: 4–5 hours

Vertical Rise: 800 feet

Rating: Moderate to difficult, depending on creek water levels

Maps: Smokies map; USGS Wear Cove

Water flows, tumbles, cascades, trickles, and seeps down this narrow, sheltered valley. Spring and summer flowers, big trees, and privacy add to the attractions. Creek crossings will be difficult during and after rain; in cold rainy weather choose another hike. Children will enjoy the lower part of this hike in summer; take towels.

How to Get There

From Sugarlands Visitor Center drive 11.3 miles west on Little River Road, past Metcalf Bottoms Picnic Area, to the Sinks parking area on the left just before a bridge. There is a CONGESTED AREA sign on a curve before the Sinks. From the Townsend entrance to the park, drive 6.1 miles east on Little River Road.

The Hike

On summer weekends many people visit the Sinks, a set of rapids and a deep pool at a sharp curve of the Little River. The hardest part of this hike may be finding a parking place, but once you have, the trail will take you away from the crowds to enjoy water in safer and more private places. Prettier, too. *Caution:* Hidden rocks and currents make it dangerous to swim at the Sinks; people have drowned or been injured.

Meigs Creek was named for Return Jonathan Meigs, a surveyor who drew boundaries of Cherokee lands after the American Revolution. New treaties eventually erased the boundaries and settlers moved in, but farming was difficult in this steep land. In the 1920s the Little River Lumber Company bought the land and built rail lines along the

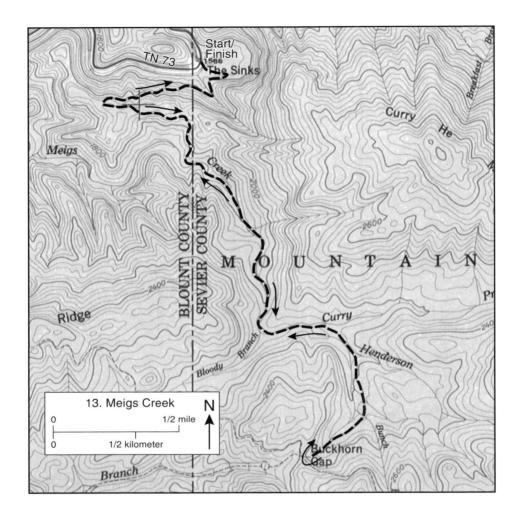

Little River (using the same route you now drive on Little River Road) and up some of the side creeks. They cut most of the virgin timber, but in a few steep pockets, such as parts of Meigs Creek, some big trees survived. The logging railroad was also used for tourist excursions from Knoxville to Elkmont. A popular, scenic ride, the trip passed through Townsend and took several hours.

From the back of the large gravel parking area, find the trail sign and swing right to climb above the eroded dirt paths to rocks overlooking the rapids. Continue on rough trail to a rock outcrop and turn left, leaving just about everyone else behind. A short descent leads to a relatively rare habitat for the Smokies: a flat, moist bottomland with rich soil. The Little River once flowed through here but left for the deeper channel at the Sinks. Swamp plants such as bamboo, pawpaw, and sedges grow here, and occasional patches of standing water foster mosquito and other larvae.

Turn right and climb the second ridge, a

much higher one that forces Meigs Creek to twist and turn west before it can join the Little River. This side of the ridge faces north, and its moist soil supports rhododendron, doghobble, mosses, ferns, and wildflowers. Look for jack-in-the-pulpits on the trail bank in April—usually hard to spot, but so abundant here that you can't miss them.

> ➤ *Jack-in-the-pulpits are fully formed underground, then push up inside a tough sheath. Next the three-part leaves and the peculiar hooded flower unfold like butterfly wings from a chrysalis, and the flower is ready for the coming-out ritual of pollination. Each plant can be male one year and female another, depending on the resources garnered during the previous year. Flies and beetles entering the male plant get a dusting of pollen and crawl out a hole in the bottom. The female plant has no such opening, but she doesn't care; all she wants is the pollen from insects that have already visited a male flower. In summer female plants produce a cluster of fleshy green fruits; these turn bright red in fall.*

Early-spring flowers here include bloodroot, round-leafed violets (yellow), and hepatica. In April foamflower, yellow mandarin, blue cohosh, true and false Solomon's seal, and sweet cicely bloom amid unfurling fiddleheads of Christmas, maidenhair, and wood ferns. Summer flowers include black cohosh and asters.

At the top of the ridge the trail swings right onto a south-facing slope with different trees and flowers: mountain laurel, sourwood, pine, and oak, with trailing arbutus, galax, wintergreen, and dry lichens along the bank. Rocks to the right of the trail provide sunning spots for fence lizards or garter snakes. After descending to cross a side creek, the trail goes through a rhododendron tunnel at about 1 mile and emerges in the Meigs Creek Valley with the first and worst stream crossing straight ahead. In low water there may be stepping-stones; otherwise you'll have to wade, but the creek bottom has sand and pebbles between a few slippery rocks. As always, don't attempt to cross in high water.

The trail swings back and forth, crossing Meigs Creek about 18 times and crossing two side creeks. You're never far from the creek, and in two spots rock faces push the trail almost into the creek. The valley becomes deeper and narrower, with each creek crossing easier than the last (but remember, you have to come back down). Several cascades sparkle through the rhododendron, and cardinal flower blooms in the few sunny spots. Large beech and hemlock trees grow above the rhododendron, and about halfway up (after maybe eight or nine crossings) look for the biggest beech tree on the left—so big that it has developed buttress roots extending far from its base.

At about 3 miles a spring on the left contributes water to the top trickle of Meigs Creek and the valley opens to deciduous second-growth woods—logged about 70 years ago. The few hemlocks here, tiny compared to the ones below, struggle to catch up with tulip trees, oaks, and maples that colonized the bare ground. Some of the hemlocks will win in the end and become taller than their neighbors.

At 3.5 miles Meigs Creek Trail reaches a four-way intersection at Buckhorn Gap. Meigs Mountain Trail goes left toward Elkmont; Lumber Ridge Trail goes right to Tremont, and a faint, unmaintained trail goes straight. This is your turnaround point.

The Sinks along Little River

Other Hiking Options

1. At the Sinks parking lot go left instead of right onto a 0.3-mile level trail through an old creek channel that now holds standing water. Most water in the Smokies tumbles downhill, so woodland ponds are rare. Frogs, toads, and salamanders come here, perhaps from miles away, to lay eggs, and their larvae eat delicious pond scum or the larvae of mosquitoes and gnats. The trail continues past a hillside of boulders (look for tall blue phacelia and stonecrop in spring) and goes around the top end of the frog pond. After a level stretch with many ferns and wildflowers, this alternate trail joins Meigs Creek Trail as it starts to climb the ridge.

2. If you arrange a car shuttle between Metcalf Bottoms and the Sinks, you could turn left at Buckhorn Gap onto Meigs Mountain Trail. In 2 miles, just past a small cemetery, turn left again onto Curry Mountain Trail to reach Metcalf Bottoms in 3.3 miles (total mileage: 8.8).

3. A similar car shuttle between the Sinks and Tremont would allow you to turn right onto Lumber Ridge Trail and descend 4 miles to Tremont. To park at Tremont, turn right at the Townsend park entrance and turn left almost immediately at a sign for GREAT SMOKY MOUNTAINS INSTITUTE at Tremont. Drive 2 miles, turn left across a bridge, and left again to park. Lumber Ridge Trail starts just above a dormitory building up to the right. With options 2 and 3, you won't have to make all those creek crossings again.

III

Southern Unaka Mountains

14

Fodderstack–Cold Spring Gap–North Fork Citico Creek Loop

Total Distance: 9.9 miles

Hiking Time: 6–7 hours

Vertical Rise: 1,300 feet

Rating: Very difficult

Map: USGS Whiteoak Flats

Trail Marking: Cutbark blazes

This loop starts along the Tennessee–North Carolina border, drops into the old-growth forest of the Citico Wilderness Area, and then returns by way of 5,180-foot Fodderstack Mountain. It's an all-season hike, but excellent wildflower displays and high elevation make it especially good in spring and summer. The North Fork Citico Creek section goes along and in the creek so would not be safe in high water or ice. Bad winter weather may make TN 165 icy. Wear long pants and long sleeves because of high-elevation coolness and abundant nettles.

How to Get There

The road to this hike has four names: Tellico-Robbinsville Road, the Cherohala Skyway, TN 165, and NC 143. From Tellico Plains, Tennessee, drive east 23 miles to Beech Gap on the Tennessee–North Carolina border. From Robbinsville, North Carolina, drive west 20 miles to Beech Gap. Park at the gate on the north side of the road or at a pullout across it.

The Hike

Rugged, overgrown, and possibly the most challenging hike in this book, this loop introduces a vast remote wilderness where you can wander in peace while other folks sit in summer traffic jams. Use this description to plan your own hike and to learn about the area and its trails. Blazes are hard to see, and some parts of the trail are hard to follow; don't attempt this hike without a compass (and experience in using one) and a good map. There are USFS post signs at the trail junctions. Many Citico trails follow old log-

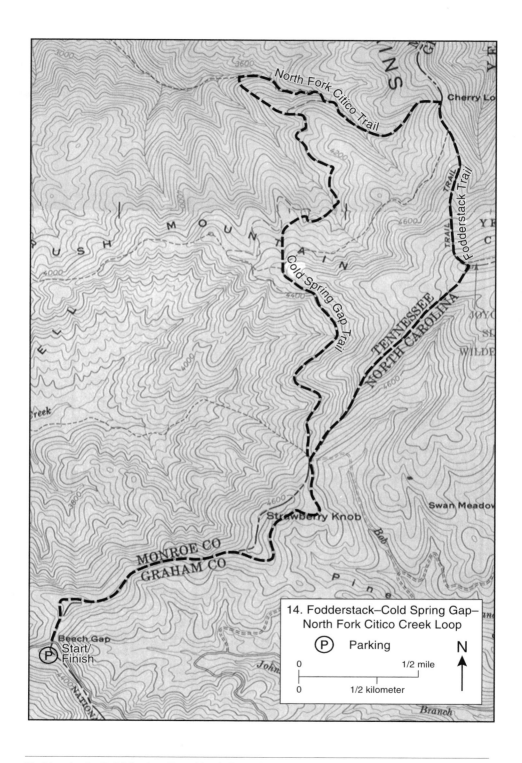

North Fork Citico Trail

Cherry Lo

Fodderstack Trail

TRAIL

Cold Spring Gap Trail

TENNESSEE
NORTH CAROLINA

JOYC

SI

WILDE

PUSH MOUNTAIN

Creek

Swan Meadow

Strawberry Knob

Bab

Pine

MONROE CO
GRAHAM CO

Beech Gap
Start/
Finish
(P)

John

Branch

14. Fodderstack–Cold Spring Gap–
North Fork Citico Creek Loop

(P)   Parking

N

0   1/2 mile

0   1/2 kilometer

An old cutbark blaze on a yellow birch

50 Hikes in the Tennessee Mountains

ging roads. If possible, stop at the Tellico District Ranger Station on USFS 210 for current conditions and maps.

Congress designated 16,000 acres of the Citico Creek drainage as a wilderness area in 1984; combined with 17,000-acre Joyce Kilmer–Slickrock Creek Wilderness, it makes up one of the largest protected wilderness areas in the East, with miles and miles of remote trails and campsites. While the Smokies, just a few miles to the north, endured farming and intensive logging, this part of the Cherokee National Forest was sparsely settled, and the loggers left many pockets of virgin forest.

The road from Beech Gap (USFS 95) to Cold Spring Gap was closed recently, so now there's a 1.9-mile road walk along the ridgetop to the Cold Spring Gap trailhead to warm you up for the real part of this hike. Beyond the gates you'll go uphill for about 0.2 mile, past two meadows, and then start a long, easy descent. At first exotic plants such as plantain, heal-all, and clover line the trail, but native summer wildflowers soon replace them: three colors of bee balm, jewelweed, turk's cap lilies, meadow rue, and wild sunflower. Spring flowers include violets, hepaticas, and anemones on the roadbank. A view to the right shows the undulating mountains of North Carolina, which should be richly colored in October. (Though this is a high-elevation hike, there are just a few views, but other high places nearby have good views.)

The trail enters a wetter area of hemlocks, roadside nettles, and possibly muddy spots. At 1.9 miles it reaches the old parking area and junction of three trails: South Fork Citico Creek (USFS 105), sharp left; Fodderstack (USFS 95), straight; and Cold Spring Gap (USFS 149), in the middle but slightly left.

Head down the roadbed of Cold Spring Gap Trail, which is wide enough to foster exuberant growths of nettles, yellow sunflowers, and other tall plants that can reach out and soak you. You may not be able to see the trail in some spots, but your feet will have no doubt where it is. The wealth of summer and fall flowers—crimson bee balm, blue lobelia, snakeroot, jewelweed—will take your mind off the nettles. Honeybees, bumblebees, wasps, and butterflies feed on sunny days. Old road culverts keep water from numerous springs off the trail except where the springs and creeklets have overflowed and made gullies. The rhododendron becomes thicker as you descend, and its bloom here is lovely in June or July.

After some rocky trail, you can hear a larger creek on the left and may see leaves or blossoms of spring wildflowers on the trailbank: dwarf-crested iris, false Solomon's seal, large-flowered trillium, several kinds of violets. Wild hogs also like wildflowers, and you may see results of their digging for the roots. At an open place (possibly a loading area or turnaround for loggers) blackberries join the mix. Road gullies increase as you descend, but the trail becomes less choked at the same time. A larger creek flows through a culvert, and then, after some rougher spots, the trail swings right at an opening and a possible campsite.

Here the trail is clearer in moist woods, dominated by doghobble and rhododendron as undergrowth and hemlocks as the shading canopy. Wood ferns line the walkway. After a small dirt hump, the trail twists left and begins to look more like a trail than an old road. Big hemlocks, maples, beeches, and multitrunked Fraser magnolias indicate more mature woods.

Descend steeply to the North Fork Citico Creek and cross it. A small sign identifies

USFS 98, North Fork Citico Creek Trail and the end of Cold Spring Gap Trail. (If the sign is gone, watch for a rock cairn on the far side of the creek.) A left will take you about 5 miles down to USFS 345 and the trailheads for several other Citico Creek Wilderness Area hikes. Turn right to continue this hike and look for faded white blazes or cutbark blazes (some look like old, swollen branch scars). Develop a search image for these blazes; you need to be going generally west and uphill, following the creek, which you will have to cross or walk in several times. Basswood and buckeye trees tower above the rhododendron as the creek valley gets steeper and narrower. Silverbell trees grow higher on the side slope. Follow the blazes up to the right for a short, dry respite from wet walking, and then dive into rhododendron again.

At one point the trail goes up the middle of the creek through nearly 100 yards of a rhododendron tunnel—no blazes, because there was no place to put one. But you'll pick them up again on the other end of the tunnel and ascend into deciduous woods along a now-dry creekbed. A faint fork goes off to the right; stay to the left following blazes. This is a good place to rest and look back. You'll be impressed with how much rhododendron you've survived, and in July you'll enjoy a sea of its blooms.

Follow the steep streambed and climb to Cherry Log Gap and an unmarked trail junction. Large black cherry trees, prized by loggers but spared by remoteness here, can be recognized by dark, somewhat flaky bark and tall, straight trunks. Squirrels and birds harvest the fruits as soon as they ripen, so you probably won't see any.

Turn right onto Fodderstack Trail and start a mile-long climb through mature high-elevation forest to the top of Fodderstack Mountain. During rest stops, admire vibur-

num shrubs (you paid to see this plant by climbing to 5,000 feet), big silverbell trees, gnarly sugar maples, and yellow birches with twisted support roots splayed out. A few switchbacks help on the climb, and if the woods are open enough, you'll get a glimpse of Stratton Bald on the left.

After 1.1 miles of climbing, look for a huge yellow birch with a hole through its trunk and finally swing right and start down. Just past the crest is the left turn onto Stratton Bald Trail (it's less than a mile over to Stratton Bald—worth a side trip, especially since it has the great views that this trail lacks).

At first the descent goes through a large patch of billowy grass, but then it enters a blackberry jungle where your feet will do fine, though the rest of you will get scratched up some. Push on through; there are some open patches with ferns and other peaceable plants, and then more blackberries. Soon you'll come into a shaded hemlock grove, pass a WILDERNESS sign, and reach the junction in Cold Spring Gap. Return to Beech Gap and your car.

Other Hiking Options

1. A 0.4-mile side trip (adding 0.8 mile to an already strenuous loop) into North Carolina on Bob Stratton Trail (USFS 54) to Bob Stratton Bald yields excellent views from a grassy bald. The side trail goes left just after the climb (about 1 mile) from the junction of South Fork Citico Creek and Fodderstack Trails.

2. The loop described here makes several connections with other trails in Citico Creek Wilderness Area.

3. You could combine part of this trail (perhaps up to Stratton Bald without the descent along Cold Spring Gap Trail) with a hike to Jeffrey Hell (Hike 15) or Falls Branch Falls (Hike 16).

15

Jeffrey Hell (USFS 196)

Total Distance: 4.4 miles

Hiking Time: 3 hours

Vertical Rise: 600 feet

Rating: First 1.8 miles easy; last 0.5 mile difficult

Map: USGS White Oak Flats

Trail Marking: Cutbark blazes

The descent into Jeffrey Hell is delightful—open woods with banks of wildflowers, profusions of rhododendron blooms, and clear rushing creeks. High elevation makes this a relatively cool summer hike. The easy first 1.8 miles can be hiked at any time of year (snowy days are especially recommended) and by all ages. You can decide whether to do the steep part when you get there.

How to Get There

From Tellico Plains, take TN 165 (Tellico-Robbinsville Road; the Cherohala Skyway) east for 22 miles, passing first a right turn on USFS 210 to the Tellico District Ranger Station and Bald River Falls. About 10 miles farther pass a left turn to Indian Boundary Campground (USFS 345). There are several parking areas and overlooks along TN 165; find the one on the left with a sign for hikes 196 and 87 (Rattlesnake Rock Trailhead). If you reach the state line, turn around and go back 1.4 miles.

The Hike

Rhododendron, mountain laurel, dog-hobble, and greenbrier tangle together to form "hells"—easy to get into, but hard to get back out of. The shrubs and vines conspire to trip, scratch, hit, lacerate, grab, choke, and confuse. Everyone should visit at least one rhododendron hell, if only to see how easy it was to hide a moonshine still near a clean, cold water supply. Hells may have also protected some big trees from loggers and saved bears and other wildlife. The story is that Jeffrey's dogs went into this hell after a bear, and then Jeffrey went in after his dogs. Man and dogs were never seen again; the bear probably ambled out the other side. This trail follows a roadbed (part of the old route from Tellico Plains to Robbinsville) through open woods high above a creek ravine, but suddenly turns right and drops into the ravine. It won't be hard to stay on the trail—the walls of rhododendron and greenbrier give you no choice. However, you may get your feet wet.

At the Rattlesnake Rock Trailhead walk left to a gap in the stone wall and descend to a WILDERNESS sign and registration box. Forest service signs on posts usually indicate only the beginnings and ends of trails; in between you must look for cutbark blazes, some of which were made decades ago and survive as swollen vertical tree scars about head-high. The forest service plans extensive trailwork starting in 2000 and may repair and reblaze the trails.

Turn right for Jeffrey Hell Trail and descend on a wide, graded roadbed. Yellow birch, hemlock, and rhododendron favor the north-facing slopes, and toothwort and spring beauty bloom early on the banks. Cross a culvert over a tiny creek coming from a spring. The next bridge, a cement road bridge, crosses Falls Branch, which forms the falls on Hike 16. Young white pines and hemlocks grow in the road, and open spots support long, thorny blackberry canes. The trail curves to a sunnier slope; in June the rhododendrons bloom, and in winter you can predict how spectacular the blooms of next year will be by counting the fat bloom buds above the leaves. Juncos, nuthatches, chickadees, and tufted titmice sing all winter, and in spring this is a good place to learn nesting-bird calls. Beech, maple, silverbell, Fraser magnolia, and medium-sized black cherry trees grow in the open woods. Large black cherry trees are rare in cut-over forest because they were so

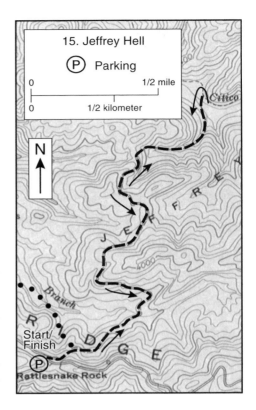

valuable as fine furniture wood.

Swing right at 1 mile; another road goes left, and you'll have to watch for the trodden path and those indistinct blazes. The trail descends a little more steeply through moist woods and a doghobble understory. In winter you can see the surrounding ridges and the other side of the deepening creek ravine to the right—a preview of the trail route to come.

At 1.8 miles you'll reach a campsite and the intersection of three old roads, none of which you get to take. Turn right beside a large hemlock with a white blaze and start the steep drop. It may be muddy or icy, which could persuade you to stop here. Continue down a creekbed trail between walls of thick rhododendron, doghobble, mountain laurel, greenbrier, and other tangly things. Masses of Dutchman's-breeches, squirrel corn, trout lily, trillium, mayapple, foamflower, and cohosh bloom here, beautifully arranged with shining club moss, princess pine, and wood ferns. Cross a creeklet for a bit of dry hiking and look for even more wildflowers in-season. Blue lobelia and cardinal flower bloom in summer. In spring look near the creeks for the orange flower clusters of buckeyes (squirrels will knock some down for you), and in fall find the mahogany brown nuts. Though poisonous, buckeye nuts are said to bring good luck if shined and kept in your pocket.

After a short rise, the trail drops again to reach South Fork Citico Creek at 3,320 feet. Cross if possible (this may be a shoes-off crossing; do not attempt it if the creek is deep) and reach the junction with South Fork Citico Creek Trail (USFS 105) in about 50 yards of dense doghobble. About 0.1 mile upstream is a pretty creekside camp-site with room for two tents.

To return, cross the creek again, climb the ravine, and stroll back to the parking area.

A U.S. Forest Service trail sign

Other Hiking Options

1. South Fork Citico Creek Trail (USFS 105) in either direction features mature woods and creek cascades. Turn right on South Fork Citico Creek and climb 2.3 miles (difficult for the last 0.5 mile) to Cold Spring Gap. A left on the trail takes you 6 miles down to Indian Boundary Campground and a junction with many other Citico Creek Wilderness Area trails.

2. This hike could be combined with Falls Branch Trail (Hike 16) for a good day's outing.

3. The Cherohala Skyway goes by several trailheads. Some of the trails are hard to follow; check with the Tellico Ranger Station for maps and trail updates.

16

Falls Branch (USFS 87)

Total Distance: 2.6 miles

Hiking Time: 1½–2 hours

Vertical Rise: 450 feet

Rating: Moderate to difficult

Map: USGS Whiteoak Flats

Trail Marking: Cutbark blazes

A rough scramble leads to a high, wispy (or roaring in wet weather) waterfall in old-growth forest. Parts of the trail have excellent spring wildflowers, and the elevation is enough to keep this area cool in summer, so it's an all-season hike. Avoid it in ice, snow, or heavy rain, however, because the steep sections will be slippery.

How to Get There

From Tellico Plains, take TN 165 (Tellico-Robbinsville Road; the Cherohala Skyway) east for 22 miles, passing first a right turn on USFS 210 to the Tellico District Ranger Station and Bald River Falls. About 10 miles farther pass a left turn to Indian Boundary Campground (USFS 345). There are several parking areas and overlooks along TN 165; find the one on the left with a sign for hikes 196 and 87 (Rattlesnake Rock Trailhead). If you reach the state line, turn around and go back 1.4 miles.

The Hike

At the Rattlesnake Rock Trailhead (see Hike 15) walk left to a gap in the stone wall and descend to a WILDERNESS sign and registration box. Forest service signs on posts usually indicate only the beginnings and ends of trails; in between you must look for cutbark blazes, some of which were made decades ago and survive as swollen vertical tree scars about head-high. The forest service plans extensive trailwork in 2000 and may repair and reblaze the trails.

Turn left at the registration box (Jeffrey Hell Trail goes right) and go down a

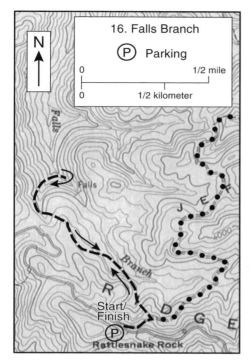

16. Falls Branch
ⓟ Parking

Start/Finish

➤ Nurse Logs

In mature or old-growth forest big trees fall and rot, with the enthusiastic help of fungi, slime molds, termites, beetles, and other wood eaters. In moist areas, such as the north-facing slopes of Hikes 15 and 16, the dead trees, now called nurse logs, decay into soft, crumbly wood that supports organisms that have trouble finding a place on the forest floor: lichens, mosses, and fungi at first, then flowers, rhododendrons, and small trees. Yellow birches and hemlocks have tiny, inconspicuous seeds without many food reserves (a fat, protein-stuffed acorn would be eaten by a squirrel before it could sprout on an exposed rotten log) and find food and support on logs with soil prepared by the decomposers. As these trees grow, however, they need to reach the real soil, so they send roots around the nurse log to find space. Sometimes they have to search for the right spots, and the result is elaborate patterns of aboveground roots.

When the nurse logs rot away, the trees are left standing on those stilt roots; you may see yellow birches with space enough underneath to crawl into. Another result of nurse log germination is a straight line of yellow birches or hemlocks that look as if the forest service planted them.

Salamanders, centipedes, earthworms, and many other small animals also thrive on nurse logs, helping ancient forests retain their species diversity.

woods road that was part of the old Tellico-Robbinsville Road and used for moving equipment during the construction of TN 165, the new Cherohala Skyway. The forest road curves right through hemlock and rhododendron, and you can see the main highway to the left at about 0.5 mile. At 0.9 mile look on the left for a black plastic silt fence left over from road construction. At a thin line of branches across the road, look up on the right for a white arrow on a tree that indicates a sharp right turn up on the roadbank. At the time of this writing there was a thigh-high tree trunk across the road just past the turn; if you get there, come back.

Ascend the bank into a mature hemlock grove (look for inch-long hemlock cones on the ground) and go over a small rise. As you

Falls Branch in winter

50 Hikes in the Tennessee Mountains

start down, you'll enter a different world—part of 180 acres of virgin forest—with huge buckeyes and yellow birches, gnarled sugar maples, and large black cherries. Rotting nurse logs provide a soft, crumbly surface for tree sprouts to grow. Yellow birch, rhododendron, and a few small hemlocks specialize in this habitat. Viburnum, a high-elevation shrub with rough heart-shaped leaves that turn scarlet or burgundy in fall, forms the understory.

Descend steeply, using caution over muddy spots and difficult rocks, to heavy rhododendron growth and finally Falls Branch. From here, you can see the smooth rock face of the falls to the right through the trees. Cross the creek on stepping-stones, if it's safe, and squeeze through a rock crack (notice a yellow birch tree on the top of the rock that has sent its exposed roots about 10 feet down to reach soil). Clamber up rocks to see the falls; the trail disappears, so go only as far as it is safe on the rock jumble at the base. This waterfall is on the north side of Sassafras Ridge and develops fantastic ice formations in winter that persist past the cold weather. It's beautiful but possibly dangerous; watch for shifting rocks or ice clumps. Toothwort, anemones, and many other spring flowers share the moist hillside with deep, soft moss beds, and close to the falls the spray zone supports liverworts and umbrella leaf.

Retrace your steps up that steep hill.

Other Hiking Options

1. This hike could be combined with Jeffrey Hell (Hike 15) for a good day's outing.
2. The Cherohala Skyway goes by several trailheads. Some of the trails are hard to follow; check with the Tellico Ranger Station for maps and trail updates.

17

Bald River (USFS 88)

Total Distance: 10 miles, out and back

Hiking Time: 5–6 hours

Vertical Rise: 400 feet

Rating: Moderate

Map: USGS Bald River Falls

Trail Marking: White blazes

A short, steep climb takes you from a crowded waterfall to a remote wilderness walk along Bald River. Spring flowers, cold water for summer wading, cross-gorge views for fall colors, and elaborate ice formations make this an all-season walk for any hikers who can make the first climb. The first 100 yards will tell you if the trail is too icy.

How to Get There

From Tellico Plains, drive 5.3 miles on TN 165 (Tellico-Robbinsville Road; Cherohala Skyway) and turn right onto USFS 210; look for signs for the Tellico Ranger Station and Bald River Falls. After 7.1 miles along the Tellico River, cross Bald River on a bridge with the falls in sight on the right. Park after the falls on the right. (This is a popular area, and the parking lot may be full on nice weekends.)

The Hike

Bald River Falls can be seen from the road. You don't even need to get out of your car. But anyone can see the waterfall; hikers can also explore the rock formations that this river carved and have lunch on big, flat river rocks. Congress designated the Bald River Gorge Wilderness, about 4,000 acres, in 1984. Between the wilderness and the high ridges of the Tennessee–North Carolina border lie the Upper Bald River Primitive Areas. Wilderness designation offers the highest degree of protection for wild lands and cannot be changed without congressional action. Primitive areas are maintained by the U.S. Forest Service for low-impact recreational use, with no new

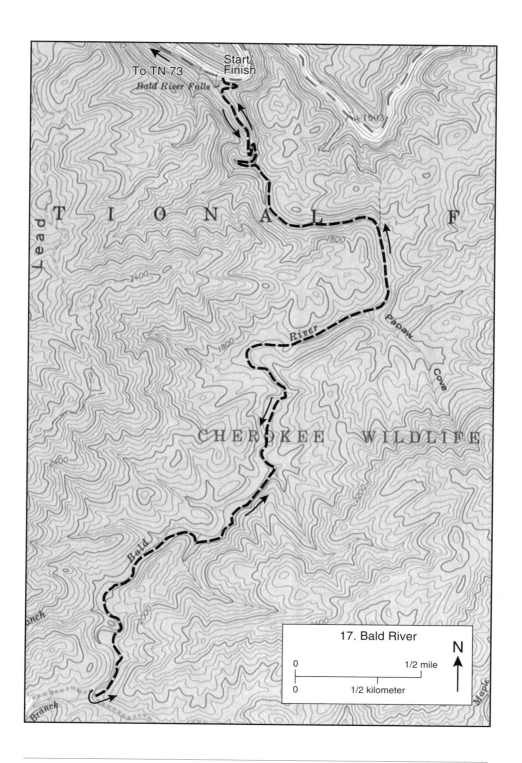

To TN 73

Bald River Falls

Start/
Finish

1503

Lead

T I O N A L   F

1800

River

Papaw

Cove

1800

2400

C H E R O K E E   W I L D L I F E

2200

2400

2400

Bald

2600

anch

Branch

Maple

17. Bald River

N

0   1/2 mile

0   1/2 kilometer

Bald River (USFS 88)

Mountain laurel

road building or off-road-vehicle use allowed. A primitive area designation can be
changed in the forest management plan,
however; conservation groups are working
now to preserve all of the Bald River drainage as wilderness.

From the far end of the parking lot (the
worn tracks beside the falls are not trails),
take a graveled trail up along a rock face,
past the gray WILDERNESS sign, to a wooden
staircase and bridges to get a view of the
top of Bald River Falls. At a picnic area with
tables find a narrow bench trail to the left
and follow it for about 0.3 mile. Look for an
inconspicuous sharp switchback to the left
onto another narrow bench; it zigzags to the
top of a jagged rock promontory. If you miss
the switchback, you drop through a small
muddy dip and come to a rock wall. Many
hikers have climbed hand over hand up
rhododendron roots. Don't do it—it erodes

the hillside and can be dangerous to both
you and the roots. Turn back and find the
turn, which is much easier to see from the
other direction.

At the top you can see a messy spot
where the root climbers crawled out. Just
past that, as the main trail curves left, find
a faint track to the right that leads to a
spiny ridge of bus-sized rock slabs pointed
toward the river. Creep a little way out—perhaps as far as the second or third point—and
look down at a long cascade over similar
rocks and across at the opposite rock wall.
It isn't safe to go much farther (in fact, if kids
are along, don't even tell them about this
side trail), but from the end of these jagged
points you'd be able to see that this huge
bulge of rock forces Bald River to make a
tight U-turn in its rush to the falls. Ten million years ago tectonic collisions pushed
masses of sandstone west; some rocks

50 Hikes in the Tennessee Mountains

went along quietly, while others shattered and tumbled over each other. This broken side ridge gives hikers a good climb to get into the gorge, and also made it difficult for loggers to lay rail lines. They had to come up on the other side of Bald River Falls and then build a bridge below these cliffs.

Return to the trail and descend to an easy riverside walk—less dramatic than the climb, but very beautiful. On the way down look for quartz veins, quartz conglomerate, overthrust slabs, and rock strata at odd angles. At 0.5 mile is a rock overhang and a small campsite; at 0.75 mile a sign at a larger campsite indicates that it's 4.5 miles more to reach USFS 126. Just past the campsite, the trail meets the old rail line from across the river. Except for a few side ridges, this grade takes you all the way to USFS 126. Sunlight on the open spots along the river allows rhododendron and mountain laurel to produce abundant blooms in May and June.

At 1.4 miles there's a small campsite to the right, and unmarked 0.8-mile Cow Camp Trail (USFS 173) goes left through thick rhododendron to rise steeply to a ridge. After meeting Henderson Trail (USFS 107) at another unmarked junction, it drops down to USFS 210 at a spot about 1 mile from Bald River Falls. For variety and extra exercise you could return this way, and possibly avoid the road walk by leaving one car at the Cow Camp Trailhead. Cow Camp Trail may be overgrown, but it's not difficult to follow.

The walls of the gorge close in as you hike upstream, past several pretty campsites and across small side creeks. The trail climbs a final easy ridge and descends to a view of small cascades and rapids. Shortly before the road is a flat rock out in the river that makes a great picnic table—and a turnaround point if you're hiking out and back.

18

John Muir Trail at Reliance (USFS 152)

Total Distance: 6 miles

Hiking Time: 3 hours

Vertical Rise: 100 feet

Rating: Easy

Map: USGS McFarland

Trail Marking: White i's (small rectangle over large one)

This easy trail offers a good introduction to a part of Tennessee with excellent recreational opportunities: hiking, rafting, canoeing, camping. Best in spring and fall, the hike could also be good in snow. Mosquitoes and ticks thrive here in summer, but on early-morning hikes the cool river mist helps. This is a good hike for children, and the first mile is a level road grade—not wheelchair accessible but good for hikers with limited mobility.

How to Get There

From Etowah, take US 411 south to TN 30. Turn left (east) and drive 5.6 miles to TN 315. Turn left, cross over the Hiwassee River, and turn right just past the bridge onto USFS 108. Look for the Childers Creek parking area on the left (the beginning of the hike). Continue past Childers Creek on USFS 108 to the Big Bend parking area (the end of the hike).

The Hike

John Muir, a Scottish naturalist (1838–1914), hiked 1,000 miles from Kentucky to the Gulf of Mexico in 1867, averaging more than 20 miles a day (with no Gore-Tex or wicking underwear). Muir later wrote a book about it, founded the Sierra Club, persuaded President Grover Cleveland to protect forest reserves, and had a hand in the creation of Yosemite and Sequoia National Parks. A long trail is planned commemorating (but probably not following) his route; some completed sections are included in this guide.

From the Childers Creek parking area,

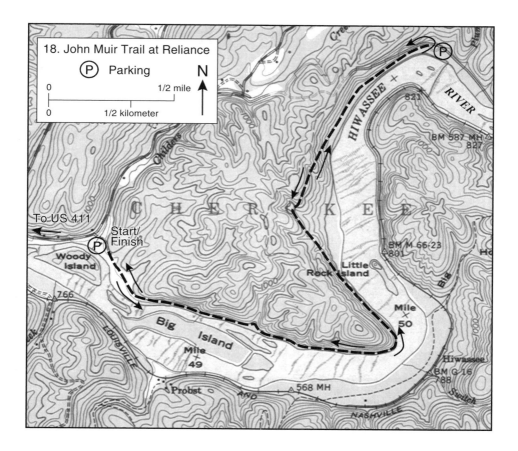

P Parking   N

0   1/2 mile
0   1/2 kilometer

cross the creek on a wooden bridge to an open, grassy spot. Plants grow here that Muir missed on his hike: honeysuckle, gill-over-the-ground, heal-all, autumn olive, ragweed—all exotics that love disturbed places. Mixed in are the native summer-blooming ironweed, queen-of-the-meadow, and wild sunflower.

The trail follows an old road with a sloped bank on the left. Curve right into the woods toward the Hiwassee River; if you start early enough, the rocks may be dry with little pools between them. Note that they form downstream-pointed ledges, one of the factors that make this an easy canoeing river. Also pay attention to warning signs; when

the Apalachia Dam starts to release water, these rocks disappear very fast.

Thin woods of small Virginia pine and other trees soon improve to mixed hardwoods of maple, oak, and mockernut hickory. This hickory has huge husks, large nuts, and tiny kernels that taste good but are hard to get to. Umbrella magnolia and doghobble appear along the trail. And this is where the flowers start: hepatica, little brown jug, foamflower, and yellow mandarin in early spring; yellowroot, columbine, and alumroot in later spring; and wood aster, spiderwort, pipsissewa, thimbleweed anemone, lobelia, agrimony, jewelweed, harebells, and nettles in summer. Hearts-a-

John Muir Trail at Reliance (USFS 152)

Maidenhair fern

bustin' produces inconspicuous flowers in spring, but the magenta fruits "bust" open in fall, revealing bright orange seeds. Bring a flower book and a hand lens.

And a fern book. Draped over the road-bank are maidenhair fern, maidenhair spleenwort, ebony spleenwort, Christmas fern, and rock cap fern.

At about 1 mile a fractured shale side ridge intrudes on the flat trail, forming an overhang occupied by lampshade spiders. Stone steps and a rusty handrail enable you to scramble over this rock pile to return to easy road walking.

Look for cranefly orchids on the road-bank. Usually this orchid grows scattered though the woods, but on this trail there are clusters of one or two dozen plants. In spring you can recognize their oval leaves by turning them over to reveal purple bottoms, but, as with many orchids, the leaves are gone when the bloom appears. The

12- to 18-inch-tall flower stalks hold up to 24 greenish purple flowers, each with a spur longer than the petals. There are two species of this orchid in the world—one here and one in the Himalayan Mountains.

The trail swings left away from the river and rises through a quiet forest of white pines and red oaks, whose trunks hold up impressive poison ivy vines. A trail sign points you back to the river and a way to get down to the water just before the Big Bend parking area and a tangle of another plant John Muir never saw: Asiatic kudzu. Look for its grape-Kool-Aid-scented flowers in August and fuzzy beanlike seedpods later.

For the 6-mile hike, turn around here and retrace your steps. To continue on John Muir Trail, find a gap in the kudzu at the other end of the parking area. The next section is less used but easy to follow. A patch of St.-John's-wort grows near the start.

Other Hiking Options

1. A 20-mile-long section of John Muir Trail starts at Childers Creek, and there are access points along USFS 108. The upper parts receive less use and have several high river overlooks. A spring or fall backpacking trip could be arranged between Childers Creek and TN 68 with a car shuttle or pickup.

2. Wilderness and scenic areas in this part of Cherokee National Forest offer excellent hiking trails: Chestnut Mountain, Starr Mountain, Gee Creek, and Coker Creek Falls, as well as forest service campsites. Get maps and current trail information from ranger stations.

19

Copper Road

Total Distance: 4.6 miles

Hiking Time: 2¼ hours

Vertical Rise: 20 feet

Rating: Easy

Map: USGS Ducktown

A 33-mile wagon road once carried copper ore from Ducktown, Tennessee, to a rail line at Cleveland, Tennessee. The building of US 64 destroyed most of the road, but this segment remains and makes an ideal all-season walk. It's safe and easy for children, with the added attraction of a river swimming hole.

How to Get There

From Cleveland, go about 30 miles east on US 64 to the Ocoee Whitewater Center. Park near the visitors center (metered) or farther down the river in all-day parking lots (fees).

The Hike

The Cherokee People, like the Europeans settlers who followed them, built their first towns east of the Appalachians. Later they established the Overhill Towns in the fertile valleys of the Tennessee and Little Tennessee Rivers. One of those towns, Tanasi, gave its name to the state and now lies under the waters of Tellico Lake. The Ocoee River, called Toccoa where it crosses the Appalachian Trail near Dahlonega, Georgia, provided a trading and communication route between the two parts of the Cherokee Nation. Beloved Woman of the Overhill Cherokees, Nancy Ward, who made both war and peace in attempts to save tribal lands, is buried near the present-day Ocoee Ranger Station.

Prospectors discovered copper near Ducktown, Tennessee, in 1843—just five years after the Cherokee marched west on the Trail of Tears. By 1850 they had opened mines and needed a way to get the ore to a rail line; the closest was Cleveland, Tennessee, 33 rugged miles away. Copper Road, along the Ocoee River, developed slowly but soon became rutted by wagons pulled by donkeys. The trip to Cleveland usually took two to three hard days. Most of the Copper Road was destroyed by the building of US 64, but the forest service preserves this section as an archaeological resource.

The Ocoee Whitewater Center, built as the canoe and kayak venue for the 1996 Summer Olympics, provides water and nonwater recreation: canoe and kayak training, photo workshops, motorbike rallies, and guided hikes. The large stone visitors center has picnic areas, a garden with labeled plants, an information desk, shaded decks, and a gift shop. On most days the view across Ocoee Gorge presents an odd sight: a wide river with no water in it. Upstream dams impound the normal flow and release water for special events. An exhibit shows how parts of the river were sculpted with limestone and concrete faux boulders to create challenging Olympic canoe courses. They look like real boulders, and most days you can walk out to see if you can distinguish between 5-year-old rock and 500-million-year-old rock.

Ocoee power plants one and two, managed by the TVA, have small dams that capture water and send it down huge conduits, which you can see across the gorge from US 64. The water drops into the plants and turns turbines to produce electricity. This type of generation works best in long, narrow valleys. Though the dams don't fill the valley with lakes, they do redirect most of the water that would flow down the river. Because of the growing popularity of water recreation, TVA releases water on schedules to provide controlled river flow for canoes, kayaks, and rafts.

Signs along the trail and throughout the

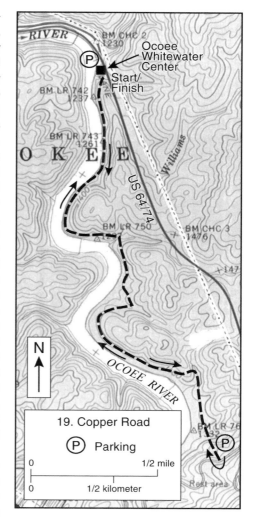

center warn of sudden water-flow increases. Take these signs seriously; check in the visitors center if any release is anticipated, and ask about recent rainfall that might raise water levels. While on the trail or the rocks, beware of water-level changes and, if you see any, call the kids.

Copper Road Trail starts at the northern end (the one nearest the visitors center) of the USFS pedestrian suspension bridge (an experience in itself). Look for a sign and a paved path going upstream. Cross a side creek on flat rocks. On a hot summer day you may see crowds of swimmers with inner tubes, but after a while you'll leave them behind. As the trail becomes more peaceful, look for cardinal flower (deep red and attractive to hummingbirds) and great blue lobelia. These two tall plants are in the same family; the flowers have similar shapes with lobed bottom lips. They both grow in open, moist places and can both survive periodic floods. The blue one is also known as *Lobelia syphilitica* because it was once believed to cure syphilis.

Pink primrose, queen-of-the-meadow, and ironweed bloom in the hottest part of summer, and may enjoy the summer sun here more than you do. Mountain laurel on the south-facing bank gets covered with cake-decorating blooms in spring; laurels exposed like this have many more blooms than those growing in shade.

Continue along a rising rock face (which may be what saved this part of Copper Road from US 64). Dogwoods and maples line the path and, in some places, shade it. A few small springs seep across the path and support stands of alders. At 1.2 miles a wooden bridge crosses a side creek, and then the bluff rises again. Look for lamp-shade spiderwebs under rock overhangs. These webs are shaped like a lampshade, with the round top of the shade against the rock surface and the skirt held out by support webs. If the spider is home, she will be flat against the rock in the center of the lampshade top.

Fence lizards and five-lined skinks hunt insects on these bluffs. Your best chance to see them comes on cool sunny days; the lizards need to bask to get enough energy to hunt. In summer you may hear them scrabble away as you approach, but you

have to be very quiet to see them.

The river valley becomes wider and flatter, and you pass through a meadow with river cane, queen-of-the-meadow, and boneset. At 2 miles cross another wooden bridge over a small creek with hepatica, violets, bluets, and toothwort blooming on the banks in spring.

A boardwalk to the right leads into a thicket of alder and willow in a flat, marshy part of the Ocoee. From a bench you may observe butterflies searching for nectar and dragonflies swooping after mosquitoes. Beavers prowl around in the evening eating vegetation—you probably won't see them, but you can find gnawed tree trunks. From here, especially in winter, there is a view up and down the Ocoee of the high surrounding mountains that this river cut through on its way from northern Georgia to the Tennessee River. Dead trees here support cavity-nesting birds such as woodpeckers, bluebirds, and screech owls.

The trail then enters shaded, moist woods with ferns along the way. After another plank bridge and another view across the gorge, the trail rises over a small hump (the only climbing you have to do) and descends to another bridge. The woods here are more mature, with maple, dogwood, sourwood, beech, and tulip tree. Closer to the river's edge look for American horn-beam, a small tree with smooth bark. This tree is also called musclewood because the bark twists and bulges as if there are muscles pumping iron underneath. Beech trees also have smooth gray bark, but none of the muscles. Beavers have been at work here, too.

The trail rises a bit to a parking area with a pit toilet. To the right, a path goes down to the river for boats to put in on a flat area shaded by hemlock and alder. This is your turnaround point.

Other Hiking Options

1. Bear Paw Loop, dedicated in 1998, is a mountain bike trail but a good walk, too. It starts at the end of the pedestrian bridge across from the visitors center and climbs to a high river-gorge overlook.

2. Thunder Rock Campground, across the bridge just below the Ocoee Whitewater Center, provides access to Benton MacKaye Trail (BMT). Benton MacKaye proposed the creation of the 2,150-mile Appalachian Trail (AT) in 1921; his vision, published in a planning magazine, became reality by 1937 and has been evolving since then. The BMT is evolving, too; the Benton MacKaye Society has built 80 miles of trail in Georgia and plans to extend this Tennessee portion of the BMT to the Smokies, providing an alternate route to the overused AT.

3. A rough but passable road from Thunder Rock Campground leads to trailheads in the Big Frog Wilderness Area.

4. The forest service plans to develop and improve trails, greenways, and bike paths. Check at the Ocoee Whitewater Center for details.

Rue anemone

20

Bays Mountain Park: Lakeside Trail

Total Distance: 2.1 miles

Hiking Time: 1½ hours

Vertical Rise: 50 feet

Rating: Easy

Map: Kingsport city map; USGS Kingsport

Trail Marking: Posts

Easy grades, bridges, a walk across a dam, lake views, ducks, turtles, and snakes: This is one of the best hikes for children in this guide. But try it even if you don't have kids. Other attractions of Bays Mountain (including a planetarium and observatory) make this an ideal all-season outing. In winter the park closes at 5 PM.

How to Get There

From the Johnson City/Kingsport exit off I-81, drive north on I-181 to exit 52B, Meadowview Conference Resort. At the exit-ramp traffic light turn left onto Reservoir Road (under the interstate) and drive 2.2 miles (passing an ostrich and llama farm) to Bays Mountain Road. Turn right and drive 0.2 mile to the park entrance on the left. There are BAYS MOUNTAIN signs at the exits and turns.

The Hike

From the beauty of pond scum to the mystery of outer space, this 3,000-acre park within the Kingsport city limits is dedicated to environmental education and hiking. During the 1800s, different owners had held large parts of the mountain and drainage basin, but left most of it in forest until the town of Kingsport bought the land in 1917 to build a reservoir. By 1968 Kingsport needed more water than its mountaintop reservoir could supply, so it was left with an unusual piece of watershed property on Bays Mountain, the northeastern end of a 115-mile ridge. Fortunately for all of us, Kingsport kept the land for education and recreation instead of selling it for development, and the result is a gem—isolated but accessible. The city built

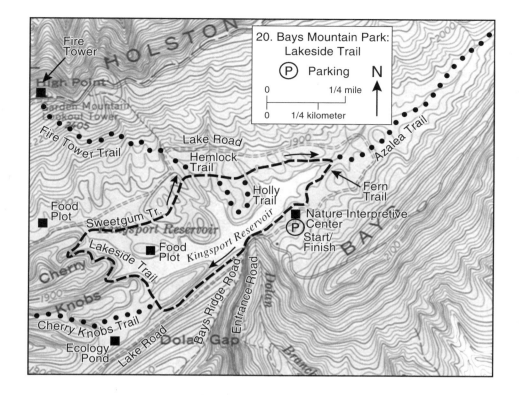

20. Bays Mountain Park: Lakeside Trail

(P) Parking N

0 — 1/4 mile
0 — 1/4 kilometer

trails, a planetarium and observatory, and a fine nature center.

One of the best things about this park is its restrictions—no pets, picnic fires, off-road vehicles, or private boats. Plenty of other natural areas provide these types of recreation. Cross-country skis and bicycles (on roads only) are welcome. Limited hours give animals and plants evenings and Sunday morning free. You won't see litter or trampled earth.

To hike Lakeside Trail clockwise, turn left at the Nature Interpretive Center and follow the paved path to the lake and over the dam. Some water is almost always cascading over the spillway, forming Dolan Branch on the left while the lake stretches off to the right. Pause here to scan the ridgeline that surrounds the basin, channeling creeks

from all directions to this outlet. You will notice many fallen trees along the shore—a heavy, wet snow in March 1996 pulled most of them over. They now provide shelter for aquatic larvae and sunning logs for turtles.

Signposts with yellow letters show the way between Lake Road and the shoreline. At about 0.1 mile Pine Trail, a connector between Lake Road and Bays Ridge Road, goes left, and at 0.2 mile Lakeside Trail drops down a bank to cross a floating bridge. Hinges allow the bridge to rise and fall with water levels. At a fork Cherry Knobs Trail goes left; continue right up a small ridge for Lakeside Trail. As you return to lake level, look for signs of beavers: knee-high stumps that look like badly sharpened pencils, trees with chunks of bark chewed off the sides, or fresh gnaw marks and shavings. A wooden

Box turtle

bridge crosses an inlet of the lake where beavers have stopped up the water to form a swampy wetland with bulrushes and other aquatic plants.

The trail swings away from the lake through mixed hardwoods, giving winter views of the lake as you climb. Sweetgum Trail, at about halfway around the loop, goes left to Lake Road, and then Lakeside Trail crosses Food Plot Road. Two food plots in the park are now growing up into forest again, but take a side trip on this road to see a beaver lodge. One tree near here once served as an osprey hacking site. Hacking is a technique of raising captive-bred birds in as natural a setting as possible. Osprey chicks lived in a facsimile osprey nest, and their human caretakers minimized contact with the birds. The project worked; the chicks fledged, and their offspring now breed in the area naturally.

The next left, Hemlock Trail, connects with Fire Tower Trail across Lake Road. As the trail crosses the last marshy inlet of this hike, more hemlocks and pines mix with the hardwoods, making this a quieter part of the forest. After Holly Trail Loop, Lakeside Trail continues along the northern shore with occasional lake views across to the barge dock and nature center. It swings around the last inlet, passes Fern Trail, and reaches the waterfowl aviary. Pintail, gadwall, scaup, teal, and other local wild ducks live in this enclosure; they dress much more elegantly than farm ducks. Also, they have a lot more to say than "quack." The wolf enclosure has five captive-born gray wolves that often sit on top of their houses like Snoopy. Otters, raccoons, birds of prey, and deer also live in enclosures; none of the animals were captured from the wild.

Continue on the paved trail, visit the animal habitats, and then complete the loop at the nature center.

Other Hiking Options

1. There are 25 miles of hikes at Bays Mountain; some of the trails connect with Lakeside Trail, and others climb ridges south of the lake. Firetower Trail adds just 1.2 miles (it's quite a climb, but there are a lot of switchbacks) to the trip around the lake and provides the highest view at 2,405 feet. Cherry Knobs Trail gives access to the Ecology Pond and to Cross Ridges Trail, one of the best spring wildflower trails in the park. Other, longer loops are possible; ask in the nature center. From the fire tower, you can see Long Island of the Holston River, which was the sacred council and treaty ground of the Cherokee and, in 1775, the starting point for Daniel Boone's Wilderness Road. Boone and 30 ax men made their way through Cumberland Gap (Hike 26), and at least 200,000 emigrants flowed through the gap to settle the West.

2. Steele Creek Park in Bristol. The best way to this Tennessee hike is through Virginia. From exit 3 off I-81 in Bristol, Virginia, take I-381 until it ends on Commonwealth Avenue (US 11E/US 19), which becomes Volunteer Avenue when it enters Tennessee. About 5 miles from the interstate turn right onto Vance Street and drive 0.6 mile to a parking lot on the left for Rooster Front Park. A short trail leads into Steele Creek Park and a 3-mile loop hike that passes wetlands, a lake, Steele Creek Nature Center, and forested Slagle Hollow, a registered state natural area with ravines, creeks, and wildflowers. There's also a short tree identification walk in Steele Creek Park and other trails off the loop in Slagle Hollow.

21

Sycamore Shoals

Total Distance: 2.0 miles

Hiking Time: 1 hour

Vertical Rise: 10 feet

Rating: Easy

Map: USGS Elizabethton

Sycamore Shoals, tucked between fast-food places and car dealerships, provides an easy hiking trail, a reconstructed fort, riverside views, and history lessons. Most of the trail is handicapped and stroller accessible; it's open all year, but on hot summer days it would be best to hike in the morning or evening. If you pass through Elizabethton on the way to strenuous hikes on the Appalachian Trail or at Roan Mountain, stop here for an hour.

How to Get There

From Johnson City, take US 23 south to the Elizabethton exit. In about 2 miles the highway ends at a cloverleaf exit. US 321 continues into Elizabethton and reaches the Sycamore Shoals State Historical Area on the left in 2 miles.

The Hike

During the summer of 1780, British armies hammered at the northern colonies, but expected little trouble from the South. General Cornwallis sent Major Patrick Ferguson to take care of a few upstart Patriots and recruit Loyalists to march northward. Ferguson wiped out much of the resistance and then issued an ultimatum to the settlers across the mountains: Pledge allegiance to King George or suffer destruction "with fire and sword." This didn't sit well with the Wataugans, who had declared independence in 1775. Six colonels and 900 men mustered at Sycamore Shoals on September 25, 1780, and hiked more than 200 miles in 12 days (try that for hiking speed, carrying weapons, ammunition, and supplies) to Kings Mountain, South Carolina. North Carolina Patriots joined them along the way, and the combined forces surrounded Kings Mountain. Rather than marching in dignified formation, they charged the slopes, dodging behind trees and yelling like "hellish banditti"—strategies that astonished the British, who had chosen the mountaintop because of its security. The battle lasted a few hours and resulted in 225 Loyalist casualties (including Ferguson), 28 Patriot casualties, and the end of Loyalist help from the South. This victory by the brash Overmountain Men is considered by some the turning point of the American War of Independence.

John Sevier, one of the leaders of the Overmountain Men, also fought battles with the Cherokee (who, for a while, supported the British), became governor of the state of Franklin, served in the North Carolina Senate, served as governor of the new state of Tennessee, and then became the first member of the U.S. Congress from west of the mountains.

This is only part of the historical significance of the Sycamore Shoals State Historical Area, where you can learn about dramatic adventures and the origins of the state of Tennessee. From the parking lot, walk to the right of the visitors center and find the gravel path through a mowed area. Pass a map erected by a Boy Scout troop and a memorial to Valentine Sevier, father of John Sevier. The trail enters woods of small maple, dogwood, and sassafras trees and continues past a bird-feeding station and some fitness equipment (and a bench to rest on after you do some pull-ups). After a left curve, the trail approaches the Watauga River at the shoals where settlers crossed to reach the Holston Valley; imagine horses picking their way across the shallow rapids and slippery stones. On

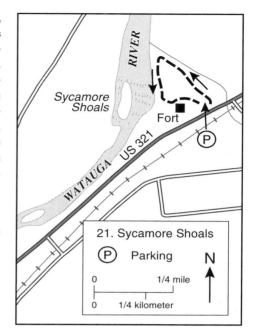

21. Sycamore Shoals

(P) Parking

N

0   1/4 mile

0   1/4 kilometer

the other side they established the first American establishment outside the 13 colonies.

Maples and elms grow larger here, but the best trees are the sycamores that lean out over the water. These trees, with patchy, peeling bark (sometimes called deciduous bark), thrive mainly near creeks. The leaves, shaped somewhat like red maple leaves but larger and less toothy, are covered with a light fuzz in spring. Try stepping gently on one of the gumball-sized fruits—if it's ready, it will break into hundreds of tiny parachuted seeds.

The trail forks; the right branch crosses a small creek and leads to a better view of the shoals and the curve of the Watauga River while the left fork continues the main trail, crosses a bridge, and, after one more view of the shoals, turns back toward the visitors center.

A reconstructed Fort Watauga tells

Fort Watauga

more stories of conflicts with the Cherokee. During one battle, John Sevier reached over the wall and yanked a young woman, Bonny Kate, to safety inside the fort. They later married. You can enter the fort, stand on a bench and plot battle strategy, or visit powder houses and officers' quarters. In summer an action-packed outdoor drama, *The Wataugans,* chronicles the history of Sycamore Shoals.

Other Hiking Options

1. Across that busy highway, the quiet town of Elizabethton offers a walking tour past restored historic features, including an 1882 covered bridge over the Doe River and the site of the syca-more tree (it died in 1987) that shaded the founders of the Watauga Association in 1772. Their Articles of Association established a democracy that predated the American Constitution. Get a brochure at the Sycamore Shoals Visitor Center.

2. About 30 miles southeast of Elizabethton lies Roan Mountain (take US 19E to TN 143 to Carvers Gap), with the largest grass bald in the Appalachians and a network of high-elevation hikes, mostly in North Carolina. The Rhododendron Gardens near Roan High Bluff attract thousands of visitors in June.

3. Hikes 3 and 4 and access to other sections of the Appalachian Trail are close to Elizabethton.

22

House Mountain

Total Distance: 4.8 miles

Hiking Time: 3½–4 hours

Vertical Rise: 900 feet

Rating: Moderate to difficult

Map: USGS John Sevier

Trail Marking: Blaze color for each trail section

About half an hour from downtown Knoxville, House Mountain juts up from the Tennessee Valley farmlands and makes you wonder, as you climb its steep sandstones, how it got there. Winter ice and summer abundance of poison ivy can be problems, but the hike provides a surprising variety of spring wildflowers and outstanding views, especially in fall. *Note:* At the time of this writing, state funding for House Mountain was uncertain. Check with the state parks office before you go.

How to Get There

From Knoxville, drive east on I-40 to the Rutledge Pike exit and turn right onto US 11W. After 10 miles turn left onto Idumea Road at a sign for HOUSE MOUNTAIN STATE PARK. In 0.6 mile turn left onto Hogskin and drive 0.8 mile to a parking area on the right.

The Hike

The House Mountain State Natural Area is shaped like a fox with a furry trail. On this hike you will climb up its front leg to its nose, the West Overlook, then hike along its spine to the tip of its tail, the East Overlook. From here, you return to somewhere near its liver and take a winding trail across its shoulder and back down to its front foot. An old trail, steep and difficult, goes down the hind leg.

One of Tennessee's newest state parks, House Mountain's trail system was built by volunteers in 1993–94. The parking area overflows on pretty fall weekends, but on weekdays or weekends in other seasons, it might be just you and the soaring vultures. Many parts of House Mountain are in an

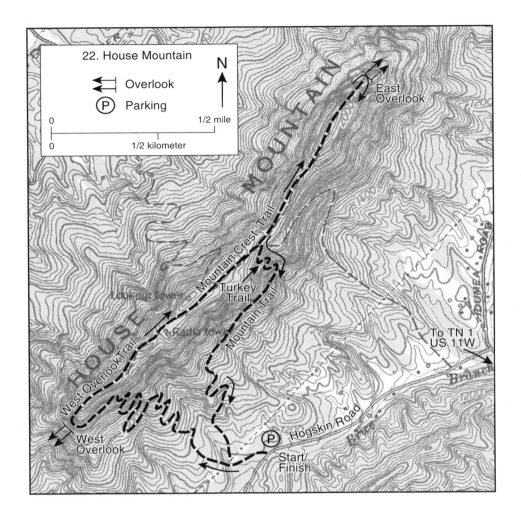

active stage of forest regrowth, and the ground cover includes saplings of the main tree species, providing lots of leaves for identification. Sapling leaves growing in shade are much larger than their counterparts on a mature tree. Bring a tree book. The open forest also provides a favorite habitat of poison ivy and Virginia creeper.

From the parking lot, start on the wide trail between the picnic tables and the information sign. Sawmill Trail Loop goes left; you continue straight to pass an open area

under transmission lines with oak, hickory, and sassafras saplings and the first thick growth of poison ivy. The trail enters the woods between a walnut (look for compound leaves, more than a foot long, with 15 to 23 leaflets) and a maple tree. For a while there's some relief from poison ivy, which doesn't grow well in shade. As the forest grows, poison ivy will diminish and wildflowers, already here to provide seeds, will increase.

At a three-way trail junction turn left for

Pawpaw leaves

West Overlook Trail (yellow blazes) and walk on rocks under hickory trees (look for compound leaves about 1 foot long with five to nine leaflets). Some of the hickory leaves have galls shaped like garbanzo beans; break one open to see a full house of aphids.

Cross a small creek with bedstraw, stonecrop, geranium, foamflower, and false Solomon's seal blooming in spring. Pawpaw shrubs grow waist- to shoulder-high along the creek. Find one of their foot-long smooth-margined leaves and rub it. Then smell your fingers—a positive pawpaw identification is a smell like burned peppers or tires. Whatever it smells like to you, you won't forget it. The leaves droop at the ends as if they're a bit too heavy. Lumpy potato-shaped fruits in fall taste delicious, but squirrels usually get them first.

Along the way, during the day in spring and summer, you can hear wood thrushes, vireos, ovenbirds, and great crested fly-catchers. These clever flycatchers, actually only about 8 inches long from the head to the ends of the tail feathers and just barely crested, decorate their nests with snakeskin.

Turn left on the established trail and start climbing through boulders, which will dominate the scenery the rest of the way up. A plant that is common on and near the rocks is alumroot, with purple and green rounded leaves that can be seen spring to fall. At a rail fence the trail switches back, and it will do so several more times to ease your climb and prevent erosion. Some folks cut across switchbacks when they see the trail above them; on this trail you can see how damaging that can be. Please don't do it.

Squawroot grows along the trail, a yellow six-inch cone-shaped stalk with white flowers in spring. This plant, which gets its food from oak roots and has no chlorophyll, turns to a scruffy black cone by fall.

The trail rises beside a ravine, where you can look down on trees. Cross the same creek again, possibly dry at this elevation, and pass a short left spur to even more rocks to look at. Farther along at another switchback you can see cliffs ahead at about 0.5 mile from the trailhead, but the trail turns away from them to make its way past rock overhangs and more huge boulders with fractures, layers, and plenty of lichens. A weedy spot contains lush poison ivy and Virginia creeper, and also spiderwort, which produces vivid blue flowers in late spring and summer.

Climb along the next rock level, swing right, follow the yellow arrow, swing right again and then left to reach the West Overlook at 0.9 mile, with a view of farms and distant Copper Ridge and the Cumberland Mountains. Here's where you meet the vultures soaring on the thermals from the steep slope you just climbed.

For the East Overlook, follow the ridgetop over more lichen-covered rocks on Mountain Crest Trail. It soon reaches a level dirt trail and then emerges onto an old road in a meadow where you can look back to see communications towers. Follow the road past private property and into woods. A large flat rock on the right would be a good picnic spot, but, as usual, be careful about poison ivy.

At 0.8 mile the trail reaches a bench and the junction with Turkey Trail. Continue on Mountain Crest Trail for another 0.8 miles through a pine forest and then out onto more lichen-covered rocks, some of which you will need to climb over and between. At the end of the ridge the East Overlook shows more neat farms and the Smokies in the distance to the right. Sourwood and pine trees surround the viewing rocks.

Return to the bench and junction and turn down the steep, winding Turkey Trail

(white blazes). After 0.3 mile, turn right onto Mountain Trail (blue blazes). This trail runs parallel to the crest trail, but beneath the cliffs and boulders. Open spots provide better views of the Smokies. After half a mile it drops down on switchbacks past more rock outcrops through open woods. At a trail fork you can take either one; the right one travels closer to the creek, but both reach the three-way junction that you passed on the way to the West Overlook. Return under the transmission lines and to the parking lot, 1.2 miles from the junction of Turkey and Mountain Trails.

Other Hiking Options

1. The Sawmill Hill loops are nearly flat and run through pretty woods with a good variety of trees and wildflowers. The right loop (0.4 mile) starts between the information sign and the parking lot, and the left loop starts about 100 yards beyond the parking lot on the main trail. Trees on the right loop have labels. Both loops would be good for children on a cool or winter day.

2. Another hike within easy driving distance of Knoxville (about 40 minutes) is the TVA's River Bluff Trail. From I-75, take the Norris exit. Turn right onto TN 61, drive about 2 miles, past the Museum of Appalachia, then turn left onto US 441 and drive about 5 miles to the Norris Dam. Cross the dam, drive up the winding road, and pass the Norris Dam Overlook. Turn left on the next road after the overlook. Immediately turn left again at a fork and drive down another winding road to trail parking on the right. The well-worn 3-mile loop passes a superb wildflower carpet in March and April, with hillsides of trout lilies, trillium, Dutchman's-breeches, celandine poppies, twinleaf, and more.

23

Ijams Nature Center

Total Distance: 1.5 miles

Hiking Time: 1 hour

Vertical Rise: 200 feet

Rating: Easy

Maps: Knoxville city map; USGS Shook Gap

Only 5 miles from downtown Knoxville, Ijams (the name rhymes with *rhymes*) Nature Center offers several miles of trails with river views, diverse habitats, abundant wild-flowers, and opportunities for nature study. Small children will like the safe, graded trails and promise of frogs and turtles. Summer days may be too hot, but cooler evenings make this an all-season hike. Special pro-grams, exhibits, and children's activities are available.

How to Get There

From downtown Knoxville, cross the Gay Street Bridge toward Baptist Hospital and turn left at a traffic light onto Sevier Avenue, where you should see the first green IJAMS sign. Drive 0.6 mile along Sevier and veer right onto Island Home Avenue. Follow the green signs for 2 miles to the Ijams entrance on the left.

The Hike

After exploring the nature center and pools, head back on River Trail, swinging left and left again down the wide path carpeted with wood chips. The trail runs below the nature center through a growth of kudzu, an Asian import that has covered much of the South-east in tree-killing masses of big leaves and vines. In August peek under the leaves to find purple-blue blossoms that smell like grape Kool-Aid. The nature center building site and its surrounding landscapes were once choked with kudzu; people chopped, dug, bulldozed, and hired goats to clear the land. Cross a wooden bridge and head down a slope that can be a little slippery in rain. At a fork where the trail starts to level out, turn right and continue toward the river. (The left fork leads to a network of trails in the old section of the park, also worth a visit.)

Then comes the best feature of this trail—a long boardwalk along the base of the river bluff and just a few feet above the water. The boardwalk curves in and out with the bluff, even leaving holes for trees that hang out over the river. This is the Tennessee River, or Fort Loudon Lake; a TVA dam downstream controls the water level and allows barge traffic. Just upstream from here the French Broad River from North Carolina and the Holston River from Virginia join to form the Tennessee River. This fork is now the site of an industrial area called, of course, Forks of the River. During the siege of Knoxville in the Civil War, suppliers of food and other necessities slipped down the French Broad to sustain the Union army in Knoxville. A map mistake showed the fork below Knoxville instead of above, and the Confederates had no idea where the supplies were coming from.

Honeysuckle, tree-of-heaven, and a few other alien plants crowd the beginning of the boardwalk, but farther along pawpaws, American hornbeams, elms, spleenwort, and resurrection fern represent native plants. Mud dauber wasps build clay houses for their larvae on the rock face, and blue-tailed skinks run up and down the bluffs. These 5- to 8-inch lizards wave their bright blue tails over their backs when they come out where they might be spotted by predators. If a bird grabs the conspicuous tail, it breaks off, leaving the rest of the lizard wounded but alive.

Just past a bench is a bat cave with iron bars; you can peer in at a sandy floor and tiny spring. The bats have been disturbed here in the past, but the iron bars keep

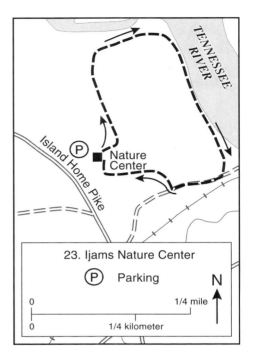

23. Ijams Nature Center

(P) Parking   N

0   1/4 mile

0   1/4 kilometer

explorers (the human ones with flashlights) out. The cave should be more bat-friendly now, and evening visitors may see bats catching food on the wing. There are other small caves and cracks in the rock face; enjoy them from a distance.

Continue along the boardwalk and look for dragonflies, great blue herons, kingfishers, and geological folds in the limestone. At the end of the boardwalk the trail travels along the river on the level, turns right at a limestone-crushing plant, and ascends a grassy road. A signed trail to the left crosses railroad tracks and makes a loop on another smaller boardwalk along a forest creek.

Back on the main trail watch for a NORTH COVE AND TOWER sign on the right (Tower Trail is a longer and steeper way to get back to the nature center), and then the SOUTH COVE sign. South Cove Trail leads to Beech Trail, which curves left back to the center. Notice

Peering into the bat cave

the beech trees with smooth gray bark and toothy leaves. Relatives of oak trees, they share the habit of keeping their brown leaves for most of the winter.

Emerge into a sunny meadow with mowed lawn on the right and sumac and meadow flowers on the left. This portion of trail is paved and handicapped accessible. Visit the butterfly house, then check again for frogs and dragonflies at the pools or have a picnic in the pavilion.

Other Hiking Options

You can spend all day or an hour hiking here. Trails in the old part of the park go by rich wildflower areas, a pond with turtles, frogs, and water snakes, meadows, cultivated gardens, and an excellent forested river view. The center provides maps. A new paved trail (Will Skelton Greenway) links the Ijams trails to another network of trails at the Eastern State Wildlife Management Area, which has open fields, pleasant woods, and one of the few healthy marshes in the Knoxville area. In spring many species of frogs, red-spotted newts, and snapping turtles breed there.

24

North Ridge

Total Distance: 7.5 miles (one way)

Hiking Time: 4-5 hours

Vertical Rise: 200 feet

Rating: Moderate

Map: USGS Clinton/Windrock

Trail Marking: White blazes, with blue blazes on access trails

A National Recreational Trail, North Ridge Trail is part of an extensive greenway system in Oak Ridge. It runs roughly parallel to Outer Drive along the north side of Black Oak Ridge. This description covers western sections of the trail and their accesses, as well as directions to other accesses. Definitely a cool-weather hike, the trail has a good variety of wildflowers, ferns, and trees. It runs up and down side ridges, steeply in some places.

How to Get There

The access to North Ridge Trail that's easiest to find is at the junction of TN 62 (Illinois Avenue) and Outer Drive. From the junction of Oak Ridge Turnpike (TN 95) and TN 62, drive 2 miles on TN 62 to the top of the ridge at a traffic light. Turn right onto West Outer Drive and then immediately left to park on the left side of a gas station and convenience store. Look for a NORTH RIDGE TRAIL sign straight ahead; the access trail is about 40 yards to the right of the sign.

To reach the western terminus of the trail, turn left onto West Outer Drive from the same intersection and go 1.4 miles. The trail starts at a rusty metal gate on the right opposite Mississippi Avenue. Parking is difficult here; use this access if someone can drop you off.

For the Walker Lane access, turn right onto West Outer Drive and go 0.9 mile to Walker Lane; turn left and drive 0.1 mile to a trail sign on the left, where there's room for two cars. The eastern end of the trail on Endicott Lane has room for several cars. Drive about 3 miles east on Outer Drive until

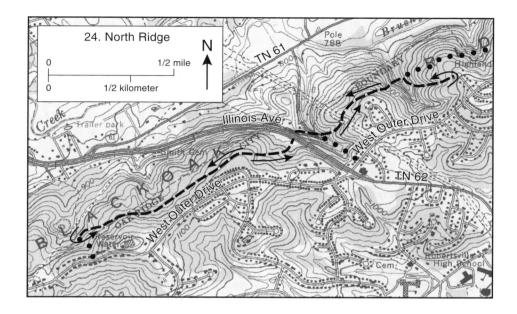

24. North Ridge

N

0 _____ 1/2 mile

0 _____ 1/2 kilometer

it becomes East Drive; drive 1 mile more and turn left onto Endicott (the next street after Enfield). Park on the left at a large NORTH RIDGE TRAIL sign.

The Hike

Built in the 1970s by the Oak Ridge–based Tennessee Citizens for Wilderness Planning, North Ridge Trail runs entirely within the boundaries of Oak Ridge and, except for two road crossings, stays in the forest all the way. Several accesses run from Outer Drive down to the trail, some with difficult parking. The route described here starts on the western end and focuses on the western half of the North Ridge Trail and its access trails; car shuttles or backtracking will be necessary. One way to see most of the trail (6.1 miles) with easy parking on both ends is to arrange a car shuttle between Illinois Avenue and Endicott Lane.

The western end of the trail, from Mississippi Avenue to the Walker Lane access, shows a variety of habitats and is far below the houses of Outer Drive. The Walker Lane access trail east of Illinois Avenue goes up a pretty valley with as many wildflowers and big trees as the main trail. From a few viewpoints you can see Pine Ridge, the next ridge west in the Great Valley, and, in the distance, Walden Ridge, the beginning of the Cumberland Plateau.

The TN 62 access trail enters the woods about 40 yards to the right of the NORTH RIDGE TRAIL sign; look for large blue blazes on telephone poles and then on trees. A false trail begins from the back of the sign, possibly made by people who didn't see the blazes.

Once in the woods the trail, clear and well blazed, passes between big white oaks and then descends steeply on an old, eroded road. Bloodroot and Solomon's seal line the trail. At first traffic noise from TN 62 is loud, but it fades as a small ridge separates the road and trail. In 0.2 mile you'll reach a hairpin turn on Old Batley Road.

To go west from here, turn left and walk

up Old Batley Road to busy TN 62 and cross. Look for a green post with a white blaze about 50 yards uphill on the other side and enter the woods. There are several turns on this section, all well marked with double blazes, and a few old roads cross the trail. Climb through oak and hickory woods with a sassafras and pawpaw understory; notice the extra-large shade leaves of young trees. A few American chestnut saplings grow here but will succumb to chestnut blight when they get larger.

The trail crosses two gullies, passing a variety of spring wildflowers: jack-in-the-pulpit, yellow oxalis with edible shamrock-shaped leaves, bedstraw, false and true Solomon's seal, and mayapple. Patches of Virginia creeper alternate with patches of poison ivy; these two ground covers (and tree climbers) almost never grow together, and the poison ivy usually prefers more sunlight.

Dead fallen logs and tree trunks show the roughly rectangular holes of pileated woodpeckers (sometimes with freshly scattered chunks of wood), and you may hear these crow-sized birds cackling as they fly through the woods.

At 1.4 miles the trail reaches a power line, with trees characteristic of drier, more open areas: sourwood, cherry, and red cedar, along with introduced plants such as multiflora rose and honeysuckle. From here you can backtrack to Illinois Avenue or climb a rutted road 0.2 mile to West Outer Drive opposite Mississippi Avenue.

To go east from the TN 62 access (for one of the prettiest sections of the trail), go down the access from the gas station and convenience store as described above. Look for white blazes to the right up the roadbank on Old Batley Road. The trail climbs a small valley and swings left through dry, open woods, reaching a powerline opening at 0.2 mile. Bracken fern and saplings of sassafras, oak, hickory, and maple trees line the trail, which has few blazes and gets tricky to follow in the open area. Several trails and tracks may mislead you. Ignore a grassy trail to the right and go straight under the first set of power lines on wooden poles. At the next fork turn right and go under the metal power-line poles and toward the woods, where the blazes resume. If you come to a pile of wooden telephone poles, go downhill a few yards to find the path into the woods.

From here, the trail starts down through maple, oak, and hickory woods. Look for umbrella magnolia saplings, 2 to 3 feet high, with all the leaves radiating from the top like spokes of an umbrella. Deciduous magnolias have soft, flexible leaves instead of the rigid, waxy leaves of southern magnolias. After you find a small one, look up and find larger ones with smooth gray bark and an umbrella at the end of each branch. In summer you may see magnolia leaves with neatly scalloped edges. Leafcutter bees snip out 1/2-inch D-shaped pieces of leaf, roll them up like cigars, lay an egg inside and provision it with food, and then tuck the cigar into a bark crevice. The bees like redbud leaves, too.

The trail goes level along a rich hillside with jack-in-the-pulpit, Solomon's seal, anise root, and bloodroot (spring flowers), along with black cohosh, pipsissewa, and rattlesnake plantain (summer flowers). A special spring flower here is twinleaf—a single stalk with two leaves (actually one leaf constricted in the middle) on top like the wings of a butterfly. The white flower, on its own stalk, blooms for a day or so in March and drops its petals at the slightest disturbance. The leaves and the peculiar fruit capsule with a lid like a teapot keep

Stonecrop

growing well into summer. Blue cohosh and mayapple, also found on this trail, are in the same family (barberry) as twinleaf. American chestnut, redbud, and mulberry saplings grow along the trail.

With two quick switchbacks, the trail drops to limestone boulders at its lowest point. Ridges in the Great Valley are made of ancient, hard sandstone, while the valley floor consists of more recent limestone. Alumroot, blue phacelia, and stonecrop live in rock cracks, along with a covering of moss. Black cohosh and yellow leaf cup bloom in summer. Look for four kinds of ferns here: ebony spleenwort and walking fern up on the rocks, and Christmas fern and rattlesnake fern on moist soil near the base.

After a few more boulders, cross a small creek. At 0.5 mile from Illinois Avenue, white-blazed North Ridge Trail goes on straight; the blue-blazed Walker Lane access trail turns right to climb 0.3 mile. Orange-flowered jewelweed, up to 3 feet tall, crowds the creek and produces ex-

ploding seedpods in late summer; cup your hand around a mature one and catch the seeds before they fly out. Eat them; they taste like black walnuts and are much less trouble. Foamflower, toothwort, and more twinleaf also bloom along the creek, and large beeches and basswoods stand above its banks. Carrion flower, dwarf-crested iris, small persimmon trees, and large chestnut oaks occupy the drier habitats of the climb, and soon you see the backs of houses. After a sinkhole on the right, pass through a patch of Virginia creeper to the trail parking lot on Walker Lane.

To continue on North Ridge Trail to Endicott Lane, pass the Walker Lane access and climb a long hill, then descend to Key Springs Road at 2.2 miles from Illinois Avenue. Cross at a sharp curve and look for steps and blazes a few yards downhill. The next 4 miles of trail are also well blazed and easy to follow. The only exception is one crossing of a woods road, where you must turn left to find the continuation of the trail.

25

Audubon Acres

Total Distance: 3 miles

Hiking Time: 1½–2 hours

Vertical Rise: 100 feet

Rating: Easy

Map: East Chattanooga

Audubon Acres, a 120-acre sanctuary less than 3 miles from I-75, has a network of hikes along South Chickamauga Creek, and the birds know all about it. Two loop trails lead from a suspension bridge to river views, the site of a Native American village, a wetland, and wooded hillsides.

How to Get There

From I-75 in Chattanooga, take exit 3A to East Brainerd Road. At the second light turn right onto Gunbarrel Road and drive 1 mile to Sanctuary Road. Turn right and follow signs 0.6 mile to Audubon Acres. Park in a large gravel lot; do not drive across the railroad tracks.

The Hike

Stop at the interpretive center to get a map and see what has been sighted recently. Then walk across the railroad tracks and follow the road past Spring Frog Cabin and a commemorative tree for the Trail of Tears in 1838. Straight ahead, an open area looks like a small clear-cut—which it is, because the pines here became infested with pine bark beetles. The trees had no chance to survive, so they were cut to prevent spread of the beetle. Scouts and other volunteers are currently planting replacement trees. Audubon Acres has a network of trails and connectors; one possible route is described here. By the time you read this, the trails through the pine area will have been rebuilt.

After visiting the cabin (and a big sequoia tree nearby), return to the road, cross it, and walk along a line of oaks toward South

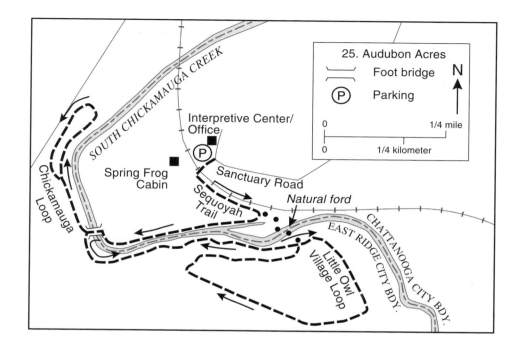

Chickamauga Creek. Enter the woods on Sequoyah Trail and swing right beside the creek. *Sequoia* and *Sequoyah* are alternate spellings of the name of the Cherokee man who invented a Cherokee alphabet in 1828 by identifying and classifying syllables: the Cherokee became literate within months and started publishing newspapers in their own language. When the trail gets to the river, its name changes to Dragging Canoe Trail, named for a Cherokee chief who opposed land treaties with European settlers in 1775.

Continue past two sinkholes and large sycamore trees to a bend in the creek and cross a suspension bridge built in 1948. Turn left and walk along the creek (possibly muddy, with bridges over the lowest spots). Foamflower, phlox, mayapple, and little brown jug bloom in spring, but honeysuckle and multiflora rose crowd the undergrowth. Kingfishers swoop up and down the creek,

and warblers, titmice, woodpeckers, and nuthatches call from the woods, even at midday. Wood-duck nest boxes may have customers.

Pass a spot where you could ford the creek back to Sequoyah Trail if you had to, and turn right through the woods to an open field. Little Owl Village once sat on this fertile area, just above the floodplain, and the site may represent 7,000 years of occupation, first by Woodland Indians and then by the Cherokee. A large sign describes the village and its history.

Continue along the right edge of the meadow, past yellow mustard, fleabane, and blue-eyed Mary. Turn right at a large tulip tree and climb a hill along a fence. Look for sessile (with the flower sitting right on the leaves) red trillium, toothwort, and Solomon's seal (pretty earringlike flowers in spring and hard green seeds that taste like raw peas in summer). Reach the crest and

Yellow trillium

50 Hikes in the Tennessee Mountains

descend on stairs through better woods—big trees and no honeysuckle. Another crop of flowers lives here: bloodroot, geranium, rue anemone, and yellow mandarin. Turn right along a woodland pond, where you might hear frog songs or see basking turtles. Reach Little Owl Village Trail and turn left to return to the bridge.

You can return on the bridge or continue on Chickamauga Loop (0.6 mile), a woodland trail with no mud. Squawroot and fire pink do well on this drier hillside, along with ash, maple, and sourwood trees. Turn right at a fork and descend to a short spur at 0.3 mile that leads to a comfortable rock above the creek, surrounded by poison ivy. Return to trail and climb past hickories and large chestnut oaks. Spiderwort, with bright blue flowers and leaves like wide grass blades, grows abundantly here.

Pass a residential area and descend to the bridge and return, along the creek or possibly on one of those new trails through new trees.

Other Hiking Options

1. Several other trails meander on both sides of the creek. Near Spring Frog Cabin is an eagle enclosure and a demonstration orchard.
2. Lookout Mountain, Chickamauga Battlefield, and several associated Civil War historical sites offer miles of hiking trails between the Tennessee River Gorge and the Georgia Border.

V

Northern Cumberland Mountains

Stone steps at Gentlemen's Swimming Hole

26

Cumberland Gap: Tri-State Peak and Cumberland Trail

Total Distance: 7 miles

Hiking Time: 4 hours

Vertical Rise: 900 feet

Rating: Moderate

Map: USGS Middleboro South (TN/KY)

Trail Marking: White blazes (CT)

This all-season hike includes two climbs—one from the iron furnace to Cumberland Gap and the next to the mountain crest above the gap. Though steep in spots, it's well graded and provides excellent views along with historical perspectives.

How to Get There

From I-81 in Morristown, travel 50 miles on US 25E/TN 32. Turn right onto US 58 and, in 0.4 mile, turn left at a sign for the town of Cumberland Gap. Turn left again immediately, cross the railroad tracks, and follow Cumberland Drive into town. Turn left on Pennwyn and then right in less than a block into the parking area for Iron Furnace.

From I-75, take the Cove Lake/LaFollette/US 25W exit and drive 8 miles to La-Follette. Where 25W turns left, stay straight on TN 63, drive 32 miles to US 25E, and follow the directions above.

Cumberland Gap National Historical Park Visitor Center is at the first exit on the Kentucky side of the tunnel.

The Hike

Cumberland Gap has been a gateway to the West for hundreds of years—as the Warrior's Path, later as Daniel Boone's Wilderness Road of 1775, and today as the site of a high-tech 4,000-foot straight-bore tunnel from Tennessee to Kentucky. The Cumberland Gap National Historical Park preserves these sites and the ridge-line of Cumberland Mountain that runs along the Kentucky-Virginia border; the mountain continues south to Cove Lake in Tennessee through public and private land.

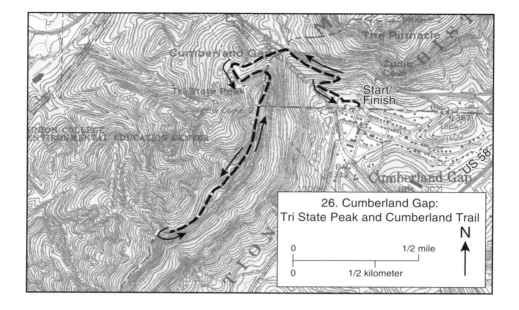

26. Cumberland Gap:
Tri State Peak and Cumberland Trail

N

0   1/2 mile

0   1/2 kilometer

Cumberland Mountain and its southern extension, Walden Ridge, form the eastern rim of the Cumberland Plateau, which contains about half of the hikes in this book. The tunnel, opened in 1996, passes under the gap (and this hike) and will allow restoration of the gap as Boone and the thousands of settlers who followed him saw it.

Between 1800 and 1880 the iron furnace at the beginning of the hike produced 150-pound ingots, sometimes 6 tons per day, using charcoal for fuel and a waterwheel for cooling. The ingots went by train to blacksmiths in Chattanooga. Charcoal workers stripped the hillsides of trees, and miners dug ore, leaving eroded pits. The waterwheel is gone, but you can see the opening where it used to be. The trees are growing back, and the mining pits have reclaimed themselves. The iron furnace and the first part of this trail are in Virginia, and you are bound to step into Kentucky a few times. This is the northern terminus of the Cumberland Trail (CT); from here, when the

CT is complete, you will be able to hike 280 miles to Signal Point near Chattanooga (the trailhead for Hike 50).

Walk up the paved trail to the furnace and turn left up a graveled path. Several switchbacks lead up to the abandoned gap road; look for depressions and old ditches from pit mining along the way. Climb a bank to the road and the BOONE'S TRACE historical sign 0.7 mile from the furnace. You can take a side trip up the road to the crest of the gap and imagine seeing the West for the first time. The pavement will soon be removed—possibly by the time you read this book—and the trail will give access to Cudjo Cave across the road. Where erosion or cracks broke through the hard sandstone of the ridge, water could seep through the underlying softer rock to carve out caves and underground rivers. Cudjo Cave and the connected Soldiers and King Solomons Caves were opened in 1890 for commercial tours; the park service has now gated the caves and plans to restore

Honeycomb erosion and one-foot-wide cave on bluff face

them for more traditional lantern tours that will preserve cave formations and habitats.

Return to the trail (now an old roadbed) to a sign that commemorates the Royal Colonial Boundary of 1665 (a short-lived boundary that allowed Native Americans to live in peace west of the mountains) and the survey from the Atlantic to the Mississippi River (which took nearly 100 years). The trail swings left past sites of the Union commissary and military storehouse and then turns right to climb the knob of Tri-State Peak. Here, in a gazebo, you can stand in three states at once (actually, only Tennessee is a state; Kentucky and Virginia are commonwealths) and learn the state songs, birds, and so on.

Continue 0.2 mile more up to Fort Farragut (elevation 2,040 feet), which provides views of the gap and the approaches on both sides. During the Civil War, visibility was excellent because all the trees had been cut down for charcoal; this fort controlled the gap, and was held first by the Confederates and then the Union. Not only did it control passage through the gap, but it also gave the Union access to the rail lines to Chattanooga.

After Fort Farragut, descend from the flat overlook and find the first Cumberland Trail white blaze on a tulip tree to the right of the trail back to Tri-State Peak. Here the trail changes character—it becomes narrow, rocky, and little used. About 2.5 miles of the trail are maintained by the Lincoln Memorial University Hiking Club. Beyond that, much of the ridge is private property; negotiations with the landowners will be needed to complete the trail to LaFollette. So for now, hike along the CT as far as you like through a good forest of oak, hickory, and sourwood. The trail twists among lichen-covered rocks, giving occasional views of Middlesboro, Cumberland Gap, the Tennessee Valley, and the Pinnacle, the high point across the gap. About 1 mile from Fort Farragut the trail rises to two rocky peaks with rough footing and then descends along a wider and gentler ridgeline until it becomes overgrown and unmaintained.

For updates on the length of the Cumberland Trail here and the construction of access trails, contact the visitors center or the Cumberland Trail Conference.

Other Hiking Options

Some excellent Cumberland Gap National Historical Park trails, leading to Skylight Cave, Gibson Gap, the Hensley Settlement, White Rocks, and Sand Cave, start in Virginia or run along the Kentucky-Virginia border. The park visitors center at the north end of the tunnel provides maps.

27

Cumberland Trail: LaFollette to Cove Lake

Total Distance: 9.9 miles

Hiking Time: 6–7 hours

Vertical Rise: 1,000 feet

Rating: Strenuous

Map: USGS Ivydell and Demory

Trail Marking: White rectangular blazes

Wonderful views from the rocky spine of Cumberland Mountain make this one of the best fall hikes in the region. Displays of mountain laurel blooms in late spring are also an attraction. Because of exposed rocks, avoid this hike in bad weather.

How to Get There

From the Cove Lake/LaFollette exit off I-75, take US 25W north 8 miles to LaFollette. Turn north with US 25W (here called Main Street) at a traffic light that features banks on the corners. Drive 0.6 mile and turn left just before a bridge across Big Creek. Look for a brown sign—CUMBERLAND TRAIL, LAFOLLETTE ACCESS—and turn right into a large gravel lot.

The Hike

Cumberland Mountain, which runs from central Virginia to Tennesses's Cove Lake State Park, is breached only once—by Big Creek in LaFollette; all other creeks and rivers must go around this knife-edged ridge. To hike this part of Cumberland Mountain you will join an elite club with the high initiation fee of climbing the mountain from Big Creek. Once on top you will see the rolling valley floor and possibly the distant Smokies to the east and the forested Cumberland Plateau to the west. This section of the Cumberland Trail (CT) has been open for years; its continuation to Cross Mountain will be open by the time you read this. To the north is the last leg of the CT to Cumberland Gap in about 35 miles; that section has some open parts and the rest is under construction (see Hike 26). This narrative

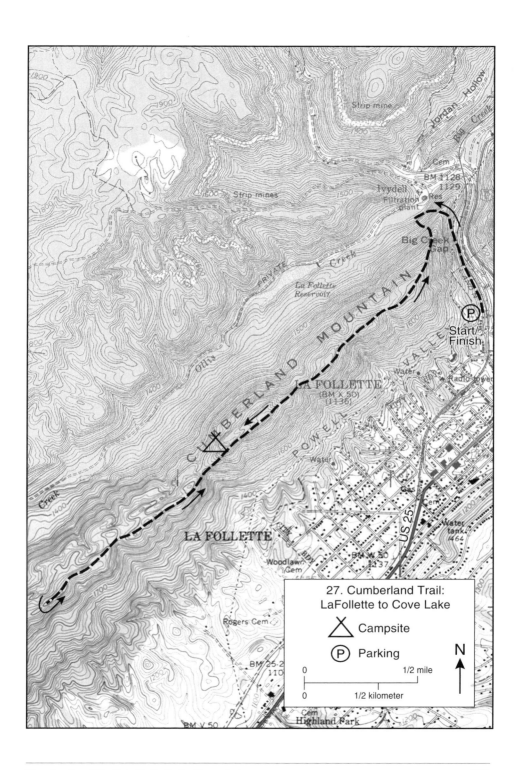

27. Cumberland Trail:
LaFollette to Cove Lake

△ Campsite

Ⓟ Parking

N

0 — 1/2 mile
0 — 1/2 kilometer

describes the hike from north to south. To do it all you will need a car shuttle, but there is a good turnaround point at 1.8 miles for a one-car hike to one of the best parts. Less than 4 miles total, this short portion of the hike can give you some exercise in a morning or afternoon; to spend all day, continue on to Eagle Bluff at 5 miles (10 miles round-trip).

Boy Scout Troop 622 of LaFollette maintains the northern 5 miles of this trail, and the Tennessee Trails Association maintains it from Eagle Bluff south.

On the left side of the parking lot Tank Springs, channeled into two pipes set in cement, provide a constant flow of sweet, clean water. Look for blazes to the right of the springs and start along a wide gravel road lined with introduced plants: kudzu, honeysuckle, clover, mullein, and Queen Anne's lace. The road runs between rocky Big Creek and a railroad embankment. There are few blazes (it's hard to blaze blackberries), so trust the road for about half a mile. Then look for a double blaze to the left on a telephone pole. Turn left, cross a pile of gravel, and go under the railroad bridge. Finally the trail switches back left to what you came for: woods, mostly sycamore and maple. Look for Solomon's seal, starry campion, jack-in-the-pulpit, mayapple, little brown jug, and, of course, poison ivy on the right bank.

Climb to a cement house platform, turn right, and climb again to an open power-line cut, passing good blazes and a patch of maidenhair fern. Watch for blazes indicating the trail to the right; this turn may be obscured by summer growth. If you start descending under the power lines, turn back and try again.

Stop often on the steep rocky climb to study lichens and rock cap fern. Yellow Tennessee Wildlife Resources Agency signs and paint marks on trees supplement the CT blazes and show property boundaries. Traffic noise from 25W and LaFollette church bells will follow you for a while.

Rock steps lead to a drier habitat with mountain laurel, a few rhododendrons, and galax, trailing arbutus, and moss carpets. After a bit more rock scrambling, you'll see a view on the right. You're on the Tennessee Valley Divide; Big Creek water flows to Norris Lake and then the Tennessee River, while creeks to the west flow into the Cumberland River. However, all the waters meet in Paducah, Kentucky, for a ride to the Gulf of Mexico.

At a double blaze on a rock turn right and descend for the first time since you left Tank Springs. After passing rhododendrons growing against a rock slab, take a quick left at another double blaze and climb again. (This ridgetop climb is not finished with you yet.) Red oak, chestnut oak, red maple, and hickory grow on wider parts of the ridgetop, and you may hear hooded warblers and vireos singing.

A geological disk set in the rock marks a high point at about 1.5 miles. Just a bit farther is an open rock with a view of downtown LaFollette and its surrounding fields and industries. Norris Lake, impounded behind the first TVA dam in 1934, can be seen to the southeast. Sit a while and watch or listen for fence lizards skittering over the rocks and doing push-ups to signal their ownership. Blue-flowered spiderwort grows in soil pockets and blooms in summer along with pokeweed. The next part of the trail may be choked with overhanging poison ivy, but a little way back in the woods sassafras and blueberry bushes form the understory. From the tops of rocks, you can look down on sweet birch (look for the catkins) and Virginia pines (look for the cones of all ages, especially the 1-inch new cones shaped like tiny pineapples).

Sassafras with four different leaf shapes on one twig—a symbol of good luck

Blazes may be scarce, but along here the trail can't hide anywhere—just follow the ridgetop. At 1.8 miles you come to the best viewing rock with a steep climb down a crevice on other side. You may want to stop here, eat lunch, and return for the one-car option.

To continue to Eagle Bluff or Cove Lake State Park, climb down the rock crevice. This could be dangerous—look it over and plan a strategy, because there are few footholds. The trail first travels along the ridge and then turns right into pretty woods to descend to a spring and campsite at about 2 miles. Two bluff walls and a small creek provide different scenery and habitat for trillium, jack-in-the-pulpit, toothwort, and hepatica. Up the slope under pine trees grow pink lady's slippers with their wide-wale corduroy leaves. Climb out of the hollow through moist woods of Fraser magnolia, maple, oak, and sassafras. After a long

stretch in a saddle between two ridgelines, you reach the rocky top again, with great views east. Then it's back to the woods. The blazes come frequently, but if you're in doubt—especially when newly fallen leaves cover the trail—look back occasionally to check the blazes behind you.

The trail emerges from the woods at 6 miles onto an eroded, possibly muddy Eagle Bluff Road that leads to Eagle Bluff, another rocky overlook, but you have already seen better views and can go on. Two miles beyond the overlook is a blazed left turn that leads down a steep section to Cove Lake State Park. However, if you have come this far, you should take the spur to Devils Racetrack, a series of vertical rock slabs. You can climb out for a wonderful view of mountains across a gap and bug-sized trucks creeping along on I-75 below.

To get to Cove Lake State Park, return to the main trail and follow the blazes down

. . . and down, until the trail comes out in a residential area. Follow the road about half a mile down into the park. The Cumberland Trail Conference plans to reroute this section to avoid private property and to make a connection with the Cross Mountain section.

Other Hiking Options

1. By the time this book appears, southern extensions of the Cumberland Trail will be ready for hiking. Across I-75 from Cove Lake State Park, the CT climbs Cross Mountain along Dunbar Creek. This difficult segment is so steep that the creek doesn't flow; it just tumbles from waterfall to waterfall. Within a year or so the CT will be complete to Frozen Head State Park (25 miles, including the trail's highest elevation) and will provide excellent backpacking trips if you can get up that first mountain. And the next ones, too.

2. North of LaFollette the CT already has a route—since there is nowhere for it to go except the narrow ridgetop—to the Cumberland Gap National Historical Park (about 35 miles). However, part of the route runs through private property, and the Cumberland Trail Conference will be working on arrangements. For maps and up-to-date trail information (and to volunteer for a work crew), consult the CT web site: http://cumberlandtrail.org.

28

Hidden Passage

Total Distance: 8.0 miles

Hiking Time: 5 hours

Vertical Rise: 150 feet

Rating: Moderate

Map: USGS Sharp Place

For a detailed study of a Cumberland Plateau bluff—over, under, along, and through—choose this Pickett State Park trail. Many ups and downs make it a moderate hike with no long, steep parts. This is an all-season hike with spring wildflowers, fall foliage, winter views, and cool rock shelters in summer, though some exposed sections can be hot. Children who have completed other 8-mile hikes will enjoy this one, but there are some unprotected bluff rims.

How to Get There

From Jamestown, drive 12 miles north on TN 154 to the Pickett State Park office. The trailhead is 0.3 mile north of the office (limited parking) on the right; it's between the office and the Group Camp, where you can also access Hidden Passage Trail if the trailhead parking is full.

The Hike

From the small parking lot, the trail descends to cross under power lines on an exposed, south-facing slope. Climbing fern and mountain laurel grow in full sun, and as soon as you get into shade, look for bigleaf magnolia, sourwood, red oak, hickory, and blueberry. Ground plants include partridgeberry, trailing arbutus, and wintergreen. Then the trail dips into a cooler creek bed that supports hemlock but not much ground cover.

At 0.5 mile the loop starts; for this hike, proceed right, or counterclockwise. The trail drops under the bluff to the hidden passage—a route through a pile of boulders underneath an overhang with a flat roof (flat because all its boulders fell off). This pat-

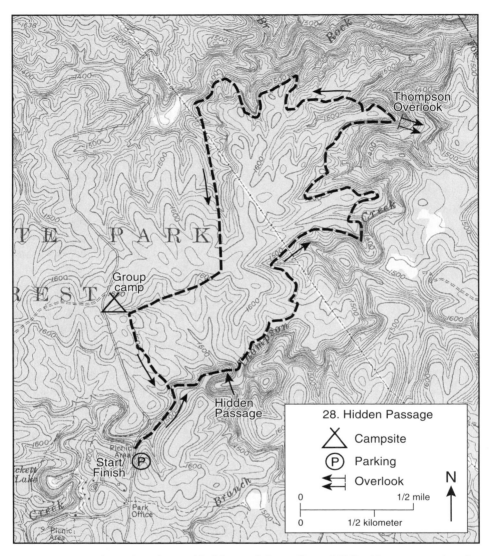

28. Hidden Passage

- △ Campsite
- Ⓟ Parking
- Overlook

N

0   1/2 mile

0   1/2 kilometer

tern repeats again and again on this hike, because softer sandstone erodes from beneath a hard rock cap, leaving cavities or rockhouses (as they are called here). South-facing rockhouses such as Hidden Passage are dry and sandy; north-facing ones are damp and grow shade- tolerant plants.

Climb to the warm blufftop again, and within 0.1 mile find the signed spur trail right to Crystal Falls. It's steep and rocky but worth the trip to a small drippy falls with a bowl-shaped pool. Return to the main trail the same way and cross the creek that formed the falls; be careful in high water. From here the trail becomes narrow and hugs the bluff rim. Keep children close to you for this short section. You can hear and perhaps glimpse Crystal Falls below.

The trail moves away from the bluff and, at 1.5 miles, crosses an old road. Trail signs help you locate the trail on both sides of the road, but the green blazes may be hard to spot. After gentle ups and downs in quiet woods, the trail returns to the bluff and a sandy rockhouse. Quartz pebbles, standing out like pimples from the sandstone, resist erosion, so the sandstone erodes around them until they drop out. Find some loose ones and help the process along. Also look for cone-shaped ant lion traps in the soft sand along the base. Ant lions (larvae of insects that look somewhat like damselflies, with long, lacy wings) burrow into the sand and then flip the grains out with their big heads. They wait for ants and other small insects to fall in and then grab them with sharp jaws. If the prey seems likely to escape, the ant lion shoots sand grains at it, making it fall. Drop a bit of sand into a pit to watch the ant lion clean house.

The trail follows the contour in and out of rockhouses, each with its own pattern of wavy lines or erosion pits, and passes under the power line again.

Creeks have cut larger channels on the bluff, and you'll hike deep into cool rockhouses and then out onto oak-covered points where you'll see the bluff across Thompson Creek Gorge. The rockhouses face north here, and the moisture fosters liverworts, mushrooms, and ferns. Wildflowers grow from cracks, and mud dauber wasps build clay nests for their larvae. After the last and somewhat drier overhang, steps on the trail lead up to a junction of Hidden Passage Trail with Double Falls Trail at 4 miles. This 1-mile side trip is strenuous and a bit hard to follow—blazes show the way down a little-traveled rocky hillside.

From the junction, Hidden Passage Trail runs under Thompson Overlook and then climbs to the top at 4.4 miles. Enjoy the view

and stay away from the edge. Then follow the trail to a gravel road that leads back to the Group Camp. Cross the road and look for a small TRAILS sign—but you have to go right and then find an opening to the left in a bank of mountain laurel. Follow Hidden Passage Trail green blazes to the junction with Tunnel Trail; this 1-mile walkway leads downhill to an old rail tunnel that you cannot enter. Hidden Passage Trail continues left along the top of the bluff, with good views of the gorge and the bluff on the other side, then cuts straight and level through woods to a road behind the Group Camp. Green blazes are hard to see here; follow the road until it curves right, then look for blazes and for a small trail sign readable from the other side. The trail crosses a lawn and then enters the woods for part of the loop. It goes over the top of a curved rock shelter that you can look back into. After some easy ups and downs, a grassy road crossing, and a small creek crossing, the trail rejoins the start of the loop near the Crystal Falls spur. Turn right to get back to your car.

Other Hiking Options

1. A strenuous side trail branches off to Double Falls just before the Thompson Overlook. The trail crosses Thompson Creek, which, in dry weather, disappears under its rocky creek bed and bubbles up farther downstream. There is an excellent campsite beside the creek, and the trail, which is a bit hard to follow, swings left at the bottom of the hill and goes by the campsite. A false trail will entice you to go right instead.

2. Rock Creek and Tunnel Trails also branch off Hidden Passage Trail. Rock Creek leads 5 miles to TN 154 and could be hiked with a car shuttle. Tunnel Trail, 1 mile long (adding 2 miles to the loop), leads to an old railroad tunnel.

29

Slave Falls and Twin Arches Loops

Total Distance: 11.2 miles

Hiking Time: 6–7 hours

Vertical Rise: 500 feet

Rating: Moderate

Map: USGS Sharp Place

Trail Marking: Red-arrow blazes on white squares; excellent signs at junctions

Sandstone arches, waterfalls, nearly a mile of bluffs and rockhouses, views for fall colors, sheltered creeks for spring wildflowers—this three-season outing would also be pleasant on cooler summer days. If the roads are open, you can probably take this hike in winter, too, with the usual cautions for ice. Children could hike parts of it and will enjoy the rockhouses, but note that there are unprotected edges on the top of the arches.

How to Get There

From the junction of TN 154 (out of Jamestown) and TN 297 (out of Leatherwood Ford), travel 1.8 miles north on TN 154. Turn right onto Divide Road (gravel), pass the Middle Creek Trailhead, and turn right onto Fork Ridge Road at 1.3 miles. Drive 1 mile to Sawmill Trailhead on the left.

The Hike

This day hike combines a piece of Slave Falls Loop, a long connecting trail, and the entire Twin Arches Loop to take you through most of the habitats, including old homesites, of the Big South Fork. It also leads to many junctions with other trails. Among the geological wonders are arches, rockhouses, and undercut waterfalls, while plant and animal species abound.

As you read about it, this route may seem confusing, but on the ground it should make sense, especially since good signs at junctions explain the choices. Other trailheads and connections allow shorter or longer hikes, for which a park map is advisable. Three creeks, Mill, Middle, and Andy, carved a gorge across the plateau; this hike goes

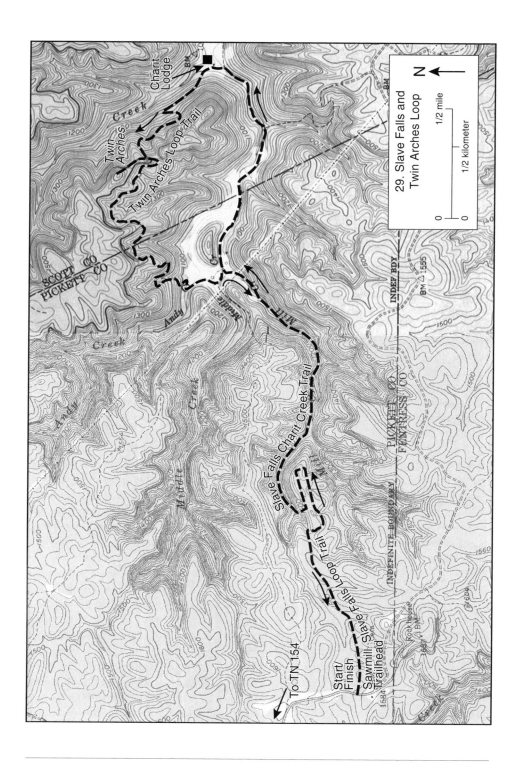

29. Slave Falls and Twin Arches Loop

N

0 ——— 1/2 mile
0 ——— 1/2 kilometer

Charit Lodge

Twin Arches

Twin Arches Loop Trail

Creek

SCOTT CO
PICKETT CO

Andy Creek

Middle

Slave Falls Charit Creek Trail

Middle Creek

Slave Falls Loop Trail

Start/Finish
Sawmill Slave Falls Trailhead

To TN 154

PICKETT CO
FENTRESS CO

INDEF BDY

BM △ 1555

INDEFINITE BOUNDARY

Rockhouse BM

down Mill Creek to the point where all three come together and join Charit Creek to form Station Camp Creek, which flows into the Big South Fork of the Cumberland River. The hike returns along a bluff formed by Andy Creek and then crosses all three creeks to return to the Sawmill Trailhead.

Turn left behind the outhouse to the sign that reads: SLAVE FALLS 1.1, CHARIT CREEK, 4.6. The trail is level and then descends somewhat through open woods of pines and hemlocks. At about 1 mile turn right onto Slave Falls Loop; just after that, a spur leads left to Slave Falls on Mill Creek. Descending into a moist valley, you will notice a change in forest type to hardwoods and rhododendrons, with some large hemlocks mixed in. Though this area was heavily logged, hemlocks were not particularly useful, and the hard-to-get individuals survived. Bigleaf magnolia, which boasts 25-inch-long leaves and 20-inch-wide creamy flowers, grows throughout the Cumberlands and thrives here. In late fall the leaves on the ground look like scattered newspapers.

Return to the main trail and descend to Needle Arch about 0.1 mile farther. An interpretive sign explains how water seeped through cracks in the not-so-solid sandstone, leaving a bridge of harder sandstone high and dry. A white pine grows in a soil pocket on top of the arch; it may help the erosion process along.

Continue down to a honeycomb bluff with moss on its floor. A bit of level trail leads to steps made of treated log sections. Be sure to step on the soil *above* the steps; the wood can be more slippery than it looks. The next bluff has quartz pebbles in the sandstone and sharp curved formations that look like the edges of peanut brittle. Softer materials between the ridges eroded; some of the deep holes developed the same way. A carpet of partridgeberry lines the trail. Its pale pink twin

flowers appear in spring and summer, and two flowers make one berry. Look for dark green rounded leaves and bright red berries with two blossom scars. Partridges live here, too, and may burst into the air as you approach.

Cross a few trickles and then one that could almost be called a creek, with a few yellow birches growing on its banks. The woods are open here because so many trees have fallen, most of them during a wet snow and ice storm in 1996. Brambles (blackberries, exotic wineberries, and greenbrier) thrive in the sunlight, and saplings grow extra-big leaves to get more sun for themselves; in a few years the brambles will have to find another opening from another storm. The downed trees feed turkey tail, witches'-butter, and other beautiful fungi, and beetle larvae and the woodpeckers that dig for them have several years of good eating ahead.

Just after the creek is another 0.2-mile spur to Slave Falls, to the other side. You can hike this now or on the way back. It leads to a fenced viewpoint of the ledge where the water flows from a crack of the curved bluff.

Continue straight after the spur past a south-facing section of trail where many more trees fell in the ice storm. Maples, whose roots often stay alive after the tree falls, send up a ring of replacement shoots; after a few years, this may form a circle of grown trees called a coppice. Mats of pussytoes and arbutus line the trail banks.

The trail descends to the moister creekside, with plantain-leafed sedge, hepatica, violets, stonecrop, and cranefly orchids on the trailbank. Jake's Place, a flat, open, grassy area with mullein, honeysuckle, and other introduced plants, appears at about 5 miles; turn right to start Twin Arches Loop counterclockwise. After negotiating muddy sections, drop down to a gravel road and turn left. A sign for TACKETT'S CABIN indicates

Wiggling through Fat Man's Squeeze

Slave Falls and Twin Arches Loops

a homesite on the left next to giant boulders. Follow the road past a new bridge up to the Charit Creek Trailhead, to come out at Charit (after a girl named Charity, who drowned here attempting to cross in high water) Creek Lodge. Cross the bridge to visit the lodge, but then come back and turn at the sign for TWIN ARCHES LOOP (left as you approached the lodge). The trail enters the woods, runs along Charit Creek, and then starts a series of switchbacks to the left—the longest steep part of this hike. But not too long—probably shorter than the 1.1 miles promised on the sign. Soon you can see the arches (sky with a roof) in front and the forbidding bluffs across Charit Creek Valley on the right. A last switchback brings you to a sign between the two arches; take a spur trail down to South Arch. Rest on the nicely arranged sitting rocks and then look for a tunnel entrance at the back left part of the arch—crawl through and then crawl back or turn left around the base of the arch.

In winter check for icicles hanging from the arches. If they're dripping, they may fall; stay out of the way.

Return to the sign and take the staircase to the top of the arches (a side trip to pass up if you're with children or it's icy). There's a great view and a chance to look at the stout twigs and compound leaves on top of a tall, straight white ash tree that grows from the floor of North Arch. Another staircase leads up to the Twin Arches Trailhead on Twin Arches Road, but to continue this hike, go back down the stairs and turn left to go under North Arch. Then turn right.

Start down the base of a long, curved bluff (of which the arches are a part). You will pass big rockhouses, trickly waterfalls, seeps that water ferns and flowers, massive chunks of rock that fell off and landed at odd angles, many erosion designs, and deep holes on the rock face that you could crawl into. There's nearly a mile of wonderful bluff. Trailing arbutus grows on both sides of the trail and blooms in March; holly, Hercules'-club (a skinny shrub with thorns on its stems and leaves), and mountain laurel also grow here. Mud daubers and ant lions live at the bluff, and fence lizards scamper across sunny spots.

Toward the end of the bluff you come to an untidy rockhouse, with rocks and boulders all over the floor, making the trail hard to see. An eroded hole through the rockhouse roof may be the beginning of a new arch. Stay close to the bluff base, looking for cairns and footprints in the sand that will show you the path where you can go around the end and to the last set of bluffs for the day. At the point look back at the long curve of bluffs.

The trail winds through boulders that rolled down the hill and then crosses a small creek with a waterfall ledge. If there's enough water, the undercut space forms a shower stall for a hot day. Mosses, cliff-brake fern, marginal shield fern, and walking fern (all evergreens) crowd the rocks, and lichens cover any space left over. At the bottom you come to Jake's Place again, from the other side, and you can see a pile of chimney rocks from Jake Blevin's house. Several walnuts grow here; though native, these trees usually indicate former home-sites, because settlers planted them. The nuts provided food and dye for wool.

From here, enter the woods on the trail you came down on and retrace your steps. If you skipped the Slave Falls spur, try it on the way back.

Other Hiking Options

Fork Ridge and Divide Roads lead to many Big South Fork trailheads and trail connections. Explore them with a Big South Fork map.

30

Angel Falls Overlook

Total Distance: 6.0 miles

Hiking Time: 4 hours

Vertical Rise: 400 feet

Rating: Moderate, with a few difficult spots

Maps: Big South Fork NRRA map; USGS Honey Creek

Trail Marking: Blue John Muir silhouettes

Three miles, three sections. The first section, along the river, is for families and plant identification; the second climbs over a ridge into the valley of Fall Branch and then climbs up the other side. The third section, up to the plateau, has difficult parts, and then offers an outstanding view. Spring for wildflowers and fall for foliage views are the best times to hike here; summer is hot with plenty of poison ivy and ticks, but offers good swimming. In winter snow and ice, the rocky sections of trail are unsafe.

How to Get There

From Oneida, take TN 297 about 10 miles to the east entrance of the Big South Fork National River and Recreation Area (BSF-NRRA). Drive 2.2 miles on a winding road to Leatherwood Ford. From the west and starting at the junction of US 127 and TN 154 just north of Jamestown, turn right and drive 12 miles north to the junction with TN 297. Turn right and drive about 10 miles more, passing the entrance to Bandy Creek Campground, to Leatherwood Ford.

The Hike

John Muir hiked 1,000 miles from Kentucky to the Gulf of Mexico, and a Tennessee trail from the Kentucky border to the North Carolina border has been designed to commemorate his feat (and feet). Not yet finished, the trail has a 50-mile section in northern Tennessee, including Angel Falls Overlook and several miles in the Cherokee National Forest (Hike 18). This hike is in the BSFNRRA, which consists of more than 100,000 acres of the Cumberland Plateau.

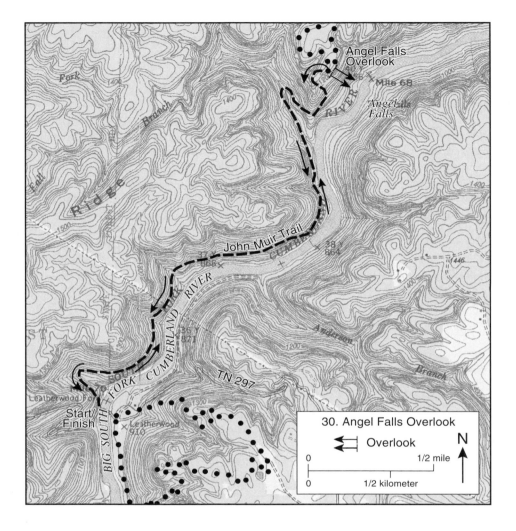

30. Angel Falls Overlook

Administered by the National Park Service, the BSFNRRA provides about 200 miles of hiking along the river, up and down bluffs, and past waterfalls and views of gorges. Several times, plans to place a dam on the river in Kentucky almost made this area into a huge lake, and in the 1960s the Tennessee Citizens for Wilderness Planning organized the Big South Fork Coalition to unite conservation groups in a tireless campaign to keep the beautiful river flowing free. The Army Corps of Engineers, which was standing by ready to build the dam, had to change gears after the resulting legislation. The corps built trails and recreational facilities, and then, in 1990, turned the land over to the National Park Service.

To start the Angel Falls Overlook hike, look for the information shelter downhill from the Leatherwood Ford bathrooms and descend to a wooden-plank bridge across the Big South Fork. Climb steps to a sign and the first Muir blaze. From here, it is 1.8 miles to Fall Branch and 2.8 miles to the beginning of Grand Gap Loop Trail; the best overlooks are within 0.2 mile of that junction.

Turn right and hike along the river for an excellent wildflower and tree walk. Though this hillside faces south, the gorge shelters it from too much direct sun, and moisture-loving plants grow here. The left bank has bloodroot, yellow ragwort, and hepatica in March; trillium, true and false Solomon's seal, lousewort, geraniums, golden Alexander, showy orchis, and some 18-inch-tall jack-in-the-pulpits in April. Spiderwort, aster, and tall yellow composites bloom in summer. Tulip tree, beech, elm, yellow birch, buckeye, and basswood thrive in the damp soil. Leatherwood, a relatively rare shrub, grows on the bank near the beginning of the trail. Strips of its tough bark were once used like leather, especially when a traveler broke a rein or other equipment. After climbing down into this gorge, repairs might well be needed, and this ford became known as a place to find leatherwood.

Cross several tributary creeks, small ones on stepping-stones, larger ones on wooden bridges. For about a mile, the trail is level and easy, with a few spots to get down to the river. Swimming and wading are possible here, but there is always a strong current; check for safety first. In high water, currents make swimming dangerous. On parts of the trail you can see evidence of floods: sand, exposed roots, and bits of debris lodged in tree branches.

After the easy part, the trail becomes more rocky and climbs into a hemlock forest with a campsite to the right. At 1.8 miles the trail turns away from the river to follow Fall Branch and then crosses it on an angled wooden bridge—stop and look up- and downstream at boulders and pools. After the bridge, turn right and climb to a large beech tree. The main trail turns left, and a smaller trail goes straight and drops to another campsite. Camping is allowed anywhere here without a permit, but practice Leave-No-Trace camping—don't establish new campsites, and don't increase damage to existing ones.

More climbing, more rocks, and several switchbacks. This section shows some of the worst examples of erosion and packed dirt caused by people cutting across switchbacks. After sets of stone steps, the trail reaches a dry, south-facing open area, with oak, hickory, and sourwood as the dominant trees. Trailing arbutus and pussytoes line the bank, and mountain laurel blooms in May.

Climb stone steps along a bluff and then turn left at a high bluff that towers over the trail. Stay left to go around this bluff (some hikers have made a trail in front of it) and walk along a shelf high above the Fall Branch Gorge. Look across to the other wall—a typical Cumberland view with vertical sandstone bluffs between hillsides of mixed hardwoods. The trail descends to a flat-roofed overhang with a sandy floor and then continues to more bluffs and a seasonal drip that waters ferns and liverworts. The difficult part of this hike starts at a right switchback with steep stone steps and a walk across possibly slippery rock with a cable to hang on to. Then more rock scrambling brings you to a passage between rock slabs. A short ladder and a few more switchbacks lead up to the trail junction and sign. A narrow trail just beyond the sign leads to a grassy campsite surrounded by mountain laurel and hidden from the trail.

Turn right at the sign to visit several overlooks. All the viewpoints are unprotected, and on some the rock slopes downward toward the edge. The first one has a spec-

Angel Falls Overlook

tacular view of the placid river to the right and the deep Fall Branch Gorge to the far right; on the left is the sheer wall of the Big South Fork Gorge and a rocky section of the river.

Return to the trail and continue on for some smaller overlooks, and finally one where you can look back at Angel Falls (actually a large rapid).

Retrace your steps to Leatherwood Ford and be careful climbing down any slippery places.

Other Hiking Options

Grand Gap Loop (6.8 miles) goes either way from the trail sign near the overlooks. If you continue 1 mile past the Angel Falls Overlook on the loop, you come to a spur to another overlook with a long view up and down the river. Then the trail winds around on the plateau, past more rock formations, to a gorge overlook, and then back to the sign. It also provides access to other Big South Fork trails. It's easy, with a few gentle climbs.

31

Leatherwood Loop

Total Distance: 3.3 miles

Hiking Time: 2 hours

Vertical Rise: 600 feet

Rating: Moderate

Map: USGS Honey Creek

Trail Marking: Blue John Muir profiles; red arrowheads

From riverside to high bluff, this trail provides views of the Big South Fork and some of its best canoeing rapids. The flat riverside section is easy, and the first part is handicapped accessible and good for children. The loop to the overlook is more strenuous. Fall colors and spring flowers excel on this trail. Heated bathrooms at the trailhead are a treat after a winter hike.

How to Get There

From Oneida, take TN 297 to the east entrance of the Big South Fork National River and Recreation Area (BSFNRRA). Drive 2.2 miles on a winding road to Leatherwood Ford. From the west and starting at the junction of TN 154 and TN 297 just north of Jamestown, drive 15 miles west on TN 297, passing the entrance to Bandy Creek Campground, to Leatherwood Ford.

The Hike

From the Leatherwood Ford parking area, go under the bridge on a gravel trail with blue Muir blazes. After 0.1 mile, the trail approaches a set of steps between massive boulders. Other steps allow access to the river; be careful in high water. In low water you can wade among the rocks. Witch hazel and mountain laurel line the riverbank, and several bigleaf magnolias grow among the boulders. In spring watch for canoes and kayaks in the rapids.

The trail moves away from the river and continues upstream on an old roadbed. Its shaded, moist bank supports spring wildflowers: bloodroot, iris, Solomon's seal, little brown jug, yellow trillium, sweet cicely, jack-in-the-pulpit. That's in March or early April; later, cucumber root, lousewort, and partridgeberry bloom. The trail becomes a little rougher, descends to cross a creek with mossy boulders, and continues upstream along a quiet part of the river. At 0.5 mile the red-arrow-blazed Leatherwood Loop Trail turns right and John Muir Trail continues straight.

The loop trail takes you away from easy hiking and moist habitats. Wooden and stone steps will help; try to stay on them to protect the crumbling trail, and do not cut across switchbacks. Sassafras, sourwood, hickory, and white pine thrive in these drier woods. Boulders broken from the bluff above lie scattered on the hillside, with tree trunks twisting around them and crops of flowers and ferns on top. As you approach the bluff, at about 1 mile, some rhododendrons line a small watercourse. At 1.2 miles you'll reach a large rock shelter made of layers of sandstone and quartz conglomerate, with sand and quartz pebbles on the floor. Hemlock, red maple, and redbud trees grow along the base, and several pawpaw shrubs grow toward the end of the shelter.

Climb left to the top of the bluff on rock steps and look for plants typical of dry, exposed habitats: wintergreen, trailing arbutus, mountain laurel, sourwood, and blueberry. At 1.5 miles a sign points left to a 0.1-mile spur to an overlook of Leatherwood Ford and Bandy Creek.

After the spur, the trail moves away from the bluff through open woods and joins an old road. Other roads and tracks cross; watch for blazes as the trail swings left to a bridge over a small pond. Listen for bullfrogs, green frogs, and spring peepers—there aren't many ponds for amphibians up on the plateau, and several species probably use this one.

After the pond, turn left into an open

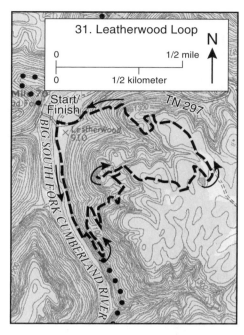

field with a few walnut trees. Blazes should be visible, but generally stay near the edge of the woods until you see blazes and the path to the left. The hike down is about as steep as the one coming up, but it travels along a creek with rhododendrons and hemlocks. Switchbacks and stone steps make it easier, and at about 3 miles you descend rock steps to TN 297. You can cross the road and return to the parking area or stay on the left for a few more steps down to the beginning of the trail under the bridge.

Other Hiking Options

1. O&W Bridge. Instead of (or before) turning up the red-blazed part of the loop, continue straight on John Muir Trail. Steps and switchbacks take you away from the river and then back down for level walking on a railroad grade with a few side-creek crossings. Continue up-

The Big South Fork under the O&W Bridge.

50 Hikes in the Tennessee Mountains

stream past a boulder in the road and a campsite (often messy—too close to the road for people to take out their trash). Just past the boulder, come out on the gravel road (an ATV, bike, and horse trail) and the Oneida and Western Bridge on the right. You can climb down around the foundations of the trestles, or you can cross the bridge and turn left onto a short trail with a good flower display. This half-mile spur goes by Devils Den, a large rockhouse with drippy waterfalls, and is the future route of John Muir Trail down to Honey Creek (Hike 33). Retrace your steps across the O&W Bridge. This option, to the bridge and back, adds 2.6 miles to the loop hike, and Devils Den adds another mile.

2. Angel Falls. From the Leatherwood Ford parking area, go downstream on an old road that becomes a wide, sandy path. It then becomes more of a trail, crossing some creeks and passing coal seams and evidence of mining. At 2.0 miles, just past steep side trails for canoe portages around the falls, you can see Angel Falls and go down to explore the river. This is not a safe place to swim, however.

32

Cumberland Trail: Nemo Bridge to Alley Ford

Total Distance: 5.0 miles

Hiking Time: 3 hours

Vertical Rise: 200 feet

Rating: Moderate

Map: USGS Lancing

Trail Marking: White blazes

This trail starts at the Obed River and winds past bluffs, up through pleasant woods, and then along a raised railroad bed before dropping back to the river at Alley Ford. It's a good cool-weather hike, but you could manage it in summer by camping at Rock Creek Campground and hiking early in the morning. As an open-ended hike (you turn around when tired), it would be good for families.

How to Get There

From the courthouse in Wartburg (worth a stop in itself) on Main Street, turn left at the NEMO BRIDGE sign and then right after one block onto winding Catoosa Road. Drive 6 miles to Nemo Bridge, cross it, and turn right into Rock Creek Campground.

The Obed Wild and Scenic River Visitor Center is around the corner from the courthouse; turn right from Main Street and look for the center on the left.

The Hike

The Obed River, like the Big South Fork, almost became a lake. A group of concerned citizens recognized its wildness, however, and worked to preserve it. The National Wild and Scenic Rivers Act, passed in 1968, seemed designed to save such resources, but it took eight years of intense conservation efforts to get the Obed included. The citizens went on to form the Tennessee Citizens for Wilderness Planning and have been leaders in regional and national conservation issues ever since. The National Park Service manages the Obed Wild and Scenic River, which offers first-class white-water, scenery, and

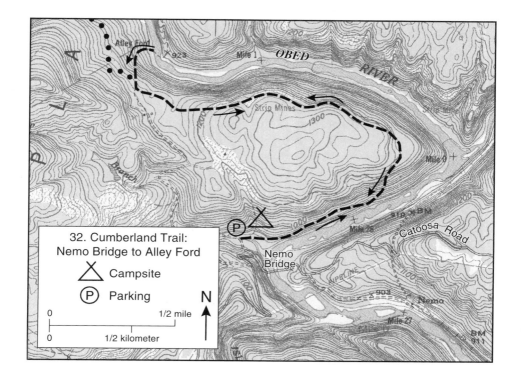

32. Cumberland Trail:
Nemo Bridge to Alley Ford

△ Campsite

Ⓟ Parking

0   1/2 mile

0   1/2 kilometer

N

hiking opportunities. Clear Creek and the Obed River flow east, join, and then turn south to meet the Emory River, which runs into the Tennessee River at Harriman. On this hike you will travel from the Nemo Bridge to the formerly proposed dam site at Alley Ford.

Turn right from the information sign and walk along the road toward the river and campground bathrooms. Keep looking left; the trail starts up a bank at a new rail fence and a trail sign. From the bathrooms, either go back and look again or find a connector trail near the river. Swing right after the sign and ascend on an easy slope.

Climb past large patches of mountain laurel to rock bluffs and overhangs. At about half a mile, turn left and climb again, onto a slope with no bluffs; you can't see the river below, but it has curved left, too, and you've entered a part of the gorge that isn't so steep.

Loggers and coal miners took advantage of this easier access; the trail joins an old logging road for a while and runs through open woods and an expanse of lady ferns.

After crossing a small side creek on a bridge, ascend to an old rail line. Steep hemlock woods drop off to the right, and on the left is the high bank that provided the dirt for the raised railbed and made this steep hill negotiable. Sandstone boulders have fallen from the excavated bank—a modern parallel of ancient bluff formation.

As the railbed curves away from a valley, it blocks a drainage and provides a rare habitat for these mountains: a woodland pond. In spring you can hear frogs and find tadpoles; somehow amphibians made their way here. Toads, newts, dragonflies, mosquitoes, and other animals lay eggs in the pond, and water-loving plants such as royal

➤ This section of the Cumberland Trail belongs to the deciduous magnolia. Umbrella and bigleaf magnolias have a circle, or whorl, of leaves at the end of each branch, and saplings have just one whorl—making them look like flat umbrellas stuck in the ground. In early spring curled-up leaves break out of long, pointed buds. Then they grow and grow and grow. The whorl of leaves may reach a diameter of 4 to 5 feet, and each branch sways with the breeze like seaweed. Mature trees produce creamy white flowers in April, and the fruit of both species looks like a cone with red berries. The leaves of umbrella magnolia are pointed at both ends, while bigleaf magnolia leaves have lobes at the bases of the leaves—somewhat like earlobes. In fall those leaves litter the ground, and in winter you can still tell the two magnolias apart: umbrella magnolia buds are green and smooth, while bigleaf buds are covered with white fuzz. A third deciduous magnolia, cucumber, has leaves less than a foot long and a fruit that looks like a lumpy pickle. Tulip tree, or tulip poplar, a dominant tree on almost every hike in this guide, is a relative of the magnolias and shares its flower shape and other traits with them.

fern and sweetgum live around it. Climbing fern (sometimes called possum paw fern from the shape of the fronds) and two kinds of club moss grow on the railbank.

A small bridge and steps bring you over another part of the railbed at about 2 miles; then you curve left into a dark hemlock grove with almost no ground cover. Descend to a small bridge over a rocky creek and climb

through open woods to an eroded road going down to the river. A sign announces the end of the trail and the beginning of the Catoosa Wildlife Management Area, which is closed during February and March and hunting seasons. From here, you can climb down the rough road for 0.1 mile to the sandy riverbank. During the hard climb back up, stop to admire jack-in-the-pulpit, trillium, blue cohosh, and other wildflowers.

Other Hiking Options

1. Two miles past Alley Ford the Cumberland Trail reaches Breakaway Bluff, an overlook on the Obed River named for the spring-break trail-building programs that helped create the Cumberland Trail. Well blazed but not yet heavily used, the trail leads through remote forest and will soon follow the Obed River, providing views from Omigod Overlook along the way, around to Daddys Creek (14 miles). At Alley Ford the Cumberland Trail enters the Catoosa Wildlife Management Area; hiking is not allowed in February and March and during hunting seasons, which are posted at the campground.

2. If you don't want to hike 14 miles, you can start at Daddys Creek and hike down the Trail of the Thousand Steps—a vast understatement—built in part by the Morgan County Correctional Facility. From the Peavine exit off I-40 (near Crossville), drive north on Peavine Road for 2 miles and turn left onto Firetower Road (paved, then gravel) for 15 miles to Daddys Creek Bridge and Devils Breakfast Table. The hike starts 50 yards up the road (away from the creek) from the parking lot and descends through a mile-long jumble of rocks, some of which have been wrestled into steps. There is a large swimming hole beside the parking lot.

50 Hikes in the Tennessee Mountains

The Cumberland Trail near the Obed River

Cumberland Trail: Nemo Bridge to Alley Ford

33

Honey Creek

Total Distance: 5.6 miles

Hiking Time: 4½–5 hours

Vertical Rise: 400–500 feet

Rating: Difficult

Maps: Big South Fork NRRA map; USGS Honey Creek

Trail Marking: Red blazes

Not for beginning hikers, this hike winds partway down a steep gorge, rises to a vista above the gorge, and then goes all the way down. Creek walking, hand-over-hand climbing, and searching for the next blaze make it a challenge; at the time of this writing, parts of the trail needed repairs. *Warning:* This trail is dangerous or impossible in ice, snow, or high water.

How to Get There

On US 27, 11 miles south of Oneida and 4.6 miles north of Elgin, look for a brown BURNT MILL BRIDGE ACCESS sign. Turn west onto Mountain View Road and follow signs to a four-way junction and Cross Roads Mission Church. Turn right and then bear left on a gravel road in 0.5 mile; reach Burnt Mill Bridge 0.9 mile from the church, and continue 3 miles to a fork. Turn right and look for a HONEY CREEK sign in about 0.1 mile; park on the left. Honey Creek Loop starts and ends here; for road access to the Honey Creek Overlook, drive 1.8 miles farther.

From Allardt, take TN 52 east 5.5 miles and turn left onto Mount Helen Road. Drive 5 miles and bear left at a fork, then drive 5 miles farther (mostly gravel road) to the left turn to the Honey Creek Trailhead.

The Hike

One way (perhaps the best) to navigate Honey Creek is to go with someone who has been there before, and most of the hiking clubs in the area schedule hikes to this popular but complicated little gorge. The other way is to make sure you have plenty

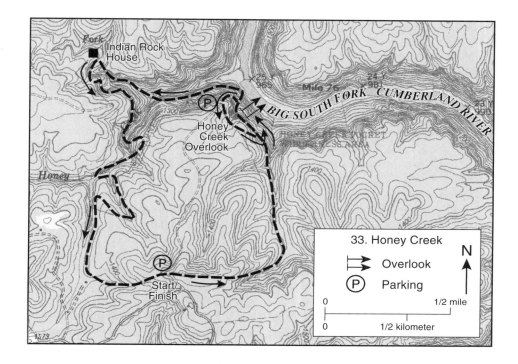

33. Honey Creek

→ Overlook

(P) Parking

N

0 — 1/2 mile
0 — 1/2 kilometer

of time, patience, and a group of people who can help each other get up and down ladders and find faint blazes. An appreciation for puzzles and obstacle courses will make this hike more fun. High bluffs (you have to go up and down them), caves, stone passages, wildflowers, and a feeling of remoteness make the effort worthwhile. Honey Creek has more waterfalls per hiking mile than any other outing in this guide.

Once a Bowater Pocket Wilderness (see Hike 38), Honey Creek is now part of the Big South Fork National River and Recreation Area (BSFNRRA). Bridges, caged ladders, red blazes and arrows, and occasional signs will help you get through twists and turns, but hikers have made confusing false trails or cut across switchbacks. Your best guide where no signs help is an established treadway. Total distance is about 6 miles, but because of loops,

options, and boulder scrambling, mileage estimates are not included here past the overlook. A heavy ice and snow storm toppled many trees in Honey Creek Gorge in 1996, and it took more than a year to get the trail open again; parts of the treadway were also damaged.

From the parking area, cross the road to wooden steps up the roadbank. John Muir Trail turns right toward Burnt Mill Bridge; keep left and ascend through dry pine woods. Pine beetles have killed many of the pines; you may see pieces of worm-eaten bark or just dead trees. Mild winters and dry summers favor the beetle, and pine plantations or hillsides with large pine groves have been hard hit. The infestation increases the risk of forest fires and forces premature harvest in commercial pine stands. Still, the Friends of the Big South Fork built a dormitory for researchers with wood from infested pines cut before it was damaged—strong wood, but with interesting blue patterns from a fungus that came after the beetles. It takes the beetles about three years to kill pines, and by then the wood can no longer be used. You will see the aftermath of pine beetle infestations on many Cumberland hikes.

After about half a mile, the trail crosses an old road and descends along a moist rock face (look up to see hemlock tree trunks growing out of cracks as if they are sitting on a fence) to a creek and bridge. This creek runs into the Big South Fork, and the trail follows it, passing a bluff (after about 1 mile), and then Moonshine Falls and several small cascades. Slippery crossings and a bridge (broken, but perhaps fixed by the time you hike) bring you to the base of a bluff with a few scattered boulders; turn left and climb to a shelf along the bluff. Erosion has made swirls and patterns on the rock face; look for mud dauber nests on the rock and ant lion pits in the sand.

Climb along the bluff to a fork at about 1.3 miles; the left fork (the more strenuous and possibly risky option) ascends a steep caged ladder (it gives you wire to hang on to, but make sure your pack straps don't get tangled). Swing left around a rock and ascend another ladder. After some switchbacks, reach a level spot and turn right to skirt the bluff's edge through blueberry bushes and mountain laurel. Small side trails lead to views, but the bluff is sheer and unprotected; you'll get a better view at the top anyway. Cross a small creek on a bridge and climb to Honey Creek Overlook at 1.8 miles. When you see the fenced platform, turn left to reach it and the gravel road—this is the continuation of the road you parked on, and from here you could walk a mile back to your car. Good parking, bathrooms, and a level ramp to the overlook make this area handicapped accessible.

From the overlook platform, look right (upstream) at the curve of the Big South Fork. It disappears under trees below, but to the left it flows north through its deep gorge. You might see canoes or kayaks—tiny colored spots. Honey Creek Gorge, obscured by trees, is below to the left.

To return to the main trail, go right (if you're facing away from the view) from the platform and then descend stairs, steeper stairs, caged ladders, and rocks back to the base of the bluff. Turn right to meet the main trail at a three-way junction.

If you took the right fork (skipping the overlook), walk along the bluff past boulders and overhangs. Climb under or through a small waterfall (or a drip, in dry times).

At the three-way junction with a sign turn downhill onto steep, possibly slippery trail, and follow several switchbacks. Mayapple, foamflower, bloodroot, hepatica, and other wildflowers bloom on the moist trailbanks, and you can see and hear the Big South Fork on the right.

The trail levels out, giving you a better chance to observe flowers (you may not get a chance to think about them again until this hike is over), and descends to your first view of Honey Creek. From here, you will travel upstream, somewhat parallel to the overlook road, until you reach a point below the parking place and climb the hill to it. But that's just a summary; you'll have to scramble back and forth across Honey Creek and its tumbling tributaries.

Squeeze around some tree roots (in very high water you may have to stop here) and continue up the left side of the creek between rhododendron-covered gorge walls and massive boulders. Signs and red arrows indicate most turns; at some points you hike in the creek on slippery rocks. In

Hiking the Burnt Mill Bridge trail

Honey Creek

a passage underneath boulders is a small waterfall. Cross Honey Creek, climb over a small rise, and drop down to North Fork (more boulders and squeeze-through passages!). A sign indicates INDIAN ROCKHOUSE LOOP straight ahead and a shortcut to the left. To visit the rockhouse, walk in the creek and up and over more obstacles to enter an open area with good rocks to sit on and the rockhouse to the left. A ladder (not in the best shape) leads 20 feet up to the rockhouse floor, which slopes upward to meet the ceiling.

Past the rockhouse signs show the way to curve left to the main trail, meeting that shortcut, and then passing Boulder Falls. The trail leaves the creek for a while and then passes a spur left for Ice Castle Falls. Return to the main trail and climb to something entirely different—Tree Top Rock, a flat, open slab of sandstone with delicate reindeer moss and other lichens, blueberry bushes, and sunlight: a chance to dry out if you need to. The trail from here on does not include any more in-the-creek walking.

Descend to the hemlock-shaded trail beside the creek, cross a bridge, and continue up Honey Creek. A left spur leads down around a curve to Honey Creek Falls, in a grotto where the sun never shines, and slippery rocks will persuade you to gaze from a distance.

Return to the main trail, cross the creek, and climb away from it, through dry plateau woods, and then up to the parking area and the real world.

Other Hiking Options

1. Burnt Mill Bridge Loop. This easy-to-moderate 3.6-mile loop goes downstream beside Clear Fork, rises to cross the road and peaceful woods, and then drops along a series of bluffs to Clear Fork again. This would be a good hike for children, and there is a riverside campsite with chances to swim or wade less than a mile upstream from Burnt Mill Bridge. If you drive out here to hike Honey Creek and find high water, hike Burnt Mill Bridge.

2. John Muir Trail. A 5-mile section of John Muir Trail connects Honey Creek and Burnt Mill Bridge Loops. Marked with the blue Muir silhouette signs, it starts about 1 mile around Burnt Mill Bridge Loop (going downstream from the parking area) and runs though pleasant woods to a spot near the right-hand beginning of Honey Creek Loop. Not nearly as pretty as the two loops, it would be a good connector if you want to do parts of both loops or, again, if the water is too high to complete Honey Creek Loop.

34

Colditz Cove

Total Distance: 1.5 miles

Hiking Time: 1 hour

Vertical Rise: 100 feet

Rating: Easy to moderate

Map: USGS Rugby

This 75-acre state natural area hides a tiny cove and waterfall like a tabletop model of the great Cumberland Plateau bluffs and rockhouses such as those of Hidden Passage Trail (Hike 28). Steep, unprotected drop-offs make it dangerous for small children, but with care, this would be a good family hike and picnic.

How to Get There

From Rugby, drive 11 miles west on TN 52 to Northrup Falls Road (with a sign for CROOKED CREEK LODGE). Turn left and drive 0.9 mile to a gravel parking area on the right. From Allardt (which has a big orange water tower), take TN 52 east for 1.2 miles, turn right onto Northrup Falls Road, and follow the directions above. On TN 52 between Rugby and Allardt is the second highest (208 feet) bridge in Tennessee, completed in 1999.

The Hike

Sluggish Big Branch flows across the plateau and springs into action at the edge of this horseshoe-shaped cove. Imagine a loop trail in which you first hike along the top of the bluff (the outer edge of the horseshoe), swing around underneath, walk under the bluff (the inner edge of the horseshoe), and then clamber up the other side. Big trees crowd the bowl of the cove, and wildflowers cling to cracks in the bluff. The Nature Conservancy helped save this Tennessee state natural area.

From the parking lot, walk straight back along a rutted old road through a field of brambles, small maples, tulip trees, and a few meadow flowers. This 0.2-mile section slopes gently downhill and can be hot and exposed in summer. The trees should grow fast and shade the path soon, however.

The trail bears right as it enters a hemlock grove and becomes narrower. A trash can appears next to a sign: LOOP TRAIL. To follow the loop counterclockwise, turn right and descend to a small wooden bridge over Big Branch. Swing left and rise to a sandstone bluff's-edge trail that gives you the first view of Colditz Cove and the tops of its trees. You can hear the waterfall and perhaps see a sparkle of the creek leading away from it.

At about 0.5 mile the trail turns left and descends steeply on rocky steps to the base of the bluff. Looking up, you can see the sharp-edged overhang where you just walked. Hemlock, rhododendron, pines, ferns, and alumroot grow from wet spots. The descent is still steep and may be muddy as you pass trickles of water that leak through the rock. Cinnamon ferns, anemones, violets, and jack-in-the-pulpits thrive along here. At one point water spurts from a ledge about 15 feet up.

The trail curves right toward Northrup Waterfall, tumbling from that quiet creek above. It drips, splashes, and may roar after rain or form long icicles in winter. Behind the falls is a deep, damp shelter with a sandy floor, and in wet weather you may have to hurry through the splash zone. Leafy liverworts, which look like soggy green cornflakes, grow in the splash zones, especially on rock faces. Once you have identified liverworts, you will see them in many places like this—wet, but often too shaded for other plants to grow. The leaves of these simple plants are one cell thick and have no way to transport water, so all cells must be in direct

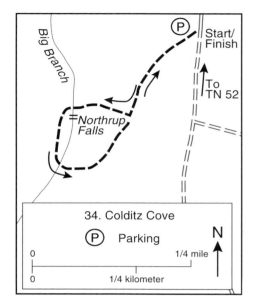

34. Colditz Cove
(P) Parking
N
0   1/4 mile
0   1/4 kilometer

contact with spray or moist dirt.

Past the waterfall you'll follow the trail along the base of the bluff through rock jumbles and drier rock shelters—great for picnics in the rain with a waterfall view. If the trail becomes obscure, just keep climbing boulders along the bluff until it shows up again.

This side of the cove faces south and has no creek. Partridgeberry, trailing arbutus, mountain laurel, and Virginia pine grow in this drier habitat. Trailing arbutus that is exposed to sun blooms earlier than almost any other flower—sometimes in February—and has a wonderful scent. Perhaps it sends a strong message to sleepy emerging pollinators: Wake up and smell the nectar! Hepatica and violets follow close behind, and many other spring wildflowers bloom here in March and April.

Scramble up to the top of the bluff and

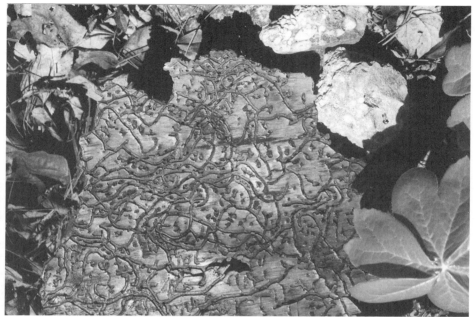

Pine bark beetle tunnels on the inner surface of bark

turn left to walk through pine, oak, and mountain laurel woods with a carpet of needles. After some views of the falls, the trail leaves the bluff's edge and drops to the loop sign; turn right to return to your car.

Other Hiking Options

This short hike could be combined with a visit to Historic Rugby or a hike and swim at the Gentlemen's Swimming Hole (Hike 35).

35

Gentlemen's Swimming Hole and Meeting of the Waters

Total Distance: 2.2 miles

Hiking Time: 1½ hours

Vertical Rise: 200 feet

Rating: Easy (swimming hole only) to moderate (Meeting of the Waters loop)

Maps: USGS Rugby; Nature guide available in visitors center or at trailhead

Trail Marking: Red arrows

This short trail runs along Clear Fork, providing swimming, wading, creek exploration, and good wildflowers. The short section to the swimming hole is an all-season trail, but the Meeting of the Waters loop should be avoided in icy conditions because of steep steps. This part of the trail could also be impassable in extremely high water. To visit the swimming hole only, take the trail to the left of the pit toilet.

How to Get There

Rugby is on TN 52 between Elgin and Jamestown. From Harrow Road Cafe in the center of Rugby, travel 0.9 mile west on TN 52; turn right onto Donnington Road (at the LAUREL DALE CEMETERY sign) and drive 0.9 mile to a parking area on the left.

The Hike

Rugby was established in 1889 by Thomas Hughes as a farming community for the younger sons of English Victorian aristocratic families. Hughes, who wrote *Tom Brown's School Days* in 1857, envisioned a class-free, self-sufficient utopia. It rose up with elegant Victorian buildings and great ambitions, but floundered after 12 years, and most of the settlers moved away. A local group has preserved and restored several buildings, which are now on the National Register of Historic Places. The town borders the Big South Fork National River and Recreation Area (BSFNRRA), and the hike is mostly within the area. A visitors center on TN 52 provides park information, maps, a museum, and tours.

This narrative describes the loop coun-

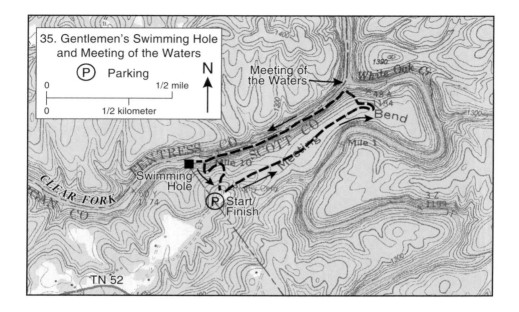

35. Gentlemen's Swimming Hole and Meeting of the Waters

terclockwise, leaving the swimming hole for last. From the parking area next to Laurel Dale Cemetery (where you'll find signs, picnic tables, and pit toilets), follow a sandy road just to the right of the toilets and descend gently, first through an open meadow and then into a thin forest of tulip tree, oak, sassafras, and sourwood. Jeeps have left tire ruts in some spots that may hold enough water in spring for toads and tadpoles. Wish them luck; they need to hustle to metamorphose before the puddles dry up.

Turn left away from the road into the woods (well marked with red-arrow blazes). Soon the easy walking ends with a switchback and a steep set of rock steps to the base of a sandstone bluff at Meeting of the Waters (0.9 mile). Clear Fork comes from the left, and White Oak Creek from the right. In summer you can wade or swim here, as many Rugby settlers did; in rain or snow you can take shelter under the bluffs. Alumroot and exuberant poison ivy grow from rock cracks, and yellowroot shrubs hug

the moist sand at the base of the bluff and the creekbank.

Swing around the end of the bluff by climbing a few well-made stone steps. This area, sheltered from the sun and cooled by Clear Fork, supports shade-tolerant plants such as hemlock, bigleaf magnolia, ferns, and leafy liverworts, while the poison ivy disappears. Pitted massive boulders in and along the creek show erosion power, and twigs and tufts of grass stuck high in trees give evidence of floods. Look for one creek boulder eroded into a giant mushroom shape.

Continue upstream for nearly a mile on the cool, moist trail and climb to a sign and junction. A spur trail down to the right leads to the swimming hole, which features the swimming hole itself and large rocks for picnics or rock-hopping adventures. (Because the Victorian gentlemen preferred skinny-dipping, the ladies had to swim somewhere else.)

High water is for canoes, though, and

Tiny waterfall erodes the base of a bluff

50 Hikes in the Tennessee Mountains

can be dangerous. Views on Clear Fork show boulders and thick creekbank forests upstream and down. On the edge of the sandy beach look for river alder, royal ferns, yellowroot, and wild phlox. Most phlox species bloom in early spring, but one, called summer phlox, stands 2 to 3 feet tall and produces many blooms through September. Behind the beach stand witch hazels, yellow birches, and a few sycamores.

Return to the sign and climb steep rock steps past shaded sandstone overhangs on the left, some with small waterfalls tumbling over them. Also notice the permanent rock waterbars that direct water off the trail and prevent erosion, possibly installed by the English settlers in the 1880s. Along here you'll find nature trail brochure numbers—in reverse if you followed this narrative. The evergreens noted in the brochure (teaberry, partridgeberry, and little brown jug) thrive in this moist, cool environment, while arbutus and iris can live in more varied environments. Rhododendron, mountain laurel, white pine, and American holly stay green in the winter woods, while sourwood, magnolia, and oak make up the deciduous canopy. Deep rock shelters on the left, including one called Witches Cave, show how the sandstone became undercut by water action. A tiny creek that runs beside the trail is probably responsible, having had several million years to do the job.

As you reach the top of the climb, the woods become drier and mostly deciduous hardwoods. Watch for a few American chestnut sprouts. It's too dry up here for rhododendron, but laurel and holly still thrive. After an easy woods walk, you come out to the parking area between the picnic tables and the pit toilet. Cross the road and

> "We have here two beautiful streams which will be a delight forever to those who dwell here if they are left free for the use and enjoyment of all. In laying out the town, we have reserved a strip of various widths along which walks and rides are being carefully laid out."

—Thomas Hughes, 1881

explore the historic cemetery.

The Big South Fork Chapter of the Tennessee Trails Association completed a trail from Laurel Dale Cemetery to Beacon Hill, about 1.5 miles round-trip, in 2000. From the Gentlemen's Swimming Hole parking area, cross to the cemetery and step over the leftmost section of a post-and-chain fence. Enter the woods on the new trail to the left, hike 0.2 mile along a ridgeline, descend to a valley, and cross a new bridge and several small creeks. At 0.5 mile climb out of the valley on an old road. This trail was built in 1999 and 2000. It winds through pretty woods with trout lily, cranefly orchid, rue anemone, gay wing, and many other wildflowers. After reaching a gravel road, retrace your steps to Laurel Dale Cemetery, where you can look for the gravestones of some of the original Rugby settlers.

The group also plans to clear and repair the old trail down to the Ladies' Swimming Hole, which starts behind the Uffington House just beyond Laurel Dale Road. The Ladies' Swimming Hole was, of course, quite a distance upstream on Clear Creek from the Gentlemen's Swimming Hole. Ask for current trail information at the visitors center.

36

North Old Mac and Panther Branch

Total Distance: 4.2 miles

Hiking Time: 2½–3 hours

Vertical Rise: 1,000 feet

Rating: Moderate

Maps: Frozen Head State Natural Area map; USGS Petros

Trail Marking: Blue (Panther Branch) and red (North Old Mac) blazes

Between Oak Ridge and Wartburg, Frozen Head State Natural Area offers well-marked trails through hilly and diverse habitats. Panther Branch Trail is the best wildflower trail in the park and should be hiked in early April for its famous trillium displays. With two waterfalls and a rippling creek for wading, it's a good trail for energetic children. Bring a flower book and a magnifying lens.

How to Get There

From Oak Ridge, take TN 62 (a continuation of Illinois Avenue) about 4 miles to Oliver Springs and turn right at a brown STATE PARK sign (still TN 62). In 8 miles turn right at the next park sign (Flat Fork Road). Go 4 miles, passing the Brushy Mountain State Correctional Facility, to the park visitors center, and then an additional 1.2 miles to the end of the road and the Panther Branch Trailhead. On the loop hike you will come out at a parking and picnic area a little less than a mile back on the road. From Wartburg, take US 27 south to its intersection with TN 62 (about 2.5 miles), turn left at a group of gas stations and fast-food stores, go 1.5 miles, and turn left to park.

The Hike

Frozen Head State Park, established in 1970, consists of 12,000 acres of wooded creek ravines and mountain peaks—a part of the Cumberland Plateau with no plateau. In 1988 the state classified most of the land (except for 330 acres at the entrance containing parking areas, campground, picnic areas, and the visitors center) as a state natural area, reserved for hiking and back-

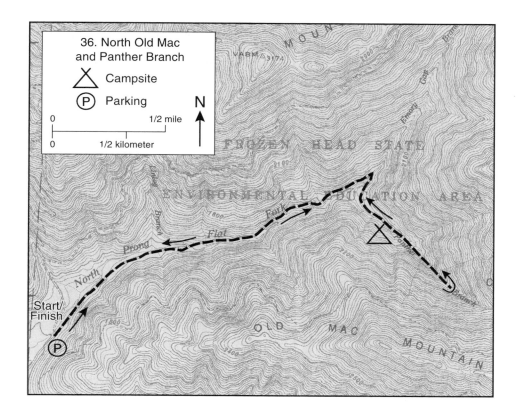

country camping (permits required). The park attracts many visitors and gets new converts every year, but no one ever gets stuck in a traffic jam coming here. Twenty trails, totaling 50 miles of hiking, receive excellent maintenance and are well marked; indeed, Frozen Head may have more blaze colors than any other Tennessee park. During the 1930s, the first Civilian Conservation Corps in Tennessee built most of these trails; currently park staff, volunteers, and state correctional facility work crews maintain the trails. The Cumberland Trail, or CT (scouted and built by volunteers), will eventually go through Frozen Head, crossing challenging and beautiful terrain that will expand the hiking opportunities. In the following description spring wildflowers are emphasized, but fall and winter hiking are good, too.

From the parking area, continue straight on the gated road across Flat Fork on a bridge. The road runs to the left of the creek, which has small rapids and big boulders. The number of spring flowers increases as you get farther from the gate; at first just a few white and yellow violets grow on the bank, then longspur violets appear. By the time you've gone half a mile you can see lousewort (or wood betony), hepatica, bloodroot, anemone, and more. As a preview of flowers to come, a few yellow trillium bloom.

Turn right for a spur trail to DeBord Falls, with an observation fence and a small trail to a shallow pool at the base of the falls. Return

---

North Old Mac and Panther Branch

Large-flowered trillium and great chickweed

to the main trail, continue up a gentle grade, and, at about 1 mile, descend to cross the creek on a wooden bridge. Panther Branch Trail makes a sharp right turn where Panther Branch and Emory Gap Branch join to form Flat Fork. For an extra half mile (1 mile total) you can go on straight to Emory Gap Falls and then return to Panther Branch.

Cross Panther Branch and cross a flat area with a backcountry campsite. Climb the hillside on the right. You will ascend a narrowing north-facing valley that has just the right balance for wildflowers—shelter from direct sun that would dry the soil, and deciduous woods that allow in the maximum of late-winter and spring sun before they grow leaves. Trillium, geraniums, cohosh, doll's eyes, spotted mandarin, and many other wildflowers carpet the hillside. Dwarf ginseng blooms closer to the ground. Closely related to ginseng, this plant has the good fortune to have no medicinal

reputation. Male plants produce a pea-sized sphere of white flowers, while female plants have less conspicuous greenish flowers.

But even with this much diversity, trillium steal the show. Tall (for spring flowers, that is) and bright, they bloom on just about all the hikes in this book, but especially at Frozen Head. The *tri* in their name refers to three leaves, sepals, petals, and stigmas. Members of the lily family, the species can be divided into two identification categories: sessile, in which the flower sits right on the leaves with no stalk (toadshades), and stalked (wake robins). The stalked varieties have flowers either above the leaves (erect) or below (nodding). Colors vary from bright white to lemon yellow to shades of maroon; odors are absent, sweet, or stinking like rotten meat (guess which insects pollinate these!). A few species (such as the most common one at Frozen Head, the white large-flowered trillium) fit the flower book descriptions. Others hybridize or resemble each other enough to give botanists hours of entertainment arguing about them. Species at Frozen Head include sessile yellow trillium, with variegated leaves and a sweet smell; its burgundy-to-brown relative stinking Willie; maroon, stalked erect trillium (the same species is usually white in the Smokies); the large Vasey's trillium (stalked, maroon, and nodding); and the large-flowered trillium, with yellow centers and white petals that turn pink just before they wilt.

Trillium reproduce vegetatively (from the bulbs) or by seeds. Each seed has a sweet glob on one end; ants collect the seeds, carry them some distance, and then eat the sweet stuff, leaving each seed nicely planted far from its parents. It takes a germinated seed several years to mature.

Continue up the valley, passing more and more rock outcropping and boulders. A small side creek slips down a rock face and muddies the trail. You may want to turn back here or go on up a steeper section of trail past Panther Branch. Just past the junction a spur trail leads to bluffs that overlook Flat Fork Valley—a good place to make a side trip for a picnic and to dangle your feet over the edge.

From here, you can retrace your steps to see the trillium again, or you can turn right onto North Old Mac Trail (red-dot blazes) and return to the road in 2.2 miles. It comes out at the picnic area parking lot about 0.5 mile from the Panther Branch Trailhead.

Other Hiking Options

1. Turn left onto North Old Mac Trail, climb 1.1 miles to Lookout Mountain Trail, and then climb 0.6 mile to the tower for a view of all the hikes in this guide north of I-40. On a good day. Return on North Old Mac Trail to the parking lot.
2. Combine this hike with South Old Mac Trail for a total of 6 or 7 miles (depending on whether you include Judge Branch) plus that 0.5-mile road walk.
3. A section of the Cumberland Trail will be built across Frozen Head State Park using existing and abandoned trails. It will probably be a difficult route; ask at the visitors center for details, or check the CT Web page.

37

Judge Branch and South Old Mac

Total Distance: 7.3 miles

Hiking Time: 4 hours

Vertical Rise: 2,000 feet

Rating: Easy to moderate

Maps: Frozen Head State Park map; USGS Petros

Trail Marking: South Old Mac, yellow blazes; Judge Branch, white blazes

Frozen Head State Park and Natural Area, site of the first Civilian Conservation Corps in the state in 1933, has excellent, well-maintained trails and some of the best wildflowers in Tennessee. This hike combines five trails between the visitors center and Frozen Head Tower, the highest point in the park. The first half of the hike (the easy part) could be used for an all-day flower study in spring, and the entire route provides exercise and a wonderful view in fall and winter.

How to Get There

From Oak Ridge, take TN 62 (a continuation of Illinois Avenue) through Oliver Springs. TN 62 turns right from Oliver Springs Bypass; continue on it for about 8 miles and turn right onto Flat Fork Road at a FROZEN HEAD sign. Pass the Morgan County Correctional Facility and the park entrance, then leave your car at the visitors center.

The Hike

Designated in 1970, Frozen Head is the only state park that started as prison land; now Brushy Mountain State Prison and the Correctional Facility/Honor Farm flank the park's rugged mountains and valleys. The visitors center, ranger station, bathrooms, recreational facilities, and a fine wooded campground are clustered on the entrance road, and the rest of the park, managed as a natural area and a state environmental education area, is restricted to hiking and backcountry camping (permit required) only. Extensive logging and a disastrous fire in 1952 reduced the forest cover to almost nothing, but the new growth has

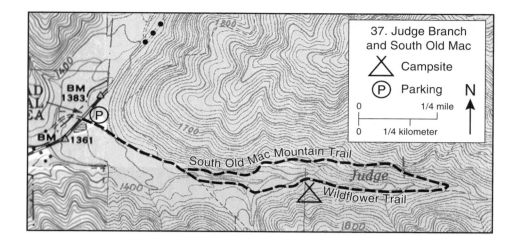

matured fast and developed a wealth of spring flowers.

From the visitors center, climb a mossy bank to a trail sign. Turn left onto Chimney Top Trail and climb over a small rise. Descending into a hemlock grove, you will see the visitors center again on the left and a creek (Judge Branch) ahead. Cross on a small wooden bridge and turn right onto the Interpretive Trail, which runs along a creek and is much prettier than the first part of South Old Mac Trail. Thick hemlocks mix with patches of deciduous trees that allow spring sunshine for wildflowers such as trillium, toothwort, and violets. Beeches, which are especially common in young forests, keep their leaves all winter, but the old ones magically disappear as new velvety bronze leaves come out in April. The bronze color is probably an adaptation to increase heat absorption from the sun; the leaves turn green as spring warms up. The bronze color returns in fall, before the leaves dry up for winter.

Pass a shale-ledge cascade across the creek and move away from the water into tulip trees, maples, beeches, oaks, and other deciduous trees. The Interpretive Trail

curves left and rejoins the main trail. Turn right and walk a few yards to a junction with South Old Mac Trail, which turns left to climb to Tub Spring and the Lookout Tower. Continue past the junction, cross Judge Branch, and turn left onto Judge Branch Trail, which runs roughly parallel to South Old Mac Trail for a mile before rejoining it to make your loop. You could skip the loop by taking the first turn onto South Old Mac Trail, which will be a little shorter than taking Judge Branch Loop.

On Judge Branch Trail (white blazes) travel 0.5 mile along the creek to Judge Branch Campsite, a large level spot with a lot of little brown jug and hepatica, both of which bloom in March. A decaying woodpile at the campsite offers an opportunity to carefully look for salamanders and centipedes; in warm weather snakes may hide here, too. Cross a tributary of Judge Branch on a new bridge and look for running ground cedar along an avenue of hemlocks. At a double blaze descend to Judge Branch and use stepping-stones to cross to a new section of trail that connects with South Old Mac Trail. Turn right at the junction and climb to a drier hillside with mountain laurel,

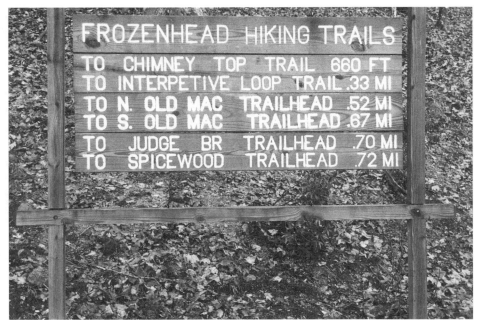

Trail sign behind visitors center

pines, and a winter view of the ridge ahead and Chimney Tops to right.

The trail continues to climb; on this south-facing slope chestnut oaks and hickories outnumber the beeches. Ascend a long sidehill, or bench, trail past rock outcrops with mosses, lichens, and alumroot, a relative of foamflower. Fence lizards and blue-tailed skinks may hunt for insects on the rocks in hot weather. Look ahead for a glimpse of the lookout tower through the trees.

At 2.75 miles from the visitors center you'll reach another sign and junction. To reach the tower, turn right onto an unblazed road and climb around the high point of Frozen Head, approaching it from the back. On top is an open grassy area, a fenced collection of communications equipment, and the tower, built in the 1930s (now showing its age). Climbing it is allowed (it may not be when you read this), but be careful about

loose or wet steps. Windy and a bit scary on top, the tower gives a 360-degree view, with Petros and Brushy Mountain State Prison directly below and the Smokies in the distance to the east on clear days.

Return to the trail sign and descend South Old Mac Trail to the parking lot, taking a left turn about 0.2 mile after the INTERPRETIVE TRAIL sign. If you miss it, by choice or accident, you come out at a different parking lot with bathrooms, signs, and a small pond with ducks, red-spotted newts, tadpoles, and mosquitoes. After the pond, turn left onto the paved road and walk about 0.2 mile to the visitors center parking lot.

Other Hiking Options

1. After visiting the tower, turn onto Chimney Tops Trail (green blazes), hike 1.1 miles to Spicewood Branch Trail (purple blazes), and return to South Old Mac and Judge Branch Trails in 2.5 miles. Spice-

wood Branch Trail is a little rough; skip it in rain or snow. But it's a north-facing slope that has a good wildflower display and closeup views of treetops in the valley below.

2. After the tower, go the other way—toward Tub Spring—and take North Old Mac Trail (3.3 miles) down to South Old Mac Trail near the parking lots. This option features bluffs, other rock formations, overlooks, and, yes, more wildflowers.

3. Be really ambitious and return via Chimney Top Trail and the highest backcountry campsite in the park. The entire trail (and you will do it all) is 6.6 miles, which will increase your total mileage to about 11 miles and give your knees a workout on the steep descent at the end.

VI

Southern Cumberland Mountains

38

Piney River Pocket Wilderness

Total Distance: 10.0 miles (with car shuttle)

Hiking Time: 6–7 hours

Vertical Rise: 250 feet

Rating: Moderate

Map: USGS Pennine

Trail Marking: White blazes, green metal tags

Piney River Trail runs beside water all the way—first Piney River and then Duskin Creek. But here's something unusual: Even with that much water, you won't have wet feet. Long bridges get you across and provide places to stand and watch cascades and ripples. Spectacular wildflowers make this one of the best spring hikes, but it's great at any time of year. Parts of this hike (out and back) would be fun for children, though some sections are rocky.

How to Get There

From US 27 at Spring City, turn west onto TN 68 and drive 1.4 miles to Shut-In Gap Road in a residential area. Turn left and drive 0.6 mile to Piney River Picnic Area on the right. To reach Newby Branch Forest Camp, the other end of the hike, drive 5 miles farther on Shut-In Gap Road (gravel with sharp turns and some timber-harvesting areas) and turn right into the camp. To shorten the hike by 1 mile, drive 1 mile past Newby Camp and park at a cement bridge; the trail crosses the road here. There's room for two or three cars; parking may be safer at Newby Camp.

The Hike

Walden Ridge, the eastern part of the Cumberland Plateau, runs from Lake City to the Tennessee River at Chattanooga. Sandstones and shales created from erosion of mountains to the east (earlier versions of the current Appalachians) were pushed westward about 250 million years ago by repeated collisions of continental plates. As the masses of rock moved, they

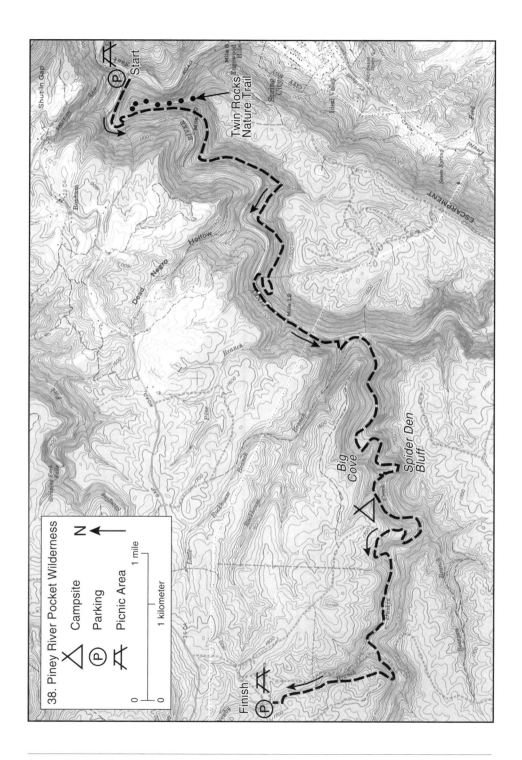

buckled, broke, bent, faulted, tumbled, and, in some places, ended up at crazy angles. A 1,000-foot escarpment, roughly parallel to the spine of western Blue Ridge and the eastern border of Tennessee, rises from the Tennessee River Valley along Walden Ridge. But even hard sandstone erodes, especially if water has 250 million years to work on it. The water also liberated enormous boulders of sandstone and quartz conglomerate. Three hikes climb the escarpment through river gorges: Piney River, Laurel Falls (Hike 39), and North Chickamauga Creek (Hike 40). All are Bowater Pocket Wildernesses—among eight recreational areas set aside by Bowater Incorporated, a paper products company (mainly newsprint). The Cumberland Trail (CT) will eventually use many of these beautiful spots and link them together with sections through Bowater or other private lands—with 32 miles of hiking you will be able to go from Piney River to Laurel Falls. Most of the CT, when it's finished, will run along Walden Ridge and take advantage of the spectacular scenery (and hiking challenge) of these gorges.

Water from two Cumberland Plateau gorges drains into Piney River, which flows through Spring City to Watts Bar Lake. On this hike you climb a gradual valley instead of the steep bluffs that you can see from US 27. If you arrange a car shuttle to Newby Branch, you'll drive up the escarpment on hairpin turns, but Piney River Trail offers an easier way up. The hike is described here going upstream from the picnic area to Newby Camp, which will be most useful to hikers with only one car or who would prefer not to shuttle cars. However, once you explore part of this hike and have to choose a turnaround point, you'll want to come back sometime and do it all. In fact, you may be able to do even more than the 10 miles:

The Cumberland Trail Conference plans to extend Piney River Trail and to connect it with Stinging Fork Pocket Wilderness.

From Piney River Picnic Area, cross the road and walk up the mowed bank to the trail sign. The trail becomes a shelf on a steep hillside with tall, straight tulip trees and other hardwoods. In winter Piney River and the other side of the gorge can be seen. At 0.2 mile Twin Rocks Nature Trail turns left, and beyond that a right spur leads to a Piney River Gorge overlook. The main trail continues to rise along the hillside, while both rocks and varieties of wildflowers increase. Trout lilies cover the hillside in March, and trillium succeeds them in April. Canada violets, plantain-leafed sedge, and foamflower also bloom in April.

Swing right to a stretch of rocky hillside with wonderful wildflowers, a few boulder-strewn side creeks, and a bit of poison ivy. Jack-in-the-pulpit, purple phacelia, true and false Solomon's seal, stonecrop, foamflower, and more poke up through rock crevices. Black cohosh blooms in summer, and female jacks as well as hearts-a-bustin' produce their bright seeds in fall. Rough footing here will give you an excuse to slow down and study the wildflowers.

At about 2 miles you'll descend to a drippy bluff and an old road with new trees growing in the middle. Anemones, Michaud's saxifrage (named for a French botanist who made a vast collection of American plants and lost them all in a shipwreck), ferns, and liverworts cling to cracks in the wet surfaces. Cross MacDonald Branch (cascades upstream and down) on stepping-stones (usually easy).

Swing away from Piney River at 4 miles and then cross it on a wooden suspension bridge—the first of several trail architectural features. There's a small campsite and good places to swim. The next section

The hikers' suspension bridge over the Piney River

Piney River Pocket Wilderness

passes more flowers (including lousewort and golden Alexander) and then follows a dinky line—a narrow-gauge railroad used to haul coal and lumber (look for cinders on the trail). The dinky line goes straight on a stone foundation to a bridge support; your trail turns right to descend to a new bridge across Rockhouse Branch. Half a mile later there's a metal bridge perched on rock supports, and then Piney River Trail turns to travel along Duskin Creek.

The trail moves away from the creek, first through a grove of large hemlocks with good sitting logs and a possible campsite, and then up into Big Cove, an open area of mixed hardwoods at 6 miles. Moist soil and sunlight flowing through leafless trees encourage spring flowers, and this is the best part of an already good wildflower trail. A tornado in 1990 flattened part of the forest, providing more open areas and jobs for termites and woodpeckers. Yellow and spotted mandarin, geranium, large patches of mayapple (a patch may be one plant with a lot of leaves; in other words, an underground tree), phlox, egg-yolk yellow wild oats, and blue cohosh—there's lots of color. Dwarf buckeye shrubs, 3 to 5 feet tall, produce bright red, orange, or yellow flower clusters.

Climb out of Big Cove and descend to a spur trail on the left to Spider Den Bluff. The spur trail drops to creek level along sandy bluffs to the largest campsite on the trail. Pink lady's slippers grow here, especially before and after a switchback.

Back on the main trail, ascend to a drier, south-facing section with sourwood trees and mountain laurel. Yellow hawkweed and fire pink also bloom here. Up to the right is an old coal mine; you can scramble up a rubble bank to see coal, timbers, and rails.

At 8.4 miles cross another bridge over Duskin Creek and continue through a quiet hemlock forest. Gay wings, a special flower of this trail, grow along the banks in mats. This plant's leaves look like partridgeberry leaves, except they're solid green instead of having white veins. In April gay wings produce showy pink flowers that look like tiny single-engine planes, with stamens as propellers.

At about 9 miles the trail emerges onto Shut-In Road, crosses the road bridge, and continues for 1 more mile to Newby Branch Forest Camp. The trail is level between the creek and the road, and then crosses the last bridge of the trail and ascends to the camp.

Other Hiking Options

1 Twin Rocks. A spur trail from Piney River Trail 0.2 mile from Piney River Picnic Area leads left for 0.6 mile to the base of a bluff and then to the top on a caged ladder. The flat sandstone slab is fenced and has a fine view of the Piney River Valley.

2. Stinging Fork. In a separate pocket wilderness in Bowater's Piney River Tree Farm, Stinging Fork Trail winds gently through pine forest to the rim of a gorge and a spur trail to an overlook. Then it descends steep rocky steps and switchbacks to a tiny campsite and a waterfall and pool. This was the first Bowater Pocket Wilderness; its trail may be extended, and part of it may be included in the CT.

Drive 4 miles past Piney River Picnic Area on Shut-In Road and look for a wide parking shoulder and a POCKET WILDERNESS sign on the right.

39

Laurel Falls Pocket Wilderness

Total Distance: 5.0 miles

Hiking Time: 3 hours

Vertical Rise: About 300 feet to Laurel Falls; 1,000 feet to top of bluff

Rating: Easy to moderate

Map: USGS Morgan Springs

Trail Marking: White blazes

An easy creekside walk and then some rocky terrain up to Laurel Falls make this an excellent year-round hike; even in hot summer, the creek is nearby and the way is shaded. This would be a good hike for children if you have plenty of time to explore rocks. This trail can be crowded on summer weekends.

How to Get There

From US 27 just north of Dayton, turn west onto Walnut Grove Road and then left onto Back Valley Road in less than a mile. In 0.7 mile look for a POCKET WILDERNESS sign and turn right onto Richland Creek Road (Pocket Wilderness Road). It reaches the gravel parking lot in 0.8 mile.

The Hike

Laurel Falls is another of eight Bowater Pocket Wildernesses (see Hike 38), recreational areas set aside by Bowater Incorporated, a paper products company (mainly newsprint). The Cumberland Trail (CT) will eventually use many of these beautiful spots and link them together with sections through Bowater or other private lands—with 32 miles of hiking you will be able to go from Piney River to Laurel Falls. The 2.5-mile section described here is short and relatively easy, good for a family outing or a beginner backpack. The other hiking options here, described at the end, both involve climbing up to the plateau. Both are rated difficult.

From the parking lot, continue up the road beside Richland Creek, which can be murmuring or rushing fast enough for kayakers. Look for a sign-in box on the left and register; Bowater needs to know how popular its trails are. Dinky lines (narrow-gauge railroads) once carried coal on the roadbed you are walking; look for fine supporting rock work, discarded railroad ties, and mine openings. Up to the right is a brick foundation with arches. Some of the coal mined here was made into coke and used to smelt iron ore.

Cross a wooden bridge on old cement supports. Side paths through luxuriant poison ivy lead to the water and to massive boulders overlooking it. At about half a mile Morgan Creek joins Richland Creek on the other side. At the next bridged side-creek crossing look for a broken pipe that once carried water from Dayton Reservoir to Dayton. The trail turns right here and climbs a steep, possibly slippery bare dirt path. For a short side trip, you can follow the old trail along the river to see the remains of the reservoir and its dam; then return to climb the hill.

The trail runs parallel to the creek but rises high above it on switchbacks. Don't cut across them; where some people have, the trail has eroded and become gullied. Soon, however, the trail becomes rocky. Solomon's seal, false Solomon's seal, stonecrop, dwarf-crested iris, violets, and trillium bloom in spring, and in June you can look down into the rhododendron blossoms along the creek. Elms, basswoods, hickories, and oaks shove the rocks aside as they grow, and maidenhair and Christmas ferns poke up between the rocks. Poison ivy vines snake across the tops.

After leveling out along all these rocks, the trail descends a bit to cross Laurel Creek on a metal bridge installed by Bowater in 1976. Swing right and continue upstream; new blazes will help you choose a route across the rocks. The trail forks at

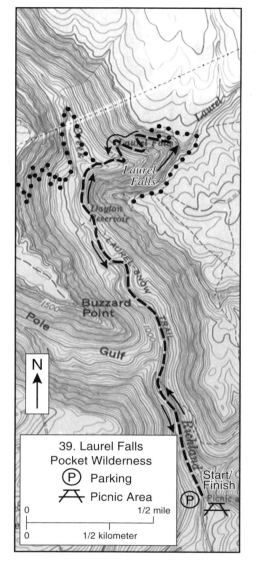

1.5 miles near a pool and a split boulder. The sharp left fork goes to Snow Falls; for Laurel Falls, continue to the right, following red arrows and white blazes. You have to wiggle between rock slabs, climb a few switchbacks for about half a mile, and finally descend to some rocks (what else?) with a

Snow Falls bridge over Henderson Creek

Laurel Falls Pocket Wilderness

good view of Laurel Falls. In heavy water the spray keeps the rocks wet and slippery—be careful, and make sure children don't go near slippery edges. In low water you can climb to the pool at the base surrounded by huge dark rocks. While you stop here to have a snack and admire the falls, you can find Fraser magnolias, white and red oaks, elms, red maples, hickories, witch hazels, and devil's walking sticks, all in plain view. Both poison ivy and Virginia creeper are abundant around the rock edges.

On the way back look for a blazed trail to the right that leads to the top of the bluff and to the falls overlook (option 1, below). To retrace your steps to the parking lot, stay left and crawl in and out of all those crevices again. On the return trip it's easy to miss the main trail blazes; if you start hiking away from Laurel Creek and pass a large, level campsite, turn back and look again. You should find blazes that lead across the rocks to the metal bridge.

Other Hiking Options

1. Laurel Falls Overlook. After visiting Laurel Falls, look for a right fork about 100 yards back. This trail climbs steeply with many switchbacks until it reaches a narrow passage to the top of the bluff. This requires finding hand- and footholds. Then you emerge into dry woods and easy walking. Turn right onto an old road and descend to where Laurel Creek slides toward the lip. You can go out on flat rocks for views down the valley, but to get a good view of the falls, cross Laurel Creek and follow the now-sandy road (used by ATVs) to an overlook about half a mile past the creek. From here you can see Laurel Falls, Buzzard Point on the opposite bluff, and the solid woods of deep creek gorges in all directions.

2. Snow Falls. At the fork just past the metal bridge turn sharply left, away from Laurel Falls Trail. Descend through shady woods for about half a mile, past the campsite. As you come to boulders again, watch for an arrow that directs you to the left to crawl around a ledge to not one, but three metal bridges perched on boulders high above Richland Creek. After the bridges, turn left and follow the creek for another half mile, until the trail takes off in ever-steeper switchbacks all the way to the bluff rim. Travel right to Buzzard Point Overlook, from which you can see Laurel Falls across the gorge and also admire the engineering feat of high-tension power lines going all the way across. Then the trail runs back into the woods until it descends to Morgan Creek. It goes straight across, but you shouldn't try unless the water is low enough. Some hikers climb all that way and can't get across to see Snow Falls.

3. The Bridges. After visiting Laurel Falls, turn onto Snow Falls Trail just far enough to cross those three bridges over Richland Creek.

40

North Chickamauga Creek Pocket Wilderness

Total Distance: 1.5 miles for Hogskin Branch Loop; 8.0 miles for Stevenson Trail

Hiking Time: 1 hour for Hogskin; 5 hours for Stevenson

Vertical Rise: 700 feet

Rating: Difficult

Map: USGS Chattanooga

Rocks, sandstone bluffs with rockhouses, a tumbling creek, and a very special lizard grace this trail. Beautiful in all seasons, it's best on cooler days. In cases of heavy rain or even the possibility of snow or ice, choose a different hike. More rocks than plain ground make this hike risky for small children and people with knee or ankle problems.

How to Get There

From US 27, take the Soddy-Daisy/Sequoyah Nuclear Plant exit (about 12 miles north of Chattanooga). Turn right at the end of the exit ramp, go to the first traffic light and turn left onto Dayton Pike (you'll see MacDonalds, Walmart, KFC, and many more on the right). Drive 3 miles to the next traffic light at a gas station. Turn right onto Montlake Road and drive 1.1 miles through a residential area; look for a BOWATER sign on the left. Park either on the left at the first wide place or down in the picnic area.

The Hike

This hike offers views, swimming holes, unusual plants and animals, and a good hiking challenge, but future plans involve even more. The adjacent state natural area, including Falling Water Falls, will protect the other side of the gorge and most of the upstream watershed. Greenway trails from Chattanooga and the Chickamauga Dam will extend from the south, and this trail will be connected to the Cumberland Trail for a spectacular, 20-mile gorge hike. These projects will take a while, but check and see how they progress.

North Chickamauga Creek Trail starts

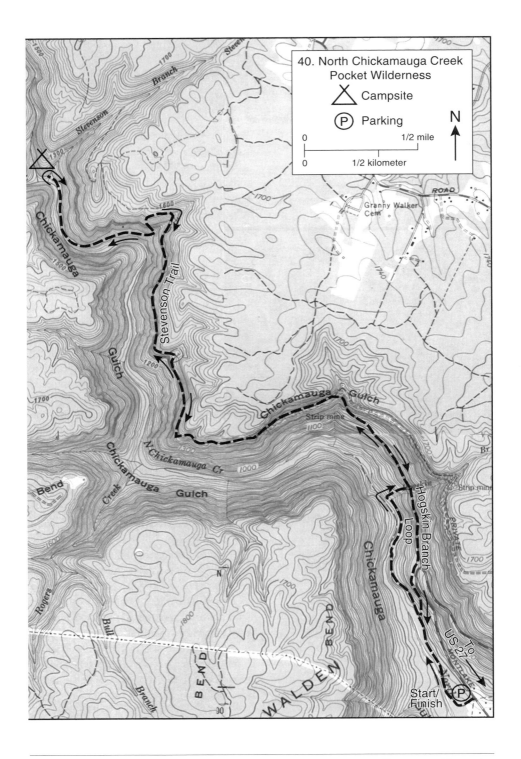

40. North Chickamauga Creek
Pocket Wilderness

△ Campsite

Ⓟ Parking

N

0   1/2 mile

0   1/2 kilometer

Chickamauga

Stevenson Trail

Gulch

Chickamauga   Gulch

N Chickamauga Cr

Chickamauga   Gulch

Creek

Bend

Strip mine

Granny Walker Cem

ROAD

Hogskin Branch Loop

Chickamauga

Strip mine

To US 27

Start/ Finish

Rogers

Bull

Branch

BEND   BEND

WALDEN

to the right of the parking area on an old road blocked by boulders. At the first picnic table on the left there is easy access to the creek and excellent sitting rocks. Continue past several picnic tables and look for white blazes on trees. Some of these are faded, and you'll need to develop a good search image for them because rock piles may obscure the trail route. (The trail will probably be reblazed by the time you hike it.) The old road (imagine building a road through these rocks!) continues higher above the creek, and you'll see a double blaze and small trail on the right. This is the return part of the Hogskin Branch Loop.

Soon the rocks take over the path, and you will be clambering up and down. Sourwoods, red maples, hickories, chestnut oaks, and cucumber magnolias will be among the trees you grab for balance. Hepaticas, violets, trillium, and ferns manage to find soil between the rocks.

Wooden steps take you higher above the creek, but then you have to go down to cross a side creek—and then up again. Continue level for a while, then follow the blazes down past another side creek (probably dry). The next side creek is Hogskin Branch, which ranges from a trickle to a tricky crossing. Cascades above and below the crossing show red iron-ore deposits.

The trail turns definitively away from the river and uses switchbacks and wooden steps to climb to a higher, more established old road that was used for logging and coal mining. To complete the 1.5-mile Hogskin Loop, turn right here, cross Hogskin Branch, and walk along the upper road. About 80 yards past the end of a bluff, turn right on a narrow trail marked by an arrow. Follow the blazes to the lower road and then back to your car.

To follow Stevenson Trail, turn left and hike up a steady grade on rubbly gravel.

Pignut hickories abound here; in fall collect a few nuts and take advantage of the best feature of this trail: rocks. Smash any nuts that look fresh (and don't feature exit holes from nut grubs). The shells are tough and thick (how do the nut grubs and squirrels do it?), but the meat is usually sweet, though it might have a hint of bitterness. Taste a bit before eating the whole thing; chances are you'll only get a bit anyway.

After a split rock slab, the trail eases a bit and approaches a fractured cliff face on the right. Look left for occasional views of the corresponding cliff across the creek. Bits of coal on the ground and the foundation of a coal tipple are a reminder of earlier activity.

Climb to a side creek with extravagant cascades to the right. It's worth a climb up to the base of the cascades on slippery rocks.

The trail continues on the roadbed but is less used—many hikers turn back at the creek crossing. The trail becomes a rocky bench along the bottom of a steep cliff with exposed bluffs alternating with overhanging rock shelters. On the right is a coal mine entrance. This is unstable and unsafe to enter—just take a look inside at the coal seam sandwiched between sandstone layers. You can hear dripping from deep in the cave, and a tiny creek flows out to form a room-sized marsh. Somehow a few marsh plants got here: netted chain ferns, some sedges, and small sweetgums with winged twigs. Bright green Saint-John's-wort, with yellow flowers in summer, grows near the mine entrance.

Moving along the base of the bluff, the trail narrows to a sandy path, sometimes going up and down like a roller coaster and marked by faded blazes. Hug the bluff. Occasional wet spots where water seeps down the rock face support midge and mosquito larvae and possibly tadpoles.

Here's where you can start to look for anolis lizards (usually brown, but green when they feel like it) running in and out of rock cracks; they will obligingly show themselves if you stand still. These lizards, like armadillos and fire ants, are gradually extending their range northward. They live on south-facing bluffs like these and come out when sun warms the rocks; they do not hibernate. Fence lizards, skinks, garter snakes, and other reptiles also take advantage of this massive solar-heated bluff. Some female hollies (the ones with berries) grow in the sandy soil, and ant lions wait in their pits.

Organ pipe mud dauber wasps build nests on the rock face. The female wasp catches spiders, anesthetizes them, stuffs them in the clay nests, and lays eggs on them: fresh food for growing wasp larvae.

When the trail seems to dead-end in a rhododendron thicket, look for blazes and a wooden ladder on the right, and climb it to a metal bridge and a fenced platform with a view across the gorge. To continue, look for blazes straight back up the hill. You may want to stop here for a snack and then return along the bluff for a 6-mile hike. There's another overlook to the left, and the trail switches back through a stand of pines until it reaches a level, grassy road. If you choose to continue the hike from here, look for landmarks to find this turn on the way back.

The last 1.5 miles of this hike include an easy, level road walk. Then the grassy road leads slightly downhill past coal mine openings and reaches an open area with several large mines reinforced with timbers, now broken. A marshy spot, probably created by earthmovers, supports cattails, sedges, and frogs. The trail swings left, and the road becomes shaded. In about 0.2 mile a dirt mound and blazes indicate a left turn down a jolting rock scramble to North Chickamauga Creek. Old rock steps, a cable across a slippery creek cascade, and trees to grab help somewhat, but this section is an adventure. Look for blazes and use caution on wet spots. The trail snakes along a bluff and then drops down to creek level before heading upstream to a campsite, probably not used much.

Retrace your steps back to the gorge rim and then across the base of the bluffs to the upper logging road to Hogskin Branch. To return by the Hogskin Branch Loop, cross Hogskin Branch to an easy road walk. Yellow paint on rocks and trees indicates pocket wilderness boundary, and a few blazes reassure you that this is the way. The road passes a rock face on the left; about 80 yards after that, look to the right for an arrow and a narrow trail down through rocks. Montlake Road can be seen and heard above a rock pile. Gentle at first, the path soon plunges into another boulder jumble with switchbacks, steps, and a few blazes. Hepatica, trillium, and cranefly orchids live along the trail; one of the common trees here is shagbark hickory, with its gray bark peels curving out. Shagbark hickory nuts taste better than pignut hickory; the squirrels know that, and take most of them.

You'll reach the lower road near the picnic tables. Turn left to return to your car or to play on creek boulders.

41

Virgin Falls

Total Distance: 8.0 miles

Hiking Time: 4–5 hours

Vertical Rise: 800 feet

Rating: Moderate to difficult

Map: USGS Lonewood

Trail Marking: Main trail, green blazes; spur trails, blue blazes; occasional metal hiker signs

A bit out of the way, Virgin Falls Pocket Wilderness nevertheless attracts many visitors on weekends; you'll have a better hike on weekdays or by starting early. Part of the trail is rocky enough to be rated difficult, but the rest is well graded. This is an all-season hike and probably too rough for small children.

How to Get There

From I-40, take exit 317 (Crossville Playhouse, US 127) and drive south about 2.5 miles to a junction with US 70/US 70N. Turn right; in 0.2 mile stay straight on US 70 while US 70N goes to the right. Go 15.6 miles to De Rossett. Turn left onto Eastland Road (less than a mile past a blue and white water tower) and drive 5.9 miles; turn right onto Scotts Gulf Road (there's a sign for Chestnut Mountain) and drive 2 miles on this gravel road past a pine plantation to the Virgin Falls parking area on the right.

The Hike

The trail starts level through thin woods of oak, hickory, and young beech. Swing left and cross a marshy hollow on flat rocks; look for tadpoles and waist-high bouquets of cinnamon fern. Climb to dry woods again and descend, first into laurel, then into rhododendron, to cross Big Branch Creek at 0.5 mile. Descend along the creek to another crossing and look for a hidden left turn to Big Branch Falls. (If you miss it, you'll find it on the way out.)

The trail forks at a trail sign and map. The right fork climbs to Caney Fork Overlook and Martha's Pretty Point on a difficult route that includes stairs, boulders, and a

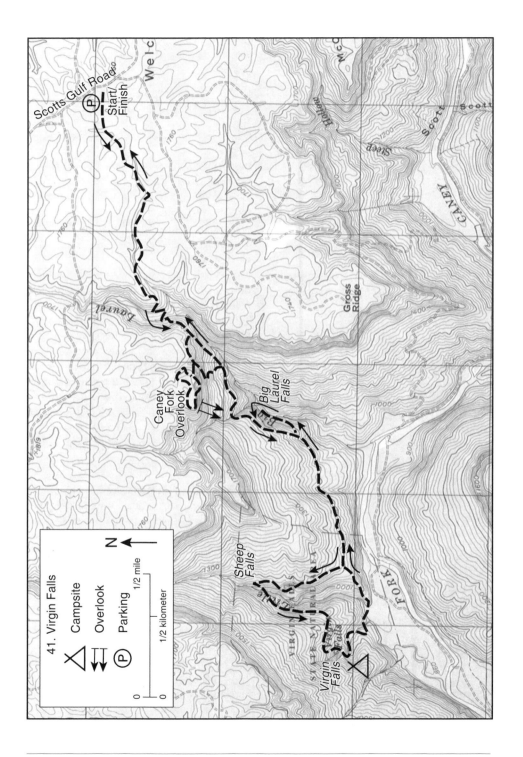

Scotts Gulf Road

Welc

Start/Finish

Holly Hollow

McC

Scott

Scott

Scott

Sheep

CANEY

Laurel

Caney Fork Overlook

Big Laurel Falls

Gross Ridge

1300

Sheep Falls

FORK

41. Virgin Falls

△ Campsite

Overlook

Ⓟ Parking

N ←

0   1/2 kilometer
0   1/2 mile

STATE NATURAL AREA

Virgin Falls

caged ladder on a rock face. After all that, it travels along the bluff rim to viewpoints of the Caney Fork River Valley and distant green hills. To return, pass a campsite, come down the ladder, and return to the fork following green blazes, or find green blazes for a rougher trail down to the connector.

The left fork, or connector, continues downstream; it connects the parking area to the pocket wilderness, which is the land around the falls. Railroad-tie steps help on steep rocky places, and after a creek crossing, the trail levels at a spur for a campsite and Big Laurel Falls, a gaping cave mouth. The creek runs over a ledge and then disappears—a preview of Virgin Falls. With winter icicles the cave looks like a hungry deep-ocean fish.

For a while after the falls, the trail is an easy, cushioned walk through beech, oak, and hickory woods. Little brown jug, hepatica, toothwort, and sweet cicely bloom in early spring, followed by trillium, mandarin, and more. Summer flowers include pachysandra and Allegheny spurge.

A rocky climb brings you to a view of Caney Fork River on the left. Turn right for the loop and climb to 10-foot-tall boulders and a sign. Sheep Cave yawns to the right down in a sinkhole and swallows its waterfall; you can get a close-up view by taking a narrow blue-blazed trail around the left side of the sinkhole. Stay left to go down into the sink; private land starts on the other side. In dry periods you can explore the cave entrance. Flowers thrive on the sinkhole banks.

Turn left onto the main trail, descend to a creek crossing, and head up the other side into oak, sourwood, and magnolia woods. Pass a flat campsite on the left in a hemlock grove. The sound of the waterfall becomes louder. Ninety-foot Virgin Falls looms ahead, pouring off a high ledge and disappearing into a sinkhole—it's a creek with no name

because there's no visible creek. Virgin Falls faces north and so receives little sunlight; huge icicles that form in cold weather may persist for weeks. The spray zone waters many ferns and flowers in spring. To reach a path to the top of the falls, continue past the falls on the main trail, turn left, and climb through a massive boulder field to the top of the falls. Well away from the dangerous lip you can cross the no-name creek on big rocks and see it roaring out of a cave like a freight train. After crossing, climb to a wonderful campsite above the falls. It looks like some hikers have tried to continue the loop around, but the rough paths lead to bluff drop-offs; return the way you came.

A simpler way to admire the falls is from a sunny spot just above the trail.

To return, you can complete the loop: Go through the lower campsite to the left of the waterfall sinkhole and descend toward Caney Fork River. ATV tracks (from outside the pocket wilderness) cross the trail; you have to watch the blazes and stay near a small creek along an old fence line. A spur right at the low point just past a crossing of Little Laurel Creek leads to another campsite. From here, turn left to climb a steep, rocky hillside. Continue to the loop fork and return, passing Big Laurel Falls, the side trail to the overlook, and the angled spur to Big Branch Falls that you may have missed the first time.

The other choice is to return from Virgin Falls the way you came, by Sheep Cave, which is longer but less rocky and steep.

As you hike this trail, think of the creeks rushing down toward Caney Fork River beneath your feet. The extensive cave system here has been explored and exists because this area is almost off the plateau. Water can break through the hard sandstone to the limestone below, which is both softer and soluble in the slight acidity of flowing water.

Quartz conglomerate

50 Hikes in the Tennessee Mountains

Other Hiking Options

Bridgestone/Firestone has donated 10,000 acres of forested land in Scotts Gulf, including bluffs, gorges, and a long corridor along Caney Fork River. The land, designated a centennial wilderness, lies adjacent to the Virgin Falls Pocket Wilderness and will be managed by the Tennessee Wildlife Resources Agency. Twelve miles of blazed hiking trails have been built to waterfalls, overlooks, and Chestnut Mountain Ranch. Trail access is from a parking area on Scotts Gulf Road beyond the Virgin Falls parking area. Future plans include more trails, campsites, and road and parking improvements.

42

Fall Creek Falls: Woodland, Gorge, and Falls

Total Distance: 2.8 miles

Hiking Time: 2 hours

Vertical Rise: 250 feet (Falls Trail)

Rating: Easy on Woodland and Gorge Trails; Falls Trail difficult

Map: USGS Billingsley

Trail Marking: Yellow, red, and orange blazes

The highest waterfall in the east, another one that's just as pretty, and a challenging climb make this one of the most popular trails in the state park. The upper parts of the hike would be fine for children, and the falls overlooks are handicapped-accessible. Spur trails lead to unprotected cliffs, and the gorge trail may be dangerous. October hikes provide excellent fall color views.

How to Get There

TN 284 runs through Fall Creek Falls State Park; directions here are for the north entrance. From Sparta take TN 111 south to Spencer, turn left onto TN 30, and drive 8 miles to the junction with TN 284. Turn right into the park and follow signs to the nature center. From Pikeville, take TN 30 west for 14 miles and turn left onto TN 284. From Crossville, take TN 101 south, turn right onto TN 30, and drive 6 miles to TN 284 and turn left into the park.

For the south entrance to the park, drive south 8 miles from Spencer on TN 111 and turn left onto TN 284.

The Hike

Fall Creek Falls State Resort Park has the largest visitation of any state park in Tennessee and was voted one of the five best state parks in the southeast by *Southern Living* magazine. As a resort park, it offers golf, conference facilities, a swimming pool, modern cabins, a restaurant, and more to accommodate families and groups. And, of course, it also offers excellent hiking and the highest waterfall in the east. More than half of the park is managed as undisturbed forest, regrowth from extensive logging and coal mining. The National Park Service bought the land in the 1930s, developed it as a model recreation area with labor from the Civilian Conservation Corps, and later transferred it to the state.

Behind the Betty Dunn Nature Center, walk down the paved path to Cane Creek Falls Overlook. Turn left and cross a swinging bridge over the top of the falls to a long set of cement steps up the plateau. One trail goes left to the campground and another heads right to Gorge Trail; keep going straight on Woodland Trail, following yellow blazes. Turkey Pen Ridge Trail goes right, and then Woodland Trail descends to a bridge over Fall Creek. Note the creek's red bottom from iron oxide deposits; upstream from here is Fall Creek Lake, and its construction released iron and other minerals. Climb a small rise and then descend to a smaller creek, Coon Creek. Both creeks seem to be hurrying to their falls. A steep climb takes you to three fenced Fall Creek Falls overlooks and a parking lot with bathrooms and benches. From the third you can see both Fall Creek Falls and Coon Creek Falls tumbling 256 feet before rushing down to their meeting with Cane Creek.

If you choose to try the difficult part of this hike (skip it in wet weather), proceed past the third overlook and head down a rocky trail with occasional handrails. At the first massive fractured rock face, look up at several large hemlock trees hanging out over the trail from cracks. They do their bit for rock erosion, too.

Swing right for an even steeper climb down a jumble of boulders, some of which are arranged into steps of sandstone and quartz conglomerate. Soon you face a cracked rock wall with cool air flowing out. Turn left and then right to go under the bluff and overhang. Soon you see the falls and

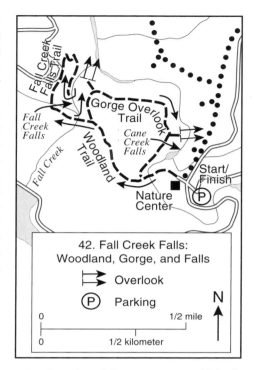

42. Fall Creek Falls:
Woodland, Gorge, and Falls

➡ Overlook

Ⓟ Parking

N

0   1/2 mile

0   1/2 kilometer

enter the edge of the spray zone, which allows plants to grow on the rock face: filmy fern, saxifrage, mosses, poison ivy, and mats of liverwort. Closer to the falls, plantain-leafed sedge and witch hazel enjoy the mist. This park, on the western escarpment of the Cumberland Plateau, has a lower elevation than many of the mountain hikes in this guide, but the creeks fall from hard sandstone and conglomerate to the softer shale of the plunge pool and carve out deep, narrow gorges.

Watch the curtains of water, be careful of slippery rocks, and then return to the top. Past the overlooks, descend to cross the two creeks again, and this time turn left onto Gorge Overlook Trail. Four overlook trails go left—each one less than 0.1 mile. From the first you can hear the falls better than you can see them. The second, Rocky Point, is well named and you'll have to climb

Fall Creek Falls

50 Hikes in the Tennessee Mountains

down one bluff and up another to get out on the point—this probably earns a rating of dangerous. Cane Creek Gorge Overlook gives a through-the-trees view down the gorge. The last overlook, around a right curve, is the best—a fenced overlook of the falls, usually sparkling in the sun.

From here, return to Gorge Overlook Trail, go back down all those cement steps, bounce across the bridge, and return to the nature center.

Other Hiking Options

Fall Creek Falls State Park has many other trails, including two overnight trails (12 and 13 miles, for longer day hikes or backpacking trips). The new Gilbert Gaul Loop (4.4 miles and named for a settler who came in 1881) starts at the gate of Group Camp #2 and runs along the rim of the gorge. Piney Creek Trail, part of the Lower Overnight Trail, leads to another great waterfall and gorge overlooks.

43

Fall Creek Falls: Pawpaw Trail

Total Distance: 4.6–5 miles

Hiking Time: 2½ hours; more if Cable Trail is included

Vertical Rise: About 100 feet; 200 feet with Cable Trail

Rating: Easy to moderate. Cable Trail: Difficult to dangerous

Map: USGS Billingsley

Trail Marking: Orange blazes (some white)

The highest waterfall east of the Rockies and the most visited state park in the system make Fall Creek Falls worth a visit. Fall is the best time, since the best features are the gorge overlooks (summer can be too hot in the open woods). Plateau trails to the overlooks are easy (though some overlooks are hard to get to and have sheer bluffs); the two trails into the gorge are challenging and should not be attempted by children.

How to Get There

TN 284 runs through Fall Creek Falls State Park; directions here are for the north entrance. From Sparta take TN 111 south to Spencer, turn left onto TN 30, and drive 8 miles to the junction with TN 284. Turn right into the park and follow signs to the nature center. From Pikeville, take TN 30 west for 14 miles and turn left onto TN 284. From Crossville, take TN 101 south, turn right onto TN 30, and drive 6 miles to TN 284 and turn left into park.

For the south entrance to the park, drive south 8 miles from Spencer on TN 111 and turn left onto TN 284.

The Hike

You don't really need a guide to these trails; in the most visited state park in Tennessee, they don't want you to get lost. Red signboards mark every junction. The creeks here on the western plateau eroded narrower and in some places steeper gorges than to the east, partly because the sandstone rock cap overlays crumbly shale, and partly because the thrust from the east 250 years ago fractured these rocks instead of pushing them. Cane Creek, which flows to Caney Fork River (which also collects the water of Virgin Falls, Hike 41), protected virgin timber on the floor of the gulf because it was too hard to get at.

From Betty Dunn Nature Center, walk right to a short rocky descent, climb up to the entrance road to cross the bridge over Rockhouse Creek, and look for two trails on the left. (You can avoid this rocky bit by simply walking on the road, especially if the trail is wet or icy.) The first left turn is for the Cable Trail, an innocent-looking path winding through mountain laurel and holly to a drop down the bluff. The park map says it's 0.25 mile long, but it looks shorter and feels longer. This trail is dangerous when dry and impossible when wet; check with a ranger in the nature center if in doubt. If you still want to do it, grab the cable and find foot- and handholds on the rock face; one spot is a straight drop, with the cable out of reach. At the bottom you are rewarded with a view of Cane Creek Falls and its green-water plunge pool. Large hemlocks and a few tulip trees grow on the small flood plain; look across the creek to a forest of larger tulip trees. You can walk upstream to get closer views of Cane Creek and Rockhouse Falls. Then return to the the cable, crawl back up, and hike back to the entrance road.

The next left turn takes you up a few steps onto a pleasant level walk through thin woods of oak, holly, dogwood, and sourwood. You can recognize sourwood by its deeply furrowed bark and its habit of changing the direction of its trunk every 15 or 20 feet. (Most other trees decide on a direction and stick with it.) Pines here have been damaged by a late-1990s infestation of the pine bark beetle. A left spur leads to Cane Creek Overlook; below are huge pointy-topped hemlocks, and farther to the right, deciduous trees are more common.

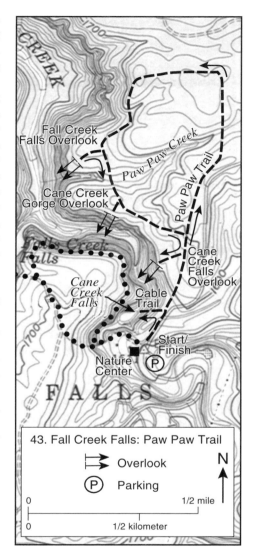

43. Fall Creek Falls: Paw Paw Trail

⊢→ Overlook

Ⓟ Parking

N

0   1/2 mile

0   1/2 kilometer

Return to the trail and reach Pawpaw Trail Loop; go right, or counterclockwise, to follow this description (with the best parts last), or go left for a shorter hike to the overlooks. Proceed through more plateau woods and look for rattlesnake plantain (an orchid, named for its scalelike leaf pattern) and rattlesnake fern (named for its repro-

Laboring up the Cable Trail

50 Hikes in the Tennessee Mountains

ductive frond that sticks up like a little rattle). Trailing arbutus grows all along this loop.

Pass the start of the overnight trail to the right and continue through a tangle of fallen pines and young maples and oaks; their big leaves take advantage of the open sky. Swing right to approach the gorge and the sound of waterfalls. Descend into a sloping creek valley with a bit of standing water that supports midges and mosquito larvae. Fall Creek Falls Overlook appears next; take a right spur to see just the lip of the falls through the trees. A view right shows how narrow this gorge is even farther downstream.

The next overlook, after another small creek crossing, is an open promontory over the gulf—a good place for lunch but unsafe for children. You can look up or down at soaring vultures and enjoy a breeze. Look for a lepidodendron fossil in one sandstone rock—this ancient tree fern looks like a patch of snakeskin. In the nature center are many larger examples.

From the overlook, take the short walk back to the beginning of the loop and then the trail back to the nature center.

Other Hiking Options

Fall Creek Falls State Park has many other trails, including two overnight trails (12 and 13 miles, for longer day hikes or backpacking trips). The new Gilbert Gaul Loop (4.4 miles and named for a settler who came in 1881) starts at the gate of Group Camp #2 and runs along the rim of the gorge. Piney Creek Trail, part of the Lower Overnight Trail, leads to another great waterfall and gorge overlooks.

44

Stone Door—Big Creek Gulf—Big Creek Rim

Total Distance: 9 miles

Hiking Time: 6 hours

Vertical Rise: 700 feet

Rating: Difficult

Maps: South Cumberland Recreation Area map, available at trailhead even when center is closed; USGS Altamont

Trail Marking: White blazes; blue blazes for side trails

The strenuous rating applies to the complete loop described here, which takes you to spectacular views across Savage Gulf and also down into (and up out of) its rocky innards. Easy-to-moderate hikes can be designed on upper sections of the loop. The plateau trails can be hiked in all seasons, but avoid the lower trails in heavy rain or any possibility of ice or snow. Stone Door Trail (0.9 mile) is graded and handicapped-accessible. Children will enjoy going through the Stone Door and hiking the easy plateau-top trails, but watch for unprotected bluffs on the Big Creek Rim Trail.

How to Get There

From Tracy City drive 21 miles north on TN 56. At Beersheba Springs, turn right at a state park sign and follow signs to the Stone Door Ranger Station (about 2 miles). From McMinnville, drive 20 miles south to Beersheba Springs.

The Hike

The South Cumberland Recreation Area, a coalition of eight parks and natural areas, includes spectacular parts of the Cumberland Plateau and superb hiking, all within an easy drive from Chattanooga. South Cumberland Visitor Center near Tracy City on TN 41 provides maps of all the areas, and ranger stations at Savage Gulf and Great Stone Door do the same. The hikes in this chapter (44–47: Stone Door, Savage Day Loop, Foster Falls, Fiery Gizzard) are just a starter kit for days and days of exploring.

Savage Gulf State Natural Area consists of three gulfs, or gorges, carved from the

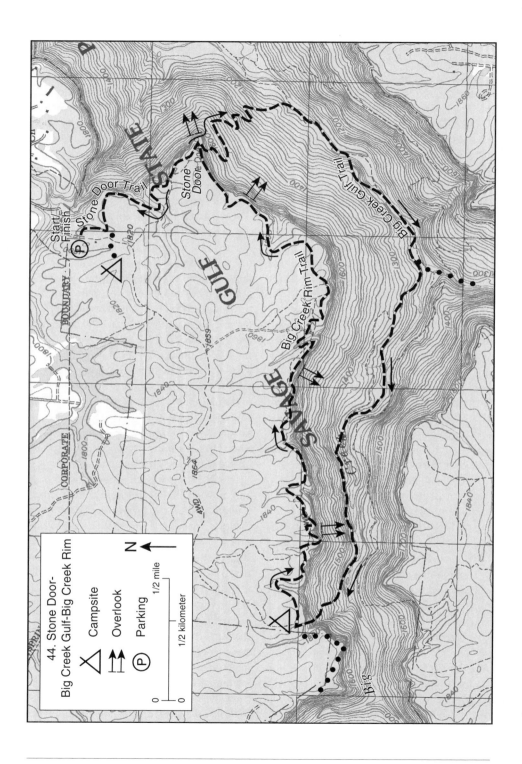

Cumberland Plateau caprock on top to beds of limestone at the bottom. Big Creek and Savage Creek (Hike 45) run through the side gulfs and join the middle gulf's Collins River, which wiggles north past McMinnville to join Caney Fork (fed by Virgin Falls, Hike 41); this in turn flows through Center Hill Lake, crosses I-40 five times, and then joins the Cumberland River at Carthage.

Stone Door Trail starts to the right of the visitor center as a wide, paved path, easily accessible to wheelchairs and baby strollers. After a sign-in box, Laurel Falls Trail goes left, and Stone Door continues down to cross a bridge. A blue-blazed trail goes right after the bridge to Stone Door Campsites, set back into the forest. The trail reaches Laurel Gulf Overlook, where you can look left up the steep canyon and across to Collins Gulf. Then it swings away from the gulf to cross small creeks before returning to the edge and the junction with Big Creek Gulf Trail. Stone Door Trail ends to the left on a wooden platform on a promontory across from seemingly endless bluffs and gorges. Don't think about the fact that you are perched out over this 700-foot-deep gulf with more air beneath you than rock.

To continue on to Big Creek Gulf, return from the platform, and wind down among rocks and trees to the Great Stone Door, which lives up to its name. Uneven rock steps help you through a narrow passage between five- to six-story rocks. You emerge in a different habitat: the gulf and the undersides of the bluffs. It's greener down here, with many kinds of trees, mosses, and wildflowers, and it feels like wilderness. Climb around rocks and switchbacks; you will need to keep track of the white blazes. At 1.9 miles from the ranger station, near the bottom of the rockiest part, the trail reaches the junction with Connector Trail, which you might use for a backpacking trip across the

gulf—15 strenuous miles would get you to Savage Day Loop (Hike 45). Look back up toward Stone Door to see the overlook point jutting out over the bluffs. Go right on Big Creek Gulf Trail through beech and hemlock woods and past a boulder field with rocks standing on end like ceramic Chinese soldiers. Quartz and sandstone conglomerate show where the rocks cracked when they fell down here as the creek eroded their surroundings.

Cross more rocks in a moist, mossy area. Even though you're on the south-facing side of the gulf, the sun doesn't dry the soil much down here, and spring flowers such as anise-root, toothwort, jack-in-the-pulpit, and foamflower bloom before tree leaves come out and take all the light. Descend to an old road (people actually cut timber down here) and a short relief from boulder hopping. The trail turns right away from the road (watch for the white blazes and a row of stones across the roadbed) and a blue-blazed trail continues on the road to a spot where Big Creek disappears into sinks when the water is low. You can walk downstream on the dry streambed to see where the creek gushes up again.

Back into rock clambering, the trail climbs a small side ridge and then drops back to creek level, where the blue-blazed Ranger Falls Trail turns left to cross the creek. Cross one rocky road and ascend right to another. Three kinds of orchids grow along and in the road: downy rattlesnake plantain, cranefly orchid, and putty root. Rattlesnake plantain flowers, following normal plant rules, grow on a stalk above the leaves. However, the other two orchids here grow leaves in winter and flower stalks in summer. Dark green oval cranefly orchid leaves have bright purple undersides, while the leaves of putty root are light green with many parallel white lines—they look some-

Yellow-bellied sapsucker holes

Stone Door-Big Creek Gulf-Big Creek Rim

what like cut and crinkled dollar bills. By the time the inconspicuous flowers come up, the leaves are gone.

Again, watch for a row of stones to indicate a right turn off the road, and climb to yet another old road, which passes a pretty cascade and then curves right as it starts climbing out of the gulf. Tulip tree, hemlock, yellow birch, American hornbeam, and witch hazel grow along the trail. As the road gets steep, you start seeing blocky sandstone bluffs. Look through the hemlocks to the left at a long cascade sliding down mossy rocks—this is Alum Creek, and its valley gave loggers one access to the gulf.

Finally, Big Creek Gulf Trail tops out at Alum Gap Camp Area and a junction with Greeter Falls, Laurel, and Big Creek Rim Trails. Turn right for Big Creek Rim Trail, which quickly establishes a pattern: Visit a bluff with a wonderful (but unprotected) view and then loop back on the plateau to cross a sloping creek valley, then ascend to another view. At the last bluff, you can see the Stone Door overlook to the left, and soon you will reach the junction with Stone Door Trail for your return.

Other Hiking Options

1. Greeter Falls. From Alum Gap it is 1.4 miles (2.8 miles round-trip) to Boardtree and Greeter Falls. The first mile is an easy, level walk, and then the trail heads down rocky hillsides and a few steep spots. Boardtree Falls, a long, ripply cascade, appears just past a swinging bridge. After some more rocky descent, the trail splits for upper Greeter Falls (right) and the larger lower Greeter Falls (left). If you get this far, don't miss the spiral staircase to the lower falls, unless there is ice on the trail. A parking lot off TN 56 about 4 miles south of Beersheba Springs provides a quicker access to Greeter Falls and could be used for car shuttles.

2. Ranger Falls Trail goes left from Big Creek Trail at the bottom of the gorge at 2 miles past the Stone Door. Only 0.4 mile long, it leads up a dry creek bed to the falls, which disappear down a sinkhole. Sometimes the water in Big Creek is too high; if in doubt, don't try to cross.

3. Laurel Falls Trail (2.9 miles) provides a shorter way between the ranger station and Alum Gap. It starts from Stone Door Trail just beyond the ranger station, goes 0.2 mile to Laurel Falls (with a viewing platform and some pretty impressive stairways), and then crosses the road to wander through plateau woods to the gap. Easy and safe (no bluff rims) and with a few marshy spots for frogs, it would be a better choice for children.

There are many other Savage Gulf trails, and the South Cumberland visitor center provides free maps.

45

Savage Day Loop, North Plateau, Mountain Oak, and North Rim

Total Distance: 8.4 miles

Hiking Time: 5 hours

Vertical Rise: 100 feet

Rating: Easy to moderate

Map: USGS Collins

Trail Marking: Signs at junctions

This easy stroll through the varied habitats of the southern Cumberland Plateau offers views deep into the wildest part of Savage Gulf. It's an all-season hike, hot in summer but mostly shaded.

How to Get There

From US 127, turn west onto TN 8 about 1 mile north of Dunlap. Turn right onto TN 399 at 4.5 miles and drive 5.5 miles to the park entrance on the right. From Spencer, take TN 111 south about 16 miles to a junction with TN 8. Continue straight on the same road, now TN 8, for 4 miles and turn right onto TN 399 to the park entrance.

The Hike

The South Cumberland Recreation Area, a coalition of eight parks and natural areas, preserves spectacular parts of the Cumberland Plateau and superb hiking, all within an easy drive from Chattanooga. South Cumberland Visitor Center near Tracy City on TN 41 provides maps of all the areas, as do branch centers at Savage Gulf. The sample of hikes in this book (Fiery Gizzard, Foster Falls, Savage Day Loop, Stone Door—Hikes 44–47) is just a starter kit for days and days of exploring. The double loop described (counterclockwise for both loops) here uses four South Cumberland Recreation Area trails to make a pleasant plateau walk and provide views into one of the wildest parts of Savage Gulf. Here's a quick overview: You'll hike a connector, swing around half of the smaller loop, take another connector to the larger loop, complete that, and return on the same connector to finish the smaller loop.

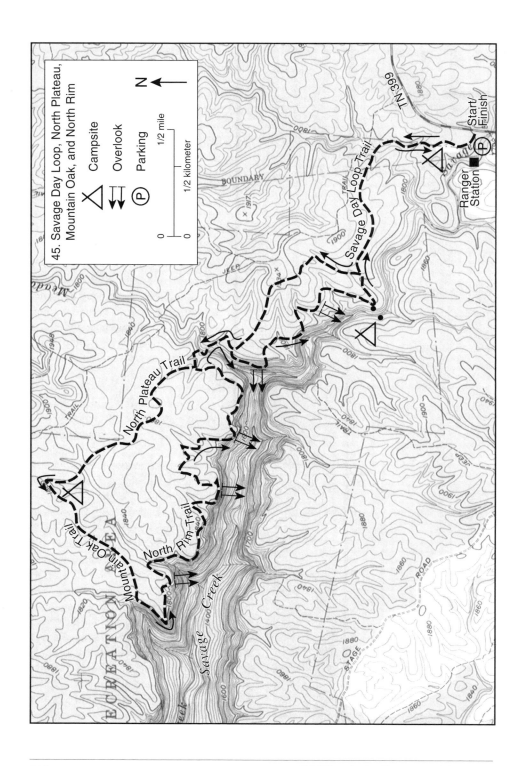

45. Savage Day Loop, North Plateau,
Mountain Oak, and North Rim

△ Campsite

▽ Overlook

Ⓟ Parking

1/2 mile
1/2 kilometer
0
0

N ←

BOUNDARY

JEEP

North Plateau Trail

North Rim Trail

Mountain Oak Trail

RECREATION AREA

Savage Creek

Savage Day Loop Trail

Ranger Station

Start/Finish
Ⓟ

TN 399

Walk to the right of the ranger station to start the 1-mile connector to the first loop, Savage Day Loop. The trail goes through thin, piney woods with some oaks and American hollies, then descends gradually, crossing two small creeks decorated with spring wildflowers. After a springy bridge over a mountain-laurel-lined creek, small sourwood, blackgum, and maple trees appear. Flat plateaus made for easy logging, but state natural area protection should soon bring back mature forests.

At 1 mile the loop of Savage Day Loop starts; turn right and continue through open forest. Running ground cedar (a type of club moss) can be seen here all year, and whorled loosestrife (which does well in young forests with plenty of light) blooms in summer with tiny yellow flowers from leaf nodes around the stem.

Cross a jeep road and reach a 2-MILE sign. Savage Day Loop turns left, and you can either return at this point or head to the right on North Rim Trail. A slightly rocky descent leads to another springy suspension bridge over Meadow Creek and more wildflowers that like moist creekbanks. Just after the bridge, North Rim Trail meets North Plateau Trail; turn right through oak and hickory woods. (Turning left at this junction and hiking out a mile or so will give you a shorter hike with the benefit of some of the North Rim views. Then backtrack to Savage Day Loop.)

On North Plateau Trail cross some overgrown woods roads and then join a narrow, raised pathway—an old dinky dine, a narrow-gauge railroad for transporting lumber and coal. A spur trail goes left to Dinky Line Campsite, with several flat sites and an outhouse. About 100 yards past the campsite Mountain Oak Trail turns left, skirts the back of the campsite, and heads 0.8 mile toward Savage Gulf. (At the time of this writing, the

Savage Gulf map showed the campsite after the trail junction rather than before, because the campsite has been relocated. Newer maps may reflect the change.) The junction is well marked. Mountain Oak Trail, which makes this moderate loop possible, was built as an Eagle Scout project by Boy Scout Troop 210. From here, you start to close the larger loop of this hike; at each sign you'll hike toward the ranger station.

North Rim Trail lives up to its promise: a pretty woods walk with several views over one of the steepest bluffs of the gulf. At Quartz Pebble Overlook, first peer down into the gulf at the tops of big old trees and a branch of the gulf, drained by Savage Creek, that has no trail. Then try to pry a quartz pebble from its sandstone bed. Quartz, harder than sandstone, protrudes as the sandstone erodes; the pebble you break a fingernail on will pop out after several thousand more rainstorms.

The trail drops into the moist hollow of Lick Creek, which holds a patch of cinnamon fern, and then returns to the rim. After flirting with the edge and retreating back to safe parts of the plateau a few times, North Rim Trail swings left along Meadow Creek to its junction with North Plateau Trail. Having completed the larger loop of this hike, you turn right, cross Meadow Creek on the swinging bridge again, and hike about 0.3 mile to Savage Day Loop. Now you turn right again to complete the other side of Savage Day Loop, the side with the good views. In 0.2 mile reach Rattlesnake Point. As the buzzard flies, it is 3 air miles west from here to the point where Savage Creek and Big Creek join Collins River, which flows through the middle gorge of the gulf. You can see Savage Creek Gorge widening, and in the distance you can see the curves of the three gorge walls. To the left you can see the head of Savage

---

Running ground cedar

50 Hikes in the Tennessee Mountains

Creek Gorge and precipitous bluffs like the one you're sitting on. A plaque honors Samuel Werner and Ellen Young Werner, who bought 3,800 acres of Savage Gulf in 1924 and protected a parcel of virgin forest. In 1973 the Tennessee State Legislature designated Savage Gulf (the gorges of all three creeks) a state natural area, restricted to hiking trails, footbridges, and campsites.

Return to the trail and continue about 0.5 mile to another steep but short spur trail, this one to an overlook of Savage Falls and its large pool. Back on the main trail, turn left at the junction with South Rim Trail, complete the loop, and turn right to return to the ranger station.

Other Hiking Options

1. For more views into the gulf, turn right at the junction of Mountain Oak and North Rim Trails and walk along the rim for another mile or so.
2. To visit Savage Falls, take South Rim Trail from Savage Day Loop and descend 0.5 mile to the top of the falls. A wooden staircase leads to the bottom of the falls. Climb back up the stairs, and from here, you can return to Savage Day Loop or turn right and explore South Rim Trail.

46

Foster Falls

Total Distance: 5.0 miles

Hiking Time: 3 hours

Vertical Rise: 50 feet (without gorge or falls options)

Rating: Easy to moderate

Map: USGS White City

Trail Marking: White blazes

Little Gizzard Creek rushes along the bottom of a narrow 60-foot gorge and then plunges another 60 feet as Foster Falls. This hike circles above the falls, giving views from both sides. Most of the hike is easy plateau walking, but overlooks are unprotected except at Foster Falls. Fall and winter views into the 1,000-foot-deep gorge are spectacular.

How to Get There

From Tracy City, drive 8 miles south on US 41/TN 150. Turn right at the FOSTER FALLS sign and drive 0.5 mile to the parking and picnic area.

The Hike

Most of this hike runs through the Small Wilds (Little Gizzard and Foster Falls Small Wild Areas) with a connection through private land, used in cooperation with the landowners. Please stay on the trail and respect their property. Foster Falls Small Wild Area (SWA) originally belonged to the Tennessee Valley Authority (TVA), which cooperated with the state to make it accessible to campers and hikers. A trail to the left of the parking area leads to a developed campground.

From the picnic shelter, hike across a strip of woods to a wooden bridge. Turn left for a good fenced falls overlook and then return to Fiery Gizzard Trail to swing right to another overlook of the top of the falls, also fenced, on a large, flat rock. The mountain laurel here gets plenty of sun and produces masses of blooms in good years. This shrub, like most plants, has a fiscal year that starts

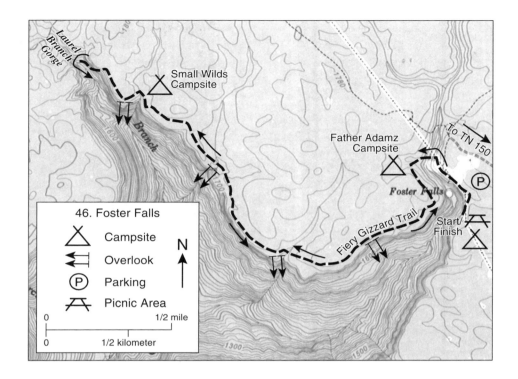

46. Foster Falls

⟁ Campsite

⇄ Overlook

Ⓟ Parking

⊼ Picnic Area

0 ————————————— 1/2 mile

0 ————— 1/2 kilometer

N ↑

around July 1, and its budget at that time determines how many bloom buds it makes for the next year. The budget depends on growing conditions of the previous year and how many resources the plant used in earlier blooms. For example, a year with scant blooms and good growing conditions will be followed by a spectacular flower display the next year. Bird's-foot violet grows around the flat rock throughout spring. With leaves shaped like a bird's foot, nearly inch-wide lavender flowers, and orange anthers, it looks different from its relatives and prefers dry, sunny spots.

Descend left through a laurel thicket to an iron bridge across Little Gizzard Creek and reach a signed fork. The right fork goes to Father Adamz Campsite. Go left to continue on Fiery Gizzard Trail and the best (but unfenced) Foster Falls overlook, this one

giving a view of the main falls and a little side falls. From here, continue on good trail with occasional rocks and roots to the other end of the campsite trail and the SWA boundary at about 2 miles. Cross a bog bridge and a large patch of ferns.

On the plateau walk to Little Gizzard SWA, listen for pileated woodpeckers and look for dead trees or logs with roughly rectangular holes. These chicken-sized woodpeckers toss wood chips around in their search for wood-boring grubs. Also look ahead and see how many white blazes you can see at one time. A score of four or five is good; try for six. Partridges may explode from their hiding places as you approach— a good strategy for startling predators. Partridges with chicks will flutter away from the chicks and distract you with pitiful cries, broken-wing acts, and even bold attacks at

Foster Falls

Foster Falls

50 Hikes in the Tennessee Mountains

knee level. Another excellent strategy, and the chicks crouch silently among the leaves.

Reach another campsite and a small creek with views on each side. From the second view, you can cautiously approach the edge and look back at the small horsetail waterfall. Hike farther to reach the edge of Laurel Branch Gorge at 3 miles and peer down into it before turning around to retrace your steps.

Two climbers' loops connect to Fiery Gizzard Trail and lead to difficult descents to the base of the first set of bluffs in the gorge. The trails do not involve rock climbing; they simply lead to good climbing areas, using rock and wooden steps on steep parts.

On the return trip you could take the trail through Father Adamz Campsite, which is about the same distance and takes you back to Fiery Gizzard Trail just before the iron bridge.

Other Hiking Options

1. Laurel Branch Gorge. Make this into a difficult hike by descending the rocky trail into Laurel Branch Gorge, with its large hemlocks, rhododendrons, and beech trees. Many wildflowers grow on the slopes and along the branch. Hike up the other side and continue along the bluff for more views (giving you four rough scrambles), or return from Laurel Branch (giving you only two rough scrambles).

2. Hike all the way on Fiery Gizzard Trail to Grundy Forest Natural Area (13 miles, with your choice of Fruit Bowl or Dog Hole Trail; see Hike 47).

3. Foster Falls Loop. For a difficult 2-mile climb around Foster Falls, turn left after the wooden bridge near the picnic area and pass the fenced falls overlook and a clearing under power lines. Turn right at a sign and climb down rugged stone steps with occasional handrails or cables. This short descent is easy to follow and reaches the large plunge pool across from the falls. To finish the 2-mile loop, cross Little Gizzard Creek (go back if the water is high) and continue through and past boulders on less used trail with occasional blue blazes; turn left at what seems to be a dead end at a bluff. Turn right at a passage through the bluff and climb to Fiery Gizzard Trail. The best way to complete this option is with someone who has done it before; otherwise, allow plenty of time and be prepared to turn back if the trail becomes too hard to follow.

47

Fiery Gizzard Trail and Dog Hole Loop

Total Distance: 8.8 miles

Hiking Time: 6 hours

Vertical Rise: 500 feet

Rating: Difficult

Map: USGS Monteagle

Trail Marking: White blazes

On this one, you need boots. Maybe knee and elbow pads, too. Somehow Fiery Gizzard Creek finds its way through a boulder jumble called the Fruit Bowl, and you will, too, but you'll feel like an ant in a gravel pit. Spring wildflowers thrive among the rocks, and Raven Point has a wonderful autumn view. Summer could be too hot for this hike, and heavy rain, snow, or ice might make it impossible. Small children can get lost between the boulders.

How to Get There

From Monteagle, drive 3 miles east on US 41 to South Cumberland Recreational Area Visitor Center for maps and other information. Fiery Gizzard Trail starts in the Grundy Forest State Natural Area; return to US 41 and continue 2.1 miles farther to a sign on the right for GRUNDY FOREST. Turn right twice at signs to drive 0.5 mile to the entrance, with picnic tables and bathrooms.

The Hike

In 1870 the owners of some coal mines wanted to know if soft southern coal could be coked—that is, made into coke good enough to fuel steel mills. They built an experimental blast furnace, which worked for three days before its chimney crashed into the "fiery gizzard" of the furnace, killing several workers. The coke passed the test, though, and workers built hundreds of coke ovens like the ones on Hike 48. The work was hard and dangerous and led to labor revolts, which became worse when the mine owners imported convict labor from Nashville.

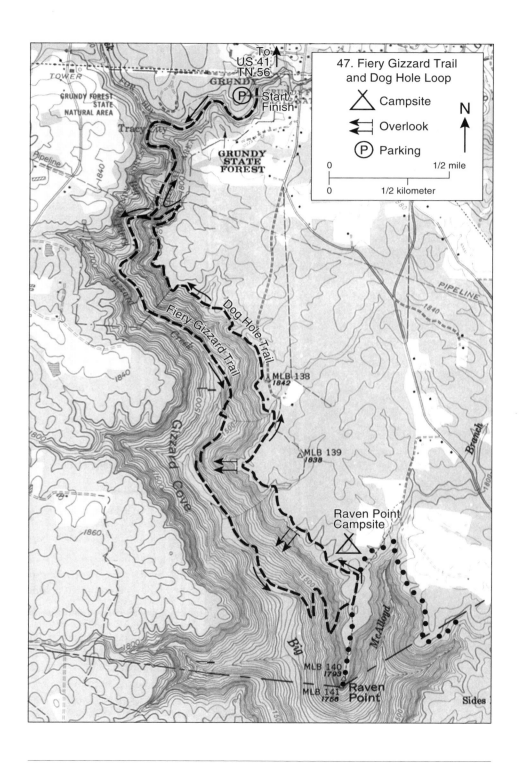

This loop starts in the Grundy Forest State Natural Area, but some of the hike is on private land, used in cooperation with the landowners. Please stay on the trail and respect their property.

From the parking lot, turn left, enter pine woods, and cross an open, flat rock overlooking Little Fiery Gizzard Creek (not to be confused with Little Gizzard Creek) on the right. Swing right down rock steps to go below the same rock, which becomes Cave Spring Rockhouse. Water seeps through mossy cracks, and the overhanging roof shows signs of past campfires. One huge and several pretty big hemlocks grow here; loggers had little interest in hemlocks.

A sandy trail leads to a bridge across muddy spots and then a small creek crossing on flat stones. American holly, hemlock, and mountain laurel cover the shady hillside, and yellowroot shrub grows by the creek, which becomes more and more like a gorge as you descend. The Civilian Conservation Corps built this trail in the 1930s, and more recently the Friends of Fiery Gizzard installed two bridges with hand rails and a set of wooden steps. Near an old cement platform Blue Hole Falls (about 8 feet high, but with a lot of water) forms a plunge pool where people swim. The trail continues along a bench over the creek and then drops down to cross on a metal bridge.

A sign tells you that Fiery Gizzard Trail continues straight while Grundy Forest Day Loop branches right and left. Continue straight as Little and Big Fiery Gizzard Creeks join at 0.9 mile and rush together through Black Canyon, a noisy cascade in a narrow rock crack; walk a few yards right of the trail for a good view. Then all that water (now called Big Fiery Gizzard Creek) flows away as you climb a rocky slope, crossing small seeps.

Rock stacks, more than 50 feet high and made of fractured rocks that look like irregular building blocks, stand at the top of the rise. They look like they could crash down at any moment, but somehow they have resisted the erosion that created this gorge. Trees grow on top of the stacks. Follow faint trails to the right to visit the bases of the stacks.

Take a rhododendron-lined avenue back toward the creek and, at 1.3 miles, reach the spur trail to Sycamore Falls (about 0.1 mile to a pretty cascade and plunge pool). From here, descend along the creek and look for bits of coal on the trail. At 1.5 miles Dog Hole Trail angles sharply left to climb a steep hillside. For the loop described here, continue straight; to complete the loop, you'll descend to this intersection.

Walk between the creek and the steep blocky bluff with coal seams and descend to a hemlock grove with a few smooth-barked beech trees. As the gorge widens a bit, look for bigleaf magnolias and many spring flowers: longspur violet, foamflower, jack-in-the-pulpit, doll's eyes, purple and white phacelia, and at least three kinds of trillium. Climb a small rock ridge and descend to more flower carpets—this begins a pattern of this trail that becomes a little more dramatic (rocky) at each repetition. Over the next ridge an old road joins the trail from the left. Admire a side-creek cascade from the other side but turn left uphill for the next ridge. Then descend to new flower and fern fields . . . and so on. The trail goes through a sandy flood zone and turns up left again; each descent is rockier than the last. You are in the Fruit Bowl—a jumble of boulders, most too big to wiggle underfoot, but some challenging to clamber over. Blazes can be hard to see; if you don't spot any for a while, go back a bit. In general, the trail stays to the right of each Fruit Bowl section and then returns to creekside.

Fiery Gizzard Creek

Fiery Gizzard/ Dog Hole Loop

At 3.7 miles look for stone steps left to the base of a bluff. Steep switchbacks lead to the top of the bluff and a level, rocky section about 0.2 mile long. Then a double blaze sends you up again through more switchbacks. From here, there are good winter views of the rocks ahead and on the other side of the creek. On this drier hillside mountain laurel replaces the rhododendron and just a few flowers grow: trailing arbutus, alumroot, bluets, hawkweed, and pussytoes. Pass along the base of some bluffs, switch back and cross a tiny creek, and finally, at 4.4 miles, angle up to a ridge crest with rock stacks in front. Just before the top, look right for a 10-foot-tall arch.

A signed trail junction offers a spur trail to the right (0.4 mile) to Raven Point, a promontory that juts out over Fiery Gizzard Gorge with excellent fall-color views and chances to see soaring buzzards. To continue the loop, return to the sign and continue to Raven Point Campsite and then another junction. Dog Hole Trail goes left and runs along the gorge rim for more than a mile, past large patches of bluets (which can bloom almost any month of the year) and good views from wide, flat rocks. The trail descends to cross creeks and then returns to the rim. Don't miss Junk Bluff on the left at 5.6 miles, where several vintage 1950s cars took their last drive. After another creek crossing, a spur trail leads about 100 yards left to Yellow Pine Falls, a two-step cascade. Then, past a clear area where a grassy road comes from the right, the trail reaches private land and a barbed-wire fence. Turn left and descend beside a creek into shady hemlock woods. Swing under the bluff, hear Fiery Gizzard Creek below, and descend steeply past a fractured rock face. A sloping ledge runs in front of the dog hole mine (don't go inside), where you'll see more coal. Dog hole mines are so small that only a dog could stand up in one, but people, sometimes children, crawled in to dig out coal from deep seams.

Other Hiking Options

1. With a car shuttle, you can hike from Fiery Gizzard to Foster Falls (13 miles). This difficult hike involves a 3-mile connector of plateau hiking on private land and deep side gorges to climb down and up. The views are spectacular. If you think you could get through the Fruit Bowl with a backpack, this would be a good overnight trip, but don't try it until you know the trail.

2. Meadow Trails. Behind South Cumberland Visitor Center is a network of easy trails through meadows and woods and around a small lake. The main trail is about 2 miles long, and several loops and cross trails provide a choice of longer or shorter hikes.

3. The 2-mile Grundy Forest Day Loop starts with Fiery Gizzard Trail but continues up Fiery Gizzard Creek instead of down at the confluence of the two creeks. It passes waterfalls and plunge pools before climbing to a level woods trail and an open, flat rock with mosses and reindeer moss lichen. In spring look for pink lady's slippers on your way back to the parking lot.

48

Lone Rock Trail at Grundy Lakes

Total Distance: 1.5 miles

Hiking Time: 45 minutes

Vertical Rise: 40–50 feet

Rating: Easy

Map: USGS Tracy City

Trail Marking: White blazes

Lone Rock Trail circles one of the Grundy Lakes, which were once used to cool coke after it came out of coke ovens. This pretty state park shows a contrast between present recreational use and the hard and dangerous coal and coke industry of the late 1800s. This easy trail would be excellent for children, with the added attraction of playgrounds and a beach; the one-way road could provide handicapped access to parts of it.

How to Get There

From the intersection of TN 56 and US 41 in Tracy City, drive south on US 41 for about 1 mile (passing a business district and a Fiery Gizzard historical marker on the right) and turn left at a GRUNDY LAKES sign. From South Cumberland Visitor Center, this turn is about 4 miles on US 41. Turn left into the main parking area in 1 mile. There are bathrooms, a beach, and a picnic area. A one-way road with a bike lane goes around the lake and provides easy access to picnic areas and views.

The Hike

Tracy City (named for Samuel Tracy, owner of the Sewanee Mining Company) was the center of a coal mining industry that provided coal and coke for iron and steel foundries in Chattanooga. After the Civil War, miners dug coal from exposed seams or from dog hole mines (narrow, unsupported mines where only a dog could stand up). An experimental furnace (the "fiery gizzard") proved that Tennessee coal could be made into high-quality coke, and workers

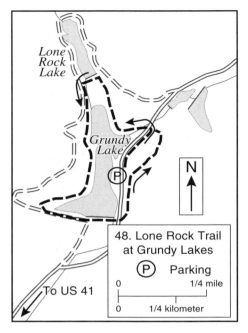

Lone
Rock
Lake

Grundy
Lake

N

48. Lone Rock Trail
at Grundy Lakes

Ⓟ Parking

0   1/4 mile

0   1/4 kilometer

To US 41

and train traffic, bursts of steam, occasional explosions, and overwhelming heat.

Coke ovens were built of brick or stone in two lines, back to back, and then covered with a level-topped mound of earth. Narrow-gauge (dinky line) trains ran along the tops of the ovens, pouring coal through roof holes onto fires on the floor. Then the ovens were closed to prevent air from entering at the base. Coal gases escaped through the holes, and in a few days workers shoveled dirt off the side openings, broke through the bricks, cooled the coke, and loaded it.

Many of the ovens in the park have been cleaned out; you can enter them to see glazed brick and the small roof vents. High school students from Sewanee–St. Andrews School volunteer in a project to clean the ovens near the entrance of the park to preserve them for demonstration.

Walk down the parking lot from the beach and start Lone Rock Trail on a wooden bridge at the end of the parking area. White blazes mark the trail as it runs along the lake and then turns right to climb a hill through oak and hickory woods. Look for bits of coal and brick on the path. Turn left to cross the dam for the upper lake, where you might see wood-duck families, and follow wooden stairs down beside the dam spillway. Jack-in-the-pulpit, foamflower, black cohosh, and other flowers bloom beside the stairs, and a large patch of field horsetail grows in a marshy area on the left. This bushy 6- to 10-inch-tall "fern ally" (not a fern, not a moss, but something in between) represents a plant family that had tree-sized members during the Carboniferous age and formed some of the coal deposits.

Climb right to a road and then return to the lake near a playground and an exercise course. Walk between two rows of coke ovens with trees and bushes growing on

built more than 500 earth-covered coke ovens. Fires on the floor of the ovens heated the coal to drive off organic compounds, leaving almost pure carbon, which burns hot enough to manufacture steel. Shortage of oxygen kept the carbon from burning in the high heat. Upon opening the ovens, workers cooled the coke with water and loaded it onto trains. It's hard to say which was worse—crawling into dog hole mines or operating the coke ovens—but local laborers eventually demanded better pay, safety, and conditions. The company crushed the revolt by importing convict labor from Nashville. Later, civil rights activists established the Highlander School to help local people fight oppressive labor practices. Grundy Lakes is on the National Register of Historic Places.

As you walk through this delightful park, imagine what it was like with no trees (they were cut to fuel the ovens), constant donkey

Coke ovens

top, and then walk out on the mowed area between the ovens and the water. Ovens on both sides of the lake give a spooky feeling, as if the eyes of giant underground creatures are watching.

Continue around the lake and climb to a road on steps. Cross the dam, then the entrance road, and follow the trail into the woods and a hollow between two more rows of ovens. More than 100 ovens are scattered through the woods and around the lakes in this park.

Turn left, cross the road, and return to your car.

Other Hiking Options

The Dunlap Ovens Historic Site, on TN 28/US 127 between Whitwell and Pikeville, has restored coke ovens and an interpretive center and trail.

49

Shakerag Hollow

Total Distance: 3.0 miles

Hiking Time: 1½–2 hours

Vertical Rise: 150 feet

Rating: Easy to moderate

Map: USGS Sewanee

Trail Marking: White blazes

This section of the 21-mile Sewanee Perimeter Trail provides an outstanding display of spring wildflowers and a view of the western Cumberland Plateau and the Highland Rim beyond. Best hiked in spring or fall, it's hot in summer.

How to Get There

From I-24, take exit 134 (Monteagle/Sewanee) and drive 4 miles west on US 41A/US 64 to the stone pillars at the university entrance. Bear right onto University Avenue, then turn right onto Greens View Road. Pass tennis courts and a golf course and reach a large gravel parking area. The other end of the Shakerag Hollow trail segment can be accessed from roadside parking just past the university entrance pillars.

The Hike

The University of the South, established in 1858 by the Episcopal Church, was destroyed in 1863 by Federal troops. In the 1880s Samuel Tracy, owner of the Sewanee Mining Company, donated funds and land to rebuild it. The university designed a new campus, patterned after Oxford and Cambridge Universities, with buildings of native sandstone. Surrounded by a 10,000-acre "domain," the university protects a large area of the southern Cumberland Plateau. The 21-mile Perimeter Trail, built partly by the Civilian Conservation Corps in the 1930s, was completed as a loop by the university. The trail passes waterfalls, bluffs, creeks, rockhouses, and views, but the Shakerag Hollow section is included here because of its spring flower display.

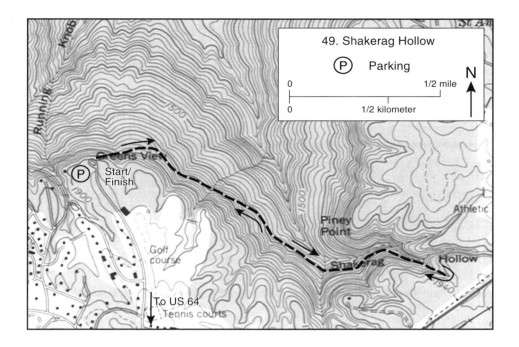

From the Greens View parking lot, walk out to stone benches on a grassy area and look north at the expanse of the Cumberland Plateau and west to the Highland Rim, stretching out but showing a few hills. Then turn left and enter the woods; the trail here is rocky with a gully across it. Scramble up to a flat rock for another view (this one framed by oak and shagbark hickory trees) or descend through the gully to a footlog and steps to the base of the rock. Saxifrage (the name means "rock breaker") clings to cracks, with its roots in tiny soil pockets. Look for inch-long hairy leaves arranged in a rosette at the base of a stalk that holds several branches of tiny white flowers in May. The leaves are often tinged with red and have teeth at the ends, like a cat's paw with a lot of extra claws.

From the base of the rock, descend steadily into the hollow, which is deep, sheltered, and north facing—all excellent conditions for spring wildflowers. Winter moisture stays in the soil, and when the sun finally reaches these slopes, it streams through leafless tree branches. The spring flowers hurry to bloom and pollinate before the leaves come out; in this cool hollow the flowers crowd together in both space and time. In March a carpet of white flowers blooms: bloodroot, hepatica, toothwort, white fringed phacelia, and sweet white violets. In early April colors and taller plants start appearing: purple phacelia, delphinium (larkspur), fire pink, burgundy trillium, blue spiderwort with orange anthers, and phlox. Irregular patches of mayapples take over some areas. Several of the umbrella-shaped leaves may come from the same root, and only double leaves produce flowers.

Continue down past a two-story boulder that must have rolled from the bluff. Shagbark hickory, chestnut oak, and buckeye trees grow along the trail, and large, straight tulip trees with smooth bark seem to be trying to reach out of the hollow. After this land was abandoned by loggers and miners, tulip trees got a head start because they can grow well in sunlight; the presence of many of them all about the same age indicates a former clearing.

Between the colored flowers, look for the well-camouflaged jack-in-the-pulpits, which will show off scarlet berries in fall when most flowers are gone.

At the bottom of the hollow celandine poppies offer a new color: bright yellow. Cross a small creek and start up the other side with just as many wildflowers. After a 0.5-mile climb, the trail levels; another trail goes left toward Sewanee–St. Andrews School. Swing right, pass under a dog hole mine, and then ascend to open woods in sight of the Sewanee entrance pillars.

Return the same way; you'll see many new flowers on the way back.

Other Hiking Options

1. Sewanee Natural Bridge. Drive about 10 miles south of the Shakerag Hollow Trailhead on TN 56 and look for a sign on the left for the NATURAL BRIDGE STATE NATURAL AREA. The hike is 100 yards or so, across the top of the bridge, or arch, and then down to its base, with wet patches and wildflowers.

2. Buggy Top Trail, Carter State Natural Area. This natural area features caves, sinkholes, wildflowers, and some difficult climbs. You can enter the caves with proper equipment, and rangers lead hikes there. Call South Cumberland Visitor Center for more information.

3. Other sections of Perimeter Trail lead to views, bluffs, and other excellent wildflower hollows.

4. While you're here, walk through the University of the South campus.

50

Cumberland Trail: Signal Point to Edwards Point

Total Distance: 5.2 miles

Hiking Time: 3½–4 hours

Vertical Rise: 1,000 feet

Rating: Difficult

Map: USGS Chattanooga

Trail Marking: White blazes

Steep and rocky, this trail starts at one Tennessee River Gorge overlook and ends at another, with a creek crossing and a swimming hole in the middle. It's best in spring (wonderful wildflowers and rhododendron) and fall (vistas for fall color); if you try this one in summer, you'll want to swim at Middle Creek. Rocks, some that shift, make this hike difficult for children or people concerned about knees and ankles. Ice, snow, or high water can make it impossible.

How to Get There

From Chattanooga, drive north on TN 8. At the junction with TN 27, continue on TN 8 (now joined with US 127) for 4.7 miles. Look for a SIGNAL MOUNTAIN PARK sign on Signal Mountain Boulevard. Follow signs left on Mississippi Avenue and left to the park entrance before the imposing Alexian Brothers retirement home (1.2 miles from US 27; you really can't miss it). If you continue straight for 0.1 mile past the Alexian Brothers building, a signed pullout on the left leads to a trail down to Rainbow Lake, which joins the Cumberland Trail.

The Hike

From Signal Point, you'll soon be able to follow the Cumberland Trail (CT) 280 miles to Cumberland Gap, but this description covers just 2.6 miles of it. During the Civil War siege of Chattanooga, the Union army under General Rosecrans held off General Bragg's Confederate attacks, getting supplies from the Sequatchie Valley up to Walden Ridge and then by river to the troops. Supply caravans moved slowly and

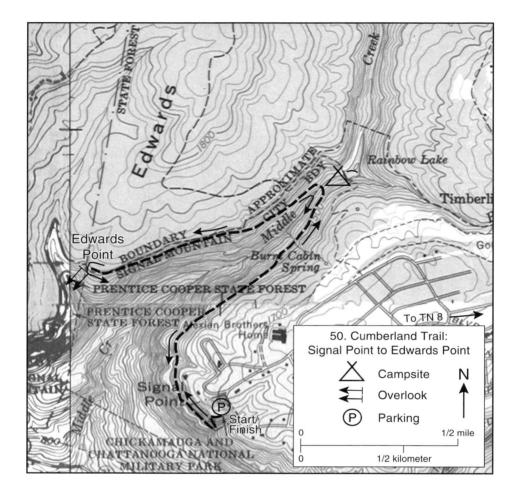

Edwards Point

Edwards

**50. Cumberland Trail:
Signal Point to Edwards Point**

△ Campsite

Overlook

Ⓟ Parking

N

0   1/2 mile

0   1/2 kilometer

Signal Point

Start/Finish

To TN 8

Rainbow Lake

Timberl

PRENTICE COOPER STATE FOREST

PRENTICE COOPER STATE FOREST

CHICKAMAUGA AND CHATTANOOGA NATIONAL MILITARY PARK

were subject to Confederate raids, so the U.S. Signal Corps used flags and flares to tell suppliers when it was safe to come. In November 1863 Grant swept in from the north, chased the Confederate army deep into Georgia, and opened the way for Sherman's March to the Sea (events described in great detail in *Gone with the Wind,* for those who read the novel slowly and carefully).

At the monument overlook you can learn the Union signal code on a plaque. Then turn left to look for the CT sign and the first white blaze. Just after entering the woods, you drop over the bluff aided by cables, bridges, a ramp, and steps of rocks and railroad ties. These hiking lifesavers were built or repaired by college students from Michigan, Florida, Illinois, and New York participating in the 1998 Cumberland Trail Conference Breakaway Program, in which the students choose hard labor over lying on a beach somewhere. Local volunteers from Cherokee Sierra Club and other groups work alongside.

Keep going right onto a level but still

rocky bench along a contour. There are boulders to climb over and crawl between, but take the time to look left for a view of Raccoon Mountain and the sides of the gorge you've entered. The TVA has built a pump storage plant on top of Raccoon Mountain—when there's extra electricity, it pumps water up to a high lake; when more electricity is needed, the water is released through turbines.

The trail crosses a creek that tumbles over Rainbow Falls, which you can visit by scrambling down a difficult and eroded side trail on the left. Sourwood, mountain laurel, and tulip trees grow on this dry, south-facing slope, and past the creek is a patch of papaw trees and some blue summer-blooming dayflower. More rocks (you can look up right to the bluff that spawned them) and two creek bridges later, you descend on a long switchback to Middle Creek and a large, pleasant campsite on the right. Walk up through the campsite to get to the swimming hole at the base of a dam that forms Rainbow Lake. Rocks and chunks of concrete make good sunning spots.

Return to the trail and cross Middle Creek on a long suspension bridge (also built by Breakaway volunteers).

Across Middle Creek, the trail rises through rhododendron and then into oak and hickory forest. At a junction with Bee Branch Loop Trail, the CT branches left at a sign for EDWARDS POINT. There's a small campsite at the base of a rock jumble, and an overhang that could provide shelter from rain (but you wouldn't want to sleep on its rocky floor). Erosion columns, arches in progress, and one large natural arch appear, and then the trail turns to the right up another rocky scramble with another rock shelter. At the top is Edwards Point, a large, rounded plateau above the Tennessee River Gorge with several rocky viewpoints.

> "The Tennessee River system begins on the worn magnificent crests of the southern Appalachians, among the earth's oldest mountains, and the Tennessee River shapes its valley into the form of a boomerang, bowing it to its sweep through seven states. Near Knoxville the streams still fresh from the mountains are linked and thence the master stream spreads the valley most richly southward, swims past Chattanooga and bends down into Alabama to roar like blown smoke through the floodgates of Wilson Dam, to slide becalmed along the crop-cleansed fields of Shiloh, to march due north across the high diminished plains of Tennessee and through Kentucky spreading marshes toward the valley's end where finally, at the toes of Paducah, in one wide glass golden swarm the water stoops forward and continuously dies into the Ohio."

–James Agee, Tennessee Valley Authority, *Fortune* magazine, 1933

The bluffs are unprotected and very high up; enjoy the several views along the trail, because at 2.6 miles you come to a gravel road to an overused, sometimes trashed campsite and bluff. From the last two or three views you will see Williams Island, where archaeologists are now studying the sites of Woodland, Mississippian, and Creek Indians. The Cherokee took over the island during the French and Indian War (1754–1763).

For the 5.2-mile hike described here, turn back at this bluff and retrace your steps, perhaps with another stop at or swim in Middle Creek. On your way back up to Signal Point you'll discover a whole new set of trail rocks.

The first blaze of the Cumberland Trail on Signal Point

50 Hikes in the Tennessee Mountains

Other Hiking Options

1. This option works best if you can get someone to pick you up at the end. If you continue on the CT around Edwards Point, you'll pass more overlooks and soon be able to see the dramatic Suck Creek Gorge—named not by backpacking teenagers, but for a massive rock that extended halfway across the narrows of the Tennessee River. Water sweeping around the rock created a suck, or boat-grabbing eddy. Soldiers blew up the rock in 1831, and the Hales Bar Dam in 1913 (later replaced by the TVA's Nickajack Dam) further improved navigation. About 3 miles past Edwards Point the CT descends to Suck Creek, which has a pretty campsite and a swinging bridge. From here, you can hike another 1.5 miles over a steep ridge to TN 27.

2. Rainbow Lake Loop. From the trailhead past the Alexian Brothers building, an excellent mapboard shows Rainbow Trail to Rainbow Lake and Bee Branch Loop (2 miles total). The blue-blazed loop starts as a cement walk beside a golf course, enters the woods, passes a spring and shelter on Bee Branch, and drops toward the lake on switchbacks. At a fork turn right and walk about 0.5 mile to a possibly difficult creek crossing, and then climb a ridge and descend to the CT just past Middle Creek. Turn left and cross the bridge, then walk left through the campsite and find a steep trail around to Rainbow Lake. Switchbacks lead up to the fork to complete the loop. You could use the trail around Rainbow Lake to add 1.5 miles to your return from Edwards Point: Turn at the BEE BRANCH LOOP sign, circle Rainbow Lake, and drop down to the Middle Creek Campsite.

Appendix

Contact these groups for information on maps, hiking club programs, trail conditions, volunteer opportunities, and more.

Appalachian Trail Conference
799 Washington Street
P.O. Box 807
Harpers Ferry, WV 25425-0807
304-535-6331
www.atconf.org

Chattanooga Hiking Club
P.O. Box 1443
Chattanooga, TN 37403
www.chattanooga.net/hiking

Cumberland Trail Conference
19 East 4th Street
Crossville, TN 38555
931-456-6259
www.cumberlandtrail.org

National Park Service
www.nps.gov

Tennessee State Parks
www.state.tn.us/environment/parks/
1-888-TN-PARKS

Tennessee Citizens for
Wilderness Planning
130 Tabor Road
Oak Ridge, TN 37830
423-481-0286
www.korrnet.org/tcwp/

Smoky Mountains Hiking Club
P.O. Box 1454
Knoxville, TN 37901
423-558-1341
www.esper.com/smhc/

Tennessee Trails Association
P.O. Box 41446
Nashville, TN 37204-1446
615-367-7881
www.tennesseetrails.org

Tennessee Wildlife Resources Agency
1-800-262-6704
www.state.tn.us/twra/

The Map Store
900 Dutch Valley Road
Knoxville, TN 37918
1-800-678-6277

Bibliography

For more trails in the mountains of Tennessee, see the following:

Upper East Tennessee

Murray, Kenneth. *Highland Trails: A Guide to Scenic Walking and Riding Trails.* Johnson City, TN: The Overmountain Press, 1992.

Cherokee National Forest

Skelton, William, Editor. *Wilderness Trails of Tennessee's Cherokee National Forest.* Knoxville, TN: The University of Tennessee Press, 1992.

The Smokies

Wise, Kenneth. *Hiking Trails of the Great Smoky Mountains.* Knoxville, TN: The University of Tennessee Press, 1996.

Big South Fork

Deaver, Brenda, Jo Anna Smith, and Howard Ray Duncan. *Hiking the Big South Fork.* Knoxville, TN: The University of Tennessee Press, 1999.

Manning, Russ. *Trails of the Big South Fork National River and Recreation Area.* Norris, TN: Mountain Laurel Place, 1995

South Cumberlands

Manning, Russ. *Tennessee's South Cumberland Recreation Area, State Parks and Forests, State Natural Areas: A Hiker's Guide to Trails and Attractions.* Norris, TN: Mountain Laurel Place, 1994.

Index

Ginger, 57
Glacial periods, 57
Gorge Overlook Trail, 205, 207
Gorge Trail, 205
Goshen Prong Trail, 78
Grandfather Mountain, 41
Grand Gap Loop Trail, 153, 155
Grapeyard Ridge Trail, 64, 69
Grass balds, 41
Great chickweed, 77
Great Smoky Mountains National Park, 13
Greenbrier Cove, 60, 62
Greeter Falls, 216
Grotto Falls, 65, 66, 67
Grundy Forest Day Loop, 228, 230
Grundy Forest Natural Area, 224, 226, 228
Grundy Lakes, 231–33

H

Hacking, 112
Heath, 36, 67–68
Heath balds, 41, 68
Hells, 89–90
Hemlocks, 32, 36, 66, 78, 94, 148, 228
Hemlock Trail, 112
Henderson Trail, 99
Hercules'-club, 150
Hickory, 28, 102, 119, 197, 198
Hidden Passage Trail, 143–45
Hikes
    with children, 18
    equipment, 14, 16
    ratings, 18
    safety on, 14, 16
    selecting, 13–14
    time to complete, 18
    weather conditions for, 14, 16
Hiking clubs, 18–19, 74
Hiwassee River, 101
Hobblebush, 71
Hogskin Branch Loop, 197, 198
Holly, 46, 198
Holly Trail Loop, 112
Holston Mountain Trail, 26–29
Holston River, 113
Holston Treaty of 1771, 74
Honey Creek, 164–68

Honeysuckle azalea, 37
House Mountain State Natural Area, 117–20
Hughes, Thomas, 172, 175
Huskey Branch, 77
Huskey Gap Trail, 78

I

Ice Castle Falls, 168
Ijams Nature Center, 121–23
Indian Gap, 73
Indian Grave Gap, 43, 48, 52
Interpretive Trail, 181
Iron Mountain, 26, 28, 30, 32, 33
Ironweed, 106

J

Jack-in-the-pulpits, 81
Jake's Creek Trail, 78
Jake's Place, 148, 150
Jeffrey Hell Trail, 89–92
Jewelweed, 127
John Muir Trail, 157, 159, 168
John Muir Trail at Reliance, 100–103
Judge Branch Trail, 180–83
Junglebrook Nature Trail, 69
Junk Bluff, 230

K

Kate, Bonny, 116
Kayaking, 105, 191–92
Kings Mountain, 115
Kingsport, 110–11
Knoxville, siege of, 122
Kudzu, 102, 121

L

Ladies' Swimming Hole, 175
Lady's slippers, 55, 141
LaFollette, 138–42
Lakeside Trail, 110–13
Lampshade spiders, 102, 106
Laurel Branch Gorge, 224
Laurel Falls, 34–38
Laurel Falls Pocket Wilderness, 191–94
Laurel Falls Trail, 216

228, 235, 236, *see also* specific flowers
Wild hogs, 33, 67, 71, 87
Williams Island, 239
Will Skelton Greenway, 123
Wintergreen, 46
Witches Cave, 175
Witch hazel, 50
Witch hobble (viburnum), 59, 94
Wolves, 112–13

Woodland Trail, 205
Woodpeckers, 126, 223

Y

Yellow birch, 25, 52, 59, 71, 78
Yellow buckeye, 56, 67, 90, 190
Yellow Pine Falls, 230
Yellow trillium, 130, 178–79

Let Backcountry Guides Take You There

Our experienced backcountry authors will lead you to the finest trails, parks, and back roads in the following areas:

50 Hikes Series

50 Hikes in the Adirondacks
50 Hikes in Connecticut
50 Hikes in the Maine Mountains
50 Hikes in Coastal and Southern Maine
50 Hikes in Maryland
50 Hikes in Massachusetts
50 Hikes in Michigan
50 Hikes in the White Mountains
50 More Hikes in New Hampshire
50 Hikes in New Jersey
50 Hikes in the Hudson Valley
50 Hikes in Central New York
50 Hikes in Western New York
50 Hikes in the Mountains of North Carolina
50 Hikes in Ohio
50 Hikes in Eastern Pennsylvania
50 Hikes in Central Pennsylvania
50 Hikes in Western Pennsylvania
50 Hikes in Vermont
50 Hikes in Northern Virginia

Walks and Rambles Series

Walks and Rambles on Cape Cod and the Islands
Walks and Rambles on the Delmarva Peninsula
Walks and Rambles in the Western Hudson Valley
Walks and Rambles on Long Island
Walks and Rambles in Ohio's Western Reserve
Walks and Rambles in Rhode Island
Walks and Rambles in and around St. Louis

25 Bicycle Tours Series

25 Bicycle Tours in the Adirondacks
25 Bicycle Tours on Delmarva
25 Bicycle Tours in Coastal Georgia and the Carolina Low Country
25 Bicycle Tours in Maine
25 Bicycle Tours in Maryland
25 Bicycle Tours in the Twin Cities and Southeastern Minnesota
30 Bicycle Tours in New Jersey
30 Bicycle Tours in the Finger Lakes Region
25 Bicycle Tours in the Hudson Valley
25 Bicycle Tours in Ohio's Western Reserve
25 Bicycle Tours in the Texas Hill Country and West Texas
25 Bicycle Tours in Vermont
25 Bicycle Tours in and around Washington, D.C.
30 Bicycle Tours in Wisconsin
25 Mountain Bike Tours in the Adirondacks
25 Mountain Bike Tours in the Hudson Valley
25 Mountain Bike Tours in Massachusetts
25 Mountain Bike Tours in New Jersey
Backroad Bicycling on Cape Cod, Martha's Vineyard, and Nantucket
Backroad Bicycling in Eastern Pennsylvania
Backroad Bicycling in Connecticut

Bicycling America's National Parks Series

Bicycling America's National Parks: Arizona & New Mexico
Bicycling America's National Parks: California
Bicycling America's National Parks: Oregon & Washington
Bicycling America's National Parks: Utah & Colorado

We offer many more books on hiking, fly-fishing, travel, nature, and other subjects. Our books are available at bookstores and outdoor stores everywhere. For more information or a free catalog, please call 1-800-245-4151 or write to us at The Countryman Press, P.O. Box 748, Woodstock, Vermont 05091. You can find us on the Internet at www.countrymanpress.com.